Forensic Cyberpsychology and the Human Side of Cybercrime

This book provides readers with an insightful and nuanced look at the human component of cybercrime. James McDowell delves into the intriguing domain of forensic cyberpsychology by exploring the complex relationship between humans and technology in the realm of cybercrime.

This groundbreaking work provides the first unifying theory of forensic cyberpsychology, weaponized affective vulnerability engineering (WAVE) theory, to illuminate the motivations, behaviors, and thought processes of both perpetrators and their targets using psychological analysis and real-world case studies. As the boundaries between the physical and digital worlds continue to blur, understanding and addressing this topic demands a nuanced approach. This book demystifies the multifaceted nature of cybercrime, investigates the duality of technological innovation, and provides practical strategies to mitigate cybercrime in an ever-evolving threat landscape. From explaining the tactics underpinning common schemes to discussing the emotional impact of exploitation, it delivers an extensive and innovative analysis of the human factor in cybercrime to support combating digital threats in an increasingly connected world.

This book is a vital resource for forensic psychologists, law enforcement professionals, business leaders, and the public in their efforts to better predict, mitigate, and respond to complex threats in the cyber arena.

James McDowell is Executive Director of the Cybercrime Research Institute and an Adjunct Professor of Cybersecurity and Cybercrime in the United States. He is a cyberpsychologist and a leader in cybercrime investigations. His insights have illuminated the intricate relationships between human behavior and cybercrime, making him a sought-after expert in the field. Dr. McDowell previously served as the Chief of Cyber Operations for a state law enforcement agency in the United States, where he led the cybercrime investigative program, several multi-jurisdictional investigations, and numerous cyber-enabled fraud task forces and working groups.

Current Issues in Cyberpsychology

Current Issues in Cyberpsychology brings together books that explore the psychology behind human interaction with digital technology, and the impact of the internet on individuals and society as a whole.

It showcases books that will be relevant to both an academic and professional market, bringing together the work of established and emerging authors. The series spans a range of topics relating to cyberpsychology; including the influence of technology on behaviour and attitudes, the effects of social media, human factors in cybersecurity, and digital identities. Ideas for new books are welcome.

The Psychology of Cybersecurity
Hacking and the Human Mind
Tarnveer Singh and Sarah Y. Zheng

Human Factors and Cybersecurity
The Psychology Behind Online Safety and Security
Lee Hadlington and Chloe Ryding

For more information about the series, please visit: https://www.routledge.com/our-products/book-series/CIIC

Forensic Cyberpsychology and the Human Side of Cybercrime
The Mind Behind the Screen

James McDowell

NEW YORK AND LONDON

Designed cover image: Getty © BlackJack3D

First published 2026
by Routledge
605 Third Avenue, New York, NY 10158

and by Routledge
4 Park Square, Milton Park, Abingdon, Oxon, OX14 4RN

Routledge is an imprint of the Taylor & Francis Group, an informa business

© 2026 James McDowell

The right of James McDowell to be identified as author of this work has been asserted in accordance with sections 77 and 78 of the Copyright, Designs and Patents Act 1988.

All rights reserved. No part of this book may be reprinted or reproduced or utilised in any form or by any electronic, mechanical, or other means, now known or hereafter invented, including photocopying and recording, or in any information storage or retrieval system, without permission in writing from the publishers.

For Product Safety Concerns and Information please contact our EU representative GPSR@taylorandfrancis.com. Taylor & Francis Verlag GmbH, Kaufingerstraße 24, 80331 München, Germany.

Trademark notice: Product or corporate names may be trademarks or registered trademarks, and are used only for identification and explanation without intent to infringe.

ISBN: 9781041091592 (hbk)
ISBN: 9781041092575 (pbk)
ISBN: 9781003649199 (ebk)

DOI: 10.4324/9781003649199

Typeset in Times New Roman
by codeMantra

This book is dedicated to the survivors of cybercrime whose experiences illuminate our understanding of psychology in the digital world and whose courage drives the advancement of forensic cyberpsychology.

Contents

1 Introduction   1
Setting the Stage 1
The Critical Problem: Why Cybersecurity Keeps Failing 1
A New Framework: WAVE Theory 2
What Is Cyberpsychology? 3
Why Does Cyberpsychology Matter? 3
The Cyberpsychological Foundation of WAVE 4
Psychological Theories for the Digital World 5
WAVE Theory in Practice: Deepfakes 6
Scope and Purpose of This Book 7
Structure of This Book 8
Conclusion 9
References 9

2 Foundations of Cyberpsychology and Cybercrime   12
Evolution of Cyberpsychology 12
Cybercrime and Cognition 15
Taxonomy of Offenses 16
Research Methods in Cyberpsychology 18
Ethical Considerations and Mitigation Tactics 20
Conclusion 21
Reflection Questions 21
Skill Builder Labs 21
References 22

3 Anatomy of Cybercrime   25
Time to Double Click 25
Classifying Cybercrime 25
Cybercrime Attack Lifecycle 28
Human Components of the Cybercrime Ecosystem 31

Contextual Factors Driving Adversary Behavior 34
Conclusion 35
Reflection Questions 36
Skill Builder Labs 36
References 37

4 Convergence of Technology and Psychology   40
Interface Psychology 40
Cognitive Impacts of Technology Use 42
Key Cognitive Biases in Interface Design 43
Weaponized Interface Design 45
Trust Calibration in Human-Technology Interaction 46
Regulatory Frameworks 47
Frictionless and Ethical Design in Cybersecurity 48
Conclusion 49
Reflection Questions 50
Skill Builder Labs 50
References 51

5 The Duality of Technological Innovation   55
The Prometheus Paradox 55
Connected Minds, Distributed Solutions 55
Mind the Gap: Digital Divides and Cultural Paradoxes 57
Economic Drivers of Technological Innovation 58
Dark Side of Innovation 59
Ethical & Regulatory Challenges 62
Conclusion 65
Reflection Questions 66
Skill Builder Labs 66
References 67

6 Evolution and Transformation of Cybercrime   71
Proto-Hacks (1960s–1980s) 71
Globalization (1990s–2010s) 73
Professionalization and Industrialization (2010s–2020s) 75
Cross-Border Policing and MLAT Limits 77
Significant Incidents: Theory in Reality 78
Emerging Trends 81
Conclusion 85
Reflection Questions 85
Skill Builder Labs 85
References 86

7 Psychological Drivers of Perpetrating Cybercrime 89
From Minecraft to Mayhem 89
Financial Drivers 90
Ideological Drivers 92
Personal Drivers 94
Rationalizing Cybercrime Behavior 98
Conclusion 99
Reflection Questions 99
Skill Builder Labs 100
References 100

8 Deceptive Tactics in Cybercrime 104
Stone Age Minds, Space Age Threats 104
The WAVE of Social Engineering 104
Digital Deception Tactics in Social Engineering Campaigns 108
Conclusion 110
Reflection Questions 111
Skill Builder Labs 111
References 112

9 Psychological Catalysts and Impacts 114
When the Expert Becomes the Target 114
Target Susceptibility Factors 115
Psychological Impact on Survivors 119
Self-Perpetuating Cycle of Chronic Exploitation 121
Ripple Effects within Communities 123
Recovery Pathways 123
Conclusion 125
Reflection Questions 126
Skill Builder Labs 126
References 126

10 Mitigating Cybercrime through Psychological Insights 130
A Digital Fortress with Open Doors 130
UX Design Interventions 131
Organizational Culture Interventions 131
Behavioral Interventions 132
Policy and Legal Interventions 133
Conclusion 135
Reflection Questions 136
Skill Builder Labs 136
References 137

11 Anticipating the Future of Cybercrime — 139
The Oracle's Dilemma 139
AI as the Perpetrator 139
Data-Driven Attacks 140
Blockchain Technology and the Decentralized Paradox of Trust 142
Quantum Horizon 143
Proactive Defense Strategies 144
Conclusion 146
Reflection Questions 147
Skill Builder Labs 147
References 148

12 Conclusion — 150
Why Security Awareness Training Often Falls Short 150
Emerging Challenges Reshaping Security Assumptions 151
Ethical Considerations That Demand Attention 152
Synthesizing the Evidence 153
Reflection Questions 154
References 154

Index — 155

1 Introduction

Setting the Stage

Jane Doe, CFO of a Fortune 500 company, stared at the email from her CEO that came in at 4:47 p.m. on a Friday: "Wire $2.3 M to the Singapore acquisition now or we lose the deal".

In 12 seconds, the money and her weekend were gone, teaching the cybersecurity world a key lesson: the most sophisticated firewall in existence still relies on three pounds of gray matter between one's ears. The email was perfect. The CEO's distinctive writing style, the Singapore acquisition they'd discussed in yesterday's board meeting, and even his habit of sending urgent requests just before his Friday afternoon flights. Every detail is precisely calibrated to bypass more than just technical defenses by also targeting a far more vulnerable system, the human brain.

This is forensic cyberpsychology in action. More than simply the study of code or configurations, it is the science of how human minds can be hacked as readily as any device. Because here's what three decades of escalating cybercrime has taught us: while we've built increasingly sophisticated digital defenses, we've barely begun to understand the psychological vulnerabilities that render them useless. Each year, the gap between exponentially advancing technology and stubbornly constant psychology grows more expensive. Yet, the real cost is measured in more than dollars. It is also measured in shattered trust, destroyed lives, and the growing realization that in the battle between targets and the adversary, we're playing by rules most do not understand. This book rewrites the rules through the introduction of weaponized affective vulnerability engineering (WAVE) theory, which shows how the adversary triggers responses by synchronously manipulating interface designs, cognitive heuristics, and social cues.

The Critical Problem: Why Cybersecurity Keeps Failing

Jane Doe's story is not an isolated incident. It is an illustration of the systemic failure costing organizations trillions of dollars each year that continues to escalate despite consistent investment in cybersecurity technologies. The uncomfortable truth is that the adversary is far more effective in exploiting psychology than technical vulnerabilities. In fact, nearly every major cybersecurity incident begins with a target making a decision that appeared reasonable at the time. A pattern illustrating that failure occurs at the intersection of humans and technology. Despite this, cybersecurity spending continues focusing on technical controls that assume humans rationally behave under pressure, remember complex procedures during crises, and maintain vigilance against increasingly sophisticated deception.

Three core assumptions underpin modern cybersecurity approaches with each assumption creating vulnerabilities that adversaries systematically exploit. The Knowledge Deficit Assumption presumes that people make poor security decisions due to lack of information or awareness. The Individual Vulnerability Model treats each person as a collection of separate weaknesses to be independently addressed. The Technical Primacy Bias assumes that cybersecurity is fundamentally a technical problem with human elements instead of recognizing the truth. It is a human problem with technical elements.

These flawed assumptions create a cybersecurity paradigm that fights yesterday's battles while adversaries invent tomorrow's exploits. Traditional approaches analyze attacks as collections of tactics, techniques, and procedures rather than recognizing them as coordinated psychological operations designed to create cognitive states where protective mechanisms fail.

A New Framework: WAVE Theory

Instead of treating psychology as auxiliary to technology, WAVE theory provides a different framework for understanding and defending against cybercrime. The foundational principle of WAVE theory is that the adversary does not succeed only through isolated manipulation techniques. The adversary succeeds through synchronized psychological orchestration. In other words, sophisticated cyberattacks create behavioral resonance by synchronizing manipulations across multiple psychological systems to overwhelm cognitive defenses, making harmful actions feel inevitable rather than chosen. An analysis of Jane's case through the lens of WAVE reveals the orchestration that made her response predictable. The familiar writing style reduced skepticism, while the Singapore acquisition context provided perceived legitimacy. Time pressure prevented verification during Friday afternoon depletion, all within the trusted environment of business email communication. This interaction of factors facilitated a cognitive state where sending money felt necessary. The adversary succeeds by synchronizing their manipulations to overwhelm cognitive defenses through coordinated amplification rather than individual exploitation (i.e., resonance over isolation); continuously adjusts their approach based on target responses creating adaptive feedback loops that evolve attacks in real-time (i.e., adaptation over static targeting); and the adversary engineers interactions that feel rational rather than manipulated (i.e., environmental orchestration vs. direct manipulation). To understand WAVE and the nuanced solution shifting cybersecurity from reactive to proactive, one must explore the scientific foundation upon which it is built.

What Is Cyberpsychology?

The world of today necessitates a comprehensive understanding of the relationship between psychology and technology, the scientific study of which is referred to as cyberpsychology. The field examines how thoughts, emotions, and behaviors vary in the digital world and focuses on understanding related phenomena, including influence, behavior, and identity.[1] Cyberpsychology as a field understandably developed alongside the expansion of the internet beyond government and academia and into the zeitgeist, which occurred circa 1993.[2] By adding the prefix "cyber-" to notate events in the digital world, researchers established the notion of cyberpsychology as the specific study of how humans behave in the digital world. While the field of cyberpsychology continues to rapidly develop, there are several alternative names used across the gestalt of academic literature, such as internet psychology, digital psychology, and web psychology. For the purposes of this book, the term cyberpsychology will be used to capture the breadth of the discipline.

Forensic cyberpsychology represents a specialized application of these broader principles. While general cyberpsychology studies all forms of digital behavior, forensic cyberpsychology specifically examines illicit and deviant activities in the digital world. By integrating theories and methods from multiple disciplines (e.g., psychology, computer science, and criminology), forensic cyberpsychology proposes a modern approach to an emerging area specifically focused on the influence of psychology on deviant behavior in the digital world. The incorporation of cognitive and social concepts from the field of psychology provides cyberpsychologists with layered perspectives into the human condition. Layering in analytical and technological insights from the field of computer science improves understanding related to the technical components of human-computer interactions.[3] When exploring the specific subset of cyberpsychology focused on cybercrime, as is the purpose of this book, criminology perspectives provide researchers a detailed understanding of cybercrime perpetration and victimization.[4] When taken in tandem, this multidisciplinary approach provides cyberpsychologists with a rich understanding of humans, computers, and the ways in which both may be exploited by the adversary.

Why Does Cyberpsychology Matter?

Every day, millions of people make decisions that seem perfectly rational at the moment, only to prove catastrophically wrong in hindsight. They click links they shouldn't, trust emails they wouldn't, and share information online that they'd never reveal in person. This isn't a failure of intelligence. Rather, it is a predictable result of human psychology colliding with digital environments designed to exploit our cognitive shortcuts. As online attention becomes increasingly fragmented through the simultaneous ingestion of multiple streams of content, in addition to the constant bombardment of notifications across applications and devices, research shows that changes in dopaminergic pathways stem partly from the reinforcement of high-stimulation interactions across sustained engagements with quickly consumable, reward-based content.[5] This ultimately taxes memory and cognitive control, leading to users identifying ways to conserve cognitive resources by over-leveraging heuristics (i.e., mental shortcuts) in online decision-making.[6]

One example of this principle in the context of cybercrime is the prevalence of imposter scams, which exploit credibility heuristics in targets. Credibility heuristics involve users over-relying on superficial clues when processing information. The adversary exploits this shortcut in imposter scams by impersonating credible institutions as a way to solicit funds or data from targets. The application of foundational cyberpsychological insights to practical applications provides important context into online behavior as it relates to cybercrime and is an important component of more nuanced discussions contained in this book. Analyzing the foundational constructs of cyberpsychology is key to understanding the synchronized orchestration underpinning WAVE.

The Cyberpsychological Foundation of WAVE

Cyberpsychology's scope is defined by four key constructs: presence, anonymity, disinhibition, and trust.[2] The concept of being there in a virtual environment is presence. This notion is important to understand the emotionally charged reactions from targets when engaging in interactions in the digital world, or why these experiences may feel strong enough to alter one's behavior in the physical world.[7] The ability to conceal one's identity in the digital world is encompassed in the construct of anonymity, which operates on a spectrum.[8] Most interactions in the digital world exist between the two extremes of total anonymity and complete transparency. For example, the Twitter Bitcoin scam of 2020 succeeded partly because verified account badges created a false sense of authenticity since the accounts were verified as belonging to the individual represented in them.[9] Social restraints rarely factor into interactions in the digital world as a result of the anonymity provided to individuals and ability to operate away from direct engagement in a process known as disinhibition.[10] This may positively manifest through increased self-disclosure and creativity, or negatively through harassment and fraud. The phenomenon clarifies why people might engage in risky behaviors online that they would avoid in physical settings.[11] Trust encompasses one's willingness to accept vulnerability based on positive expectations about others' intentions.[12] Online trust develops differently than face-to-face trust, relying more on interface cues and social proof than on nonverbal communication. Digital environments create conditions that consistently challenge human cognitive abilities, leading to predictable decision-making errors that adversaries exploit systematically.[13] The psychology of cybersecurity demonstrates how understanding human behavior patterns proves critical for developing effective digital defenses. These four constructs do not operate in isolation. Instead, they systemically interact to shape digital environments that overwhelm cognitive systems that evolved for the physical world.

Human attention systems evolved for physical environments with limited information sources. Digital environments present constant streams of competing information that overwhelm these systems. Research shows that knowledge workers check digital communication interfaces approximately every six minutes.[14] This cognitive fragmentation creates vulnerabilities that adversaries exploit through timing attacks and attention manipulation. Decision-making online relies heavily on mental shortcuts (i.e., heuristics). For example, the availability heuristic leads people to overestimate risks they've recently heard about while underestimating more common threats.[15] Authority heuristics also explain why official-looking logos and formal language make phishing emails more convincing.[16] Dual-process cognition theory distinguishes between fast, intuitive thinking (System 1) and slower, deliberative analysis (System 2).[17] Digital interfaces often trigger System 1 responses through urgency cues and social pressure, bypassing careful evaluation. This fragmented attention creates optimal conditions for the adversary to exploit, as evidenced by numerous incidents.[18]

Digital platforms amplify social influence through visible metrics like likes, shares, and follower counts.[19] These quantified feedback systems can create pressure for increasingly extreme content to capture attention in crowded information environments. Psychological manipulation in cybersecurity contexts often leverages these social proof mechanisms. Group polarization occurs when like-minded people interact primarily with others whom they feel are similar. This leads groups toward more extreme positions. Online echo chambers accelerate this process through algorithmic content curation that confirms existing beliefs while filtering out contradictory information.[20] Social proof mechanisms that help people navigate uncertain situations become vulnerabilities when apparent consensus can be artificially manufactured. Election interference efforts partly succeed by creating illusions of grassroots support through coordinated bot networks.[21] These deceptive practices highlight how behavioral analytics in cybersecurity must account for manipulation of social cues.

Emotional states significantly influence online risk-taking. Fear of missing out (FOMO) drives rapid action without adequate verification, making limited-time offers particularly effective in social engineering.[22] The GameStop trading phenomenon of 2021 demonstrated how social media can amplify FOMO beyond rational risk assessment.[23] Curiosity motivates both protective and risky behaviors depending on context. While curiosity can drive security-conscious research, it also leads to clicking suspicious links. Headlines used in items of clickbait effectively exploit this drive.[24] Moral outrage increases sharing behavior while reducing accuracy concerns. Research indicates that each moral-emotional word in social media posts increases sharing probability by approximately 20%.[25] This emotional hijacking represents a critical vulnerability in the digital world's information ecosystem.

Psychological Theories for the Digital World

Applying psychological insights to the digital world requires translating theoretical frameworks into practical applications for threat assessment and defense design. The evolution of psychological profiling in the digital age demonstrates how forensic psychology adapts to technological contexts.[26] Social Cognitive Theory (SCT) explains behavior through reciprocal interactions between personal factors, environmental influences, and behavioral outcomes.[27] In cybersecurity contexts, this theory helps understand how user confidence in their technical abilities influences security behavior, sometimes leading overconfident users to take greater risks.[28] The Theory of Planned Behavior (TPB) examines how attitudes, subjective norms, and perceived behavioral control influence intentions and actions.[29] This framework proves particularly relevant for understanding why security training often fails to translate into secure behaviors. Understanding psychological principles behind fraudulent behavior enables development of more effective defenses against manipulation and deceit.[30] Routine Activity Theory (RAT) maps traditional criminological concepts onto digital crime opportunities.[31] The theory's focus on motivated offenders, suitable targets, and absent guardians translates directly to digital environments where psychological vulnerabilities create targets.[32] Cyber offenders are motivated by financial gain, political ideology, national interests, terrorism, or personal gratification.

WAVE theory expands on these and other well-established concepts by applying a strategic, multi-level framework that operates at multiple levels (e.g., micro, meso, and macro) to establish a groundbreaking contribution to the field in the form of a unifying theory incorporating fragmented notions across multiple disciplines into a single explanatory model, reframing disparate concepts into a cohesive framework. In other words, WAVE theory represents a mosaic image comprised of principles from across multiple disciplines that, when viewed together, provide a unified pattern of the cybercrime ecosystem. Thus, WAVE theory presents an opportunity to transform forensic cyberpsychology from a collection of isolated insights into a system-level theory of the manipulation of behavior in digital environments.

WAVE Theory in Practice: Deepfakes

Deepfake technology represents an increasingly sophisticated threat to individuals, businesses, and societies. Unlike traditional fraud methods that rely on crude impersonation or generic social engineering, deepfake technology exploits fundamental human trust mechanisms by weaponizing our neurological predisposition to believe information.[33] This technology transforms cybercrime from opportunistic deception into precision-guided psychological manipulation. Deepfakes manipulate presence and trust through hyper-realistic AI-generated content that triggers the neurological predisposition to trust sensory evidence (i.e., presence overwhelms skepticism). The adversary obfuscates their actual identity via perfect impersonations that lead targets to rely on apparent confirmations. Disinhibition manifests as behavioral compliance where normal verification hesitations are circumvented.

Through SCT, it is evident how artificial intelligence (AI) sophistication erodes confidence in detecting fakes, fostering a destructive cycle. One's self-efficacy for identifying fakes decreases as sophistication increases, creating a destructive feedback loop where targets become increasingly susceptible. Analyzing deepfakes through the lens of TPB reveals the natural preference for convenience over accuracy and the social pressure to quickly share content. Social norms increasingly favor speed over verification in digital communication, while perceived behavioral control diminishes as detection becomes technically impossible for average users. RAT shows how deepfakes create perfect convergence conditions – motivated offenders with increasingly accessible AI tools, suitable targets who trust sensory evidence, and absent guardians since technical detection requires sophisticated analysis unavailable in real-time social interactions. Deepfakes exemplify WAVE theory's central insight that modern cybercrime succeeds through synchronized psychological orchestration, facilitating cognitive states where normal protective mechanisms cannot function. In other words, deepfakes undermine one's entire framework for ascertaining truth, a convergence that exemplifies the importance of WAVE theory and this book.

Scope and Purpose of This Book

This book develops and applies WAVE theory to revolutionize forensic cyberpsychology. Rather than treating human factors as auxiliary concerns, WAVE theory positions psychological understanding as the foundation for effective digital defense in an era of synchronized psychological attacks. Centering on WAVE theory's core insight that the adversary succeeds as a result of orchestrated exploitation of a variety of factors rather than isolated manipulation, the knowledge goal for this book centers on enhancing one's understanding of the systematic interaction of psychology in the digital world. Readers will also develop capabilities for behavioral resonance analysis, learning to identify when multiple psychological systems are being targeted simultaneously and designing defenses that disrupt adversarial synchronization rather than simply blocking individual attack vectors. By adopting a WAVE theory perspective that views cybercrime through the lens of psychological orchestration, this book positions individuals to recognize that sophisticated attacks succeed by creating temporary cognitive states where normal protective instincts cannot function, an approach that proves essential as cybercrime's hidden toll on mental health includes emotional distress (e.g., depression, anxiety, shame, self-isolation).[34]

Policy makers can use WAVE theory insights to develop regulations that address coordinated psychological manipulation rather than focusing solely on technical vulnerabilities, including creating legal frameworks that recognize synchronized psychological attacks as distinct adversarial behaviors requiring specialized investigation and prosecution approaches. Law enforcement benefits from WAVE theory in understanding how modern adversaries operate as psychological engineers rather than simple technical intruders. WAVE-informed investigative techniques reveal behavioral patterns in how adversaries orchestrate interface design, timing, and social proof to create cognitive resonance in their targets. Organizations can apply WAVE theory principles to design security systems that work with human psychology rather than against it. Instead of relying on individual awareness training, WAVE-informed defenses focus on disrupting adversarial synchronization through environmental design, timing protocols, and social verification systems. NGOs promoting digital rights may use WAVE theory to articulate privacy and security as fundamental safety issues, given that WAVE theory demonstrates how coordinated manipulation exploits persistent cognitive vulnerabilities to undermine human agency.

Structure of This Book

This book unfolds across 12 chapters organized into four thematic sections, each building upon previous foundations while introducing new complexities.

Part I: Foundational Knowledge

This section traces cyberpsychology's evolution from early cybernetics to contemporary digital behavior studies. Chapter 2 examines how classic psychological theories apply to digital environments, revealing both their continued relevance and limitations. Chapter 3 reviews the basics of cybercrime to establish a baseline understanding.

Part II: Understanding Cybercrime

Chapter 4 examines the relationship between technology and psychology. Chapter 5 examines the dual nature of technological innovations, with new iterations posing both positive and negative effects. Chapter 6 explores the ways in which cybercrime evolved throughout history.

Part III: The Psychology of Cybercrime

This section explores the human elements of cybercrime ecosystems, from individual psychological drivers to social structures that facilitate adversary collaboration. Understanding psychology proves essential for developing countermeasures that address root causes rather than symptoms, as is reviewed in Chapter 7. Then, Chapters 8 and 9 explore both individual susceptibility factors and broader societal impacts of cybercrime victimization. Overall, this section challenges attitudes blaming victims, who are referred to as targets or survivors throughout this book, to deliberately illustrate the importance of not victim-shaming, to demonstrate how psychological manipulation may overcome well-informed defenses.

Part IV: Defenses and Interventions

Cybercrime spans technological, educational, and policy domains. Chapter 10 examines how psychological research may inform more effective cybersecurity interventions that work with human nature rather than against it. Chapter 11 explores the future of forensic cyberpsychology examining how emerging threats (e.g., AI, blockchain technology, quantum computing) will reshape the cybercrime landscape. Finally, Chapter 12 concludes this book by providing actionable takeaways.

Each chapter of this book, aside from Chapter 1, concludes with a set of reflection questions designed to support engagement with the material by connecting theoretical concepts to experience. With the exception of the introduction and conclusion of this book (i.e., Chapters 1 and 12), every chapter also includes Skill Builder Labs consisting of an application scenario and a mini-research activity, which are designed to encourage deeper exploration and review of discussed topics. The incorporation of these components ensures that each chapter equips researchers and practitioners with actionable tools for integration into forensic, clinical, and investigative work.

Conclusion

Jane Doe's 12-second mistake cost her company $2.3 million while revealing something far more valuable: the future of cybersecurity lies in understanding the psychological orchestration that renders technical controls irrelevant. As discussed in Chapter 2, WAVE theory synthesizes findings from across disciplines into a unifying theory to provide the framework for this understanding. By revealing how the adversary creates synchronized attacks across interface design, cognitive systems, and social contexts, we can finally move beyond reactive defenses toward predictive psychological protection. The mind behind the screen remains both our greatest vulnerability and our strongest defense. This book will show how WAVE theory transforms that vulnerability into resilience through an understanding of how the adversary manipulates targets in order to design defenses that complement cognitive processes instead of attempting to circumvent them.

References

1 Attrill Smith, A., Fullwood, C., Keep, M., & Kuss, D. J. (Eds.). (2019). *The Oxford handbook of cyberpsychology*. Oxford University Press.
2 Ancis, J. R. (2020). The age of cyberpsychology: An overview. *Technology, Mind, and Behavior, 1*(1), 1–15.
3 Stanton, N. A., et al. (2016). *Human factors methods: A practical guide for engineering and design* (3rd ed.). CRC Press.
4 Wall, D. S. (2015). *Cybercrime: The transformation of crime in the information age*. Polity.
5 Oprea, D. C., Moldovan, M. A., Chirija, R., & Bolos, A. (2021). Behavioural addictions and the role of dopamine. *Bulletin of Integrative Psychiatry, 27*(4), 63–70.
6 Zucchelli, M. M., Matteucci Armandi Avogli Trotti, N., Pavan, A., Piccardi, L., & Nori, R. (2025). The dual process model: The effect of cognitive load on the ascription of intentionality. *Frontiers in Psychology, 16*, 1451590.
7 Starcevic, V., & Aboujaoude, E. (2017). Internet addiction: Reappraisal of an increasingly inadequate concept. *CNS Spectrums, 22*(1), 7–13.
8 Lapidot Lefler, N., & Barak, A. (2012). Effects of anonymity, invisibility, and lack of eye contact on toxic online disinhibition. *Computers in Human Behavior, 28*(2), 434–443.
9 Cola, G., Mazza, M., & Tesconi, M. (2024). From tweet to theft: Tracing the flow of stolen cryptocurrency. arXiv preprint arXiv:2406.18503.

10 Suler, J. (2004). The online disinhibition effect. *CyberPsychology & Behavior, 7*(3), 321–326.
11 Syrjämäki, A. H., Ilves, M., Olsson, T., Kiskola, J., Isokoski, P., Rantasila, A., ... & Surakka, V. (2024). Online disinhibition mediates the relationship between emotion regulation difficulties and uncivil communication. *Scientific Reports, 14*(1), 30019.
12 Xu, J., Le, K., Deitermann, A., & Montague, E. (2014). How different types of users develop trust in technology: A qualitative analysis of the antecedents of active and passive user trust in a shared technology. *Applied Ergonomics, 45*(6), 1495–1503.
13 Khadka, K., & Ullah, A. B. (2025). Human factors in cybersecurity: An interdisciplinary review and framework proposal. *International Journal of Information Security, 24*(3), 1–13.
14 MacKay, J. (2018). *Communication overload: Our research shows most workers can't go 6 minutes without checking email or IM.* RescueTime Blog.
15 Folkes, V. S. (1988). The availability heuristic and perceived risk. *Journal of Consumer Research, 15*(1), 13–23.
16 Greavu-Șerban, V., Constantin, F., & Necula, S. C. (2025). Exploring heuristics and biases in cybersecurity: A factor analysis of social engineering vulnerabilities. *Systems, 13*(4), 280.
17 Kahneman, D. (2011). *Fast and slow thinking.* Allen Lane and Penguin Books.
18 Frauenstein, E. D., & Flowerday, S. V. (2016). Social network phishing: Becoming habituated to clicks and ignorant to threats? In *2016 Information Security for South Africa (ISSA)* (pp. 98–105). IEEE.
19 Wang, P., & Lutchkus, P. (2023). Psychological tactics of phishing emails. *Issues in Information Systems, 24*(2), 71–83.
20 Hartmann, D., Wang, S. M., Pohlmann, L., & Berendt, B. (2025). A systematic review of echo chamber research: Comparative analysis of conceptualizations, operationalizations, and varying outcomes. *Journal of Computational Social Science, 8*(2), 52.
21 Yan, H. Y., Yang, K. C., Shanahan, J., & Menczer, F. (2023). Exposure to social bots amplifies perceptual biases and regulation propensity. *Scientific Reports, 13*(1), 20707.
22 Klütsch, J., Schwab, J., Böffel, C., Zimmermann, V., & Schlittmeier, S. J. (2024). Friend or phisher: How known senders and fear of missing out affect young adults' phishing susceptibility on social media. *Humanities and Social Sciences Communications, 11*(1), 1–14.
23 Ivantchev, B., & Ivantcheva, M. (2023). FOMO effect: Social media and online traders. *Journal of Management and Financial Sciences, 48*, 59–74.
24 Kuraku, S. (2022). *Curiosity clicks: The need for security awareness.* University of the Cumberlands.
25 Brady, W. J., Wills, J. A., Jost, J. T., Tucker, J. A., & Van Bavel, J. J. (2017). Emotion shapes the diffusion of moralized content in social networks. *Proceedings of the National Academy of Sciences, 114*(28), 7313–7318.
26 Mateo-Fernandez, P. V., & Osa-Subtil, I. (2024). The evolution of criminal profiling in the digital age: An approach from clinical forensic psychology. *International Journal of Forensic Sciences, 9*(4), 1–9.
27 Bandura, A. (1986). *Social foundations of thought and action: A social cognitive theory.* Prentice-Hall.
28 Unchit, P., Das, S., Kim, A., & Camp, L. J. (2020). Quantifying susceptibility to spear phishing in a high school environment using signal detection theory. In *International symposium on human aspects of information security and assurance,* (pp. 109–120). Springer International Publishing.

29 Ajzen, I. (1991). The theory of planned behavior. *Organizational Behavior and Human Decision Processes, 50*(2), 179–211.
30 Sommestad, T., Karlzén, H., & Hallberg, J. (2019). The theory of planned behavior and information security policy compliance. *Journal of Computer Information Systems, 59*(4), 344–353.
31 Cohen, L. E., & Felson, M. (1979). Social change and crime rate trends: A routine activity approach. *American Sociological Review*, 44, 588–608.
32 Leukfeldt, E. R., & Yar, M. (2016). Applying routine activity theory to cybercrime: A theoretical and empirical analysis. *Deviant Behavior, 37*(3), 263–280.
33 Hancock, J. T., & Bailenson, J. N. (2021). The social impact of deepfakes. *Cyberpsychology, Behavior, and Social Networking, 24*(3), 149–152.
34 Balcombe, L. (2025). The mental health impacts of internet scams. *International Journal of Environmental Research and Public Health, 22*(6), 938.

2 Foundations of Cyberpsychology and Cybercrime

Evolution of Cyberpsychology

Cyberpsychology, the interdisciplinary approach to exploring the relationship between psychology and technology, reflects the increasing importance of the continuing integration of the physical and virtual worlds.[1] By combining insights from computer science and psychology, cyberpsychology explores the frontier of knowledge related to the most pressing questions of the current era, including the implications of social media on mental health, the efficacy of virtual therapy and AI-powered therapy chatbots, and the definition of identity and self in the virtual world. This book focuses on an even more refined discipline by integrating principles from criminology into the multidisciplinary approach to explore forensic cyberpsychology and present the unified WAVE theory.

The relevance of cyberpsychology continues in an exponential trajectory as more individuals access the internet and new innovations integrate more activity between the physical and virtual worlds. Given the extent to which routine activities are carried out in the digital world (e.g., shopping, banking, working, communicating with friends and family), the ability to understand the psychological underpinnings influencing and resulting from these interactions is now a moral imperative.

Web 1.0 (Digital Self-emergence)

How one defines oneself is an essential component of how one interacts with the world. In the digital world, the concept of self is increasingly important given the ease with which one curates the digital version of self.[2] Evidence indicates that the digital definition of self is often an amalgamation of one's physical definition of self and one's experimentation with the additional aspects of personality, a finding most pronounced in the digital natives comprising Generation Z and Generation Alpha.[3] Digital communities provide areas for experimentation in identity formation, as well as cultivation of complex social interactions surrounding shared interests, regardless of geographical confines. The relationship between digital and physical self also evolved from the proto-identities of the 1970s to the integrated digital identities of the 2020s.

The emergence of the bulletin board systems (BBS) as platforms for online community interactions in the 1970s and 1980s provides the initial evidence of the creation of digital identities, with users using these platforms to connect with others. At this time in its adoption, the pseudo-anonymity of the early internet was prevalent as early adopters were more focused on connection than security. This facilitated the ability to generate digital identities that were essentially separate from one's identity in the physical world. As BBS gave way to multi-user dungeons (MUDs) in the 1980s and 1990s, the ability to generate avatars was observed.[4] MUDs were text-based environments that allowed users to construct personas and roles that would become more pronounced as technology evolved. Given that avatars form a vessel for self-expression within a digital environment, the ability to generate avatars is a key development in the history of digital identity formation with varying levels of specificity offered by different platforms (e.g., social media handles, video game characters). The evidence indicates that individuals engage more with digital environments that provide user control of avatar appearance.[5] Another perspective related to this increased engagement is that the avatars facilitate more nuanced communication in the digital world by enabling users to communicate key information in environments that limit nonverbal communication opportunities. In fact, the evidence indicates that avatars accurately communicate the creator's personality and psychological needs.[6]

MUDs served as the primary cyberpsychology laboratories in the 1990s because they allowed researchers the opportunity to study how individuals build and maintain digital identities in online communities. MUD research provided the groundwork for the formation of cyberpsychology. One of the most impactful early studies related to MUD research was Sherry Turkle's 1995 publication, which established many key concepts of cyberpsychology that are still used in 2025, including decentralization of identity.[7] Findings related to LambdaMOO, a MUD created by Pavel Curtis in 1990, revealed the importance of digital communities as another key source of early support for cyberpsychology.[8] Additionally, the work done by Richard Bartle related to classifying MUD players created a framework to understand psychological motivations for digital actions.[9] One of the most important findings related to the complex psychological relationship between digital and physical identities in the context of communication was provided by John Suler in 2004. Although individuals in physical communications are more likely to hide negative aspects of self to comply with social norms and laws, the pseudo-anonymity of digital environments often results in individuals communicating with less social inhibition, the aptly named online disinhibition effect.[10] In other words, people often feel safer saying things in digital environments that they would not communicate in person due to the lack of restraint provided by a general absence of consequences.[11] Suler's theoretical framework, outlining six key factors for individuals to behave in different ways, was the first evidence of a comprehensive explanation for this differentiation in behavior. The six factors are dissociative anonymity, invisibility, asynchronicity, solipsistic introjection, dissociative imagination, and minimization of status and authority. This effect was presented as operating along the two dimensions of benign and toxic disinhibition, with benign encompassing positive outcomes and toxic manifesting with negative implications. Suler's work generated an understanding of conceptualization of psychological traits and differing manifestations between the digital and physical worlds.

Web 2.0 (Social Connectivity and Algorithms)

Social networking sites launched in the early 2000s transformed the study of cyberpsychology as they obtained mainstream influence and became key areas of focus for researchers in the early 2000s. This included researchers initially studying the relationship between usage patterns and personality traits to identify that one's personality impacted the way in which they navigated social media platforms.[12] As mounting evidence was collected through initial research, psychological well-being in the age of social media became a key focus for researchers. This included the initial evidence indicating that social media had both beneficial and detrimental impacts on the mental health of users.[13] During this time period, social comparison theory also rose to renewed relevance with several studies exploring the role that the public nature of social media on user mental health and behaviors. The integration of real-name policies on social media platforms additionally pushed society away from pseudonymous, separate digital identities to a more blurred reality with a more integrated digital and physical identity.

The popularization of mobile phones and electronic mail represented a seismic shift in the functioning of society as the idea of constant connectivity came into the ether. Prior cyberpsychological research focused on discrete interactions for finite periods, a model that was no longer relevant in the nearly fully integrated society that began in the late 2010s. Algorithmic personalization fostered content consumption patterns where users are primarily exposed to information that aligns with established preferences and confirms existing beliefs.[14] Content similarity is prioritized over information diversity and altering perspectives fostering a cognitively rigid environment that stifles critical thinking skills.

This constant connectivity created what WAVE theory identifies as psychological conditions where individuals remain perpetually susceptible to manipulation because their cognitive defenses never have time to reset (i.e., continuous vulnerability states). The always-on nature of modern digital life means the adversary may maintain persistent psychological pressure, adapting their approaches in real-time based on user responses. This impact is not limited only to individuals. The concepts of group polarization and social identity also increasingly gained popularity as areas of cyberpsychological research in the late 2010s and early 2020s, as algorithmically based content consumption generated more complex social identities and individual perceptions of the concept of self as a member of a group. Through diminishing exposure to out-group perspectives, the perspectives of in-groups are often amplified. As a result, evidence indicates that established feedback loops with algorithmic amplification may lead to hyper-radicalization.[15] Evidence further indicates that individuals in these environments also engage in strategic positioning (i.e., performative identity behaviors that relegate authentic self-expression to a lower position behind social desirability maximization).[16]

Immersive Reality and the Singularity

Virtual reality, augmented reality, and human-computer integration represent another tectonic shift in the understanding of cyberpsychology due to the ability to influence sensory experiences and further muddying the distinction between the digital and physical worlds. The early 2020s' reality of digital environments is that the technology is capable of producing responses to stimuli that are nearly indistinguishable from physiological responses in subjects as stimuli produced in the physical world. In fact, virtual reality simulations activate the same cognitive and emotional pathways as real-world stimuli.[17] Researchers found that the brain processes information in virtual reality experiences in a similar way to information processed from the physical world and mimics anticipated responses to virtual stimuli.[18]

Leveraging theoretical frameworks, such as embodied simulation, cyberpsychologists are well-positioned to understand the rationale behind this mimicry. By maintaining ongoing, predictive simulations of the ways in which bodies interact with the physical environment, the basic cognitive processes of one's brain are primed for hijacking by virtual reality simulations. This neurological compatibility is further supported by evidence indicating the efficacy of virtual reality treatments for neurological and cognitive conditions (e.g., PTSD, anxiety, phobias).[19] The integration of virtual reality into mental health treatments illustrates the practicality of technological innovation as a tool for enhancing human life, with evidence indicating virtual reality-based exposure therapy produced comparable outcomes to in-vivo exposure while simultaneously providing enhanced safety.[20]

Cybercrime and Cognition

The two buckets that combine to create the comprehensive area of cybercrime include technology-dependent offenses and technology-enabled offenses.[21] Human psychology is a key component of this vast and dynamic threat landscape. Given that the adversary weaponizes the cognitive processes of targets, technical safeguards must be enhanced through psychological considerations.[22] WAVE fundamentally reframes this landscape by revealing that the distinction between technology-dependent and technology-enabled crimes is obsolete in the age of synchronized psychological orchestration. Modern cybercrime succeeds because the adversary creates cognitive states where protective mechanisms cannot function regardless of technical applications.

Cybercrime Fundamentals

Cybercrime is a comprehensive term encompassing a diverse array of illicit activities exploiting information and communication technologies. While legal definitions vary based on the applicable jurisdiction, legal definitions of cybercrime generally reference any offense defined by statute that requires a computer, network, or digital device either as the object or means.[23] Colloquially, cybercrime is typically used as an umbrella term to describe any illicit online activity. These range from hacking and identity theft to digital stalking and piracy. Within popular culture, the usage of the term cybercrime is often focused on the execution of activity in the digital world. Understanding cybercrime through a WAVE lens means recognizing that every successful attack involves the synchronized exploitation of interface design, cognitive biases, and social dynamics to create states where rational decision-making becomes impossible.

In the United States, the Computer Fraud and Abuse Act (CFAA) was originally enacted in 1986 and later amended to cover a wide array of illicit activities that were facilitated through a computer.[24] The United Kingdom's Computer Misuse Act of 1990 criminalized both the activity as well as the creation of tools for exploitation.[25] The Budapest Convention in 2001 was the first binding treaty attempting to harmonize cybercrime legislation across signatory states.[26] The Budapest Convention importantly categorized specific offenses into computer-specific crimes (e.g., hacking, malware), computer-related crimes (e.g., fraud, forgery), content-related offenses (e.g., internet crimes against children), and copyright infringement. The European Union's Directive on attacks against information systems continues to further refine definitions to address emerging threats.[27]

Given the juxtaposition between the speed at which technological innovations occur and the speed at which laws and regulations are enacted to govern those technologies, a wide spectrum of digital behaviors occupies what is often considered a gray zone that blurs the legality and deviance of actions. Cyber-deviance is a term to encompass behaviors in digital environments that violate social or organizational norms without always breaching formal laws or regulations.[28] An often cited example of a cyber-deviant act is online trolling that does not violate applicable laws. A common example of a gray-zone cyber act is state-sponsored disinformation campaigns that do not violate applicable laws and do not rise to the level of overt warfare. The exploitation of jurisdictional ambiguities is often a key component of gray-zone acts. The recognition of cyber-deviance and gray-zone acts is a key component of developing nuanced policies with clear violations.

Taxonomy of Offenses

In this book, cyber offenses are classified according to the role of technology in the commission of a crime. This creates a distinction between technology-dependent crimes and technology-enabled crimes.[29]

Technology-Dependent Cybercrimes

As the name implies, technology-dependent cybercrimes are offenses where the adversary is dependent on technology to perpetrate the crime. This may include directly targeting information and communications technology infrastructure or using it as a tool to facilitate the crime.[30] In contrast to technology-enabled cybercrimes, these offenses focus on technical applications (e.g., distributed denial-of-service (DDoS) attacks, malware, and the exploitation of system vulnerabilities).

Executing a DDoS attack is relatively straightforward, yet still destructive. The adversary overwhelms the endpoints of a target with a flood of fraudulent traffic, which makes the services inaccessible to legitimate users. By leveraging botnets (i.e., thousands of compromised devices used to generate fraudulent traffic), the adversary may inflict significant damage to targets at a previously unprecedented scale.[31] Even seemingly technical attacks (e.g., DDoS attacks) demonstrate WAVE principles, such as the timing of these attacks to create maximum psychological impact by launching them during critical business periods or in coordination with social engineering campaigns that exploit the chaos and urgency created by system outages.

Malware, which is the compound word for malicious software, is a comprehensive term referencing a wide variety of programs designed to infiltrate, damage, or control a target's system, such as ransomware, viruses and worms, Trojan horses, and spyware. These subsets are known as variants, and each variant is designed to accomplish a different objective of the adversary.

Encrypting a target's files and demanding payment in exchange for the subsequent decryption of them is known as ransomware. Viruses and worms represent digital parasites spreading autonomously across networks to deplete resources and destroy data. Named after the popular story of the gift horse housing enemy soldiers to obtain access to the city of Troy's impenetrable walls, Trojan horses are deceptive programs that initially appear legitimate, only to provide the adversary with unauthorized access through a hidden back door. Beyond controlling or destroying a target's data or devices, the adversary may decide to covertly gather sensitive data by deploying malware classified as spyware.

One of the most dangerous categories of technology-dependent crimes involves the exploitation of system vulnerabilities, which allows the adversary to circumvent security controls without human interaction. By allowing the adversary to seize control of resources, execute code, or escalate privileges, these attacks typically lead to prolonged data breaches with massive data exfiltration. A subset of this activity involves the exploitation of previously unknown exploits, known as zero-day exploits or zero-days. These are called zero-days because they are exploited in the wild, and targets have no time (i.e., zero-days) to fix the issue before exploitation.

Technology-Enabled Crimes

Technology-enabled crimes adapt traditional illicit behaviors to digital environments, leveraging digital capabilities to enhance scope, persistence, and psychological impact beyond what physical-world equivalents could achieve. These crimes exist in the physical world but gain new dimensions through digital amplification.

Romance scams represent sophisticated adaptations of confidence schemes that exploit digital communication capabilities to sustain long-term psychological manipulation.[32] In the context of fraud schemes, the adversary uses intermittent reinforcement through expressing affection or promising future financial incentives to foster an emotional and financial investment from the target that is reinforced through repeated compliance.[33] Given the pattern of behavior incorporates the concept of variable-ratio schedules, targets are often resistant to ceasing engagement as a result, at least in part, of past positive payoffs. Romance scams exemplify WAVE's three core principles: they create resonance by simultaneously targeting emotional attachment, financial hope, and social isolation; they adapt continuously based on target responses, evolving the relationship in real-time; and they orchestrate environmental conditions (private messaging, photo sharing, future planning) that make the manipulation feel like authentic relationship development rather than exploitation.

By impersonating trusted authorities and exploiting workplace hierarchies, business email compromise (BEC) attacks use organizational psychology against targets. Successful BEC attacks exploit psychological factors, including authority deference, time pressure, and routine workflow assumptions rather than technical vulnerabilities.[34]

Traditional forms of interpersonal aggression (i.e., bullying and harassment) are transformed in the digital world into a more psychologically destructive form due to the unique features of digital communications. Through digital persistence, audience amplification, and constant access to targets, cyberbullying and digital harassment represent amplified forms of aggression without temporal boundaries.[35] These behaviors demonstrate how digital environments can transform isolated incidents into sustained psychological campaigns with devastating consequences.[36]

Cybercrime statistics are often underreported, which obscures the ability to ascertain the true impact of the issue. Evidence indicates that approximately half of the cyber incidents that occur are reported.[37] This tendency to underreport is not strictly limited to individual targets, with organizations also found to significantly underreport occurrences.[38] Given the disparity between complaint-based metrics, surveys, and threat intelligence data, researchers often attempt to aggregate data across sources, which is known as data combination, to cross-validate estimates and analysis. This underscores the need for a multidisciplinary approach to researching cyberpsychology as a discipline.

The study of cyberpsychology is a complex area demanding nuanced, ethically informed studies. Robust OpSec is a prerequisite for this area of research. Cyberpsychologists rarely view the world through the ivory tower of academia. Rather, these individuals are operators, which requires specific considerations to maximize results while minimizing risks.

Research Methods in Cyberpsychology

Cyberpsychology is a complex discipline that explores relationships across cognition, behavior, and technology, necessitating a research approach as nuanced as the topic of study. To do this, cyberpsychologists leverage a variety of methodological approaches, such as leveraging quantitative, qualitative, and mixed methods, to study this important area.

Quantitative Research

The deployment of numerical data when examining data is quantitative research. Within the field of cyberpsychology, quantitative research may manifest through online surveys, big-data trace analytics, and field testing. By leveraging web-based platforms to collect self-reported data from participants, researchers are able to adapt traditional research approaches to the digital world with evidence supporting the notion that web-based surveys provide reliable data consistent with paper versions.[39] The automated extraction of the digital footprint (i.e., online activity) of an individual proves to provide sufficient evidence to accurately predict psychological factors such as personality traits and mental health status.[40] When this concept is applied to groups, known as social graphing, the power of community dynamics in the flow of information and content is evident, especially in online groups, regardless of whether those groups engage on the clear web or via darknets. Lab testing in controlled environments facilitates researchers to test hypotheses under prescribed conditions. Field testing allows researchers to capture real-world applications of hypotheses. Field tests in cyberpsychology manifest in a variety of ways, mimicking traditional field testing in the physical world. For example, many e-commerce and social media platforms deploy different versions of a feature to real users to determine which version is more effective in achieving a desired outcome in a process known as A/B testing.[41]

Qualitative Research

To explore the variety of ways in which individuals interpret experiences, researchers leverage contextual data that digs beyond quantifiable statistics, including participant interviews or observing and analyzing participants, including using netnography and discourse/conversation analysis. Researchers lurking within a community to obtain an immersive, first-hand understanding of the community is known as ethnography. When this concept is adapted to the digital world, this is known as virtual ethnography or netnography.[42] Netnography may include researchers obtaining access to forums on darknets to observe the patterns, customs, jargon, and rules of members of the community. The examination of the use of language in identity construction and interaction patterns refers to discourse analysis, including legitimizing behaviors through framing reality in a specific way or using language to psychologically distance oneself from the impact of one's action.[43] Conversation analysis is an even more focused application of this idea to review at the micro level through explicitly reviewing dynamics in interactions at a granular level, such as building credibility through providing time-stamped messages indicating the verification of transaction.

Mixed Methods in Research

Researchers may leverage both quantitative and qualitative methodologies in research to create mixed methods studies, which are a useful tool in cross-validating hypotheses and findings.[44] For example, researchers may survey participants to identify key quantifiable metrics to understand the extent of an issue. By also interviewing participants, researchers are positioned to uncover underlying psychological motivations driving that occurrence. Although it is more resource-intensive than engaging in a binary approach, mixed methods studies provide researchers with the ability to understand what may be occurring and why it is doing so.

Ethical Considerations and Mitigation Tactics

Obtaining informed consent from participants, protecting the privacy of those participants, and ensuring the safety of researchers are unique challenges presented to researchers conducting studies in the digital world.[45] Cyberpsychologists deploy a variety of practical mitigation strategies to minimize the risks posed by studies while simultaneously maximizing the potential benefits of the research.

Obtaining informed consent is a requirement for ethical research. This important step may be especially difficult when examining topics and individuals relying on pseudonymity (e.g., adversary communication patterns in darknet forums).[46] Transparent communication concerning the purpose of a study, usage of collected data, and withdrawal rights of participants is an ethical requirement that is increasingly complex in forensic cyberpsychology research. Data collection and processing present their own unique challenges to research, especially in the context of privacy regulations (e.g., the General Data Protection Regulation (GDPR) in the European Union and the California Consumer Privacy Act (CCPA) in the state of California in the United States). Beyond the legality of data collection, researchers are ethically bound to collect only the required data, known as data minimization, and ensure that even seemingly innocuous data is protected from facilitating the de-anonymization of participants. Studying illicit activity often leads to researchers experiencing concerns related to safety, as well as handling illicit content if encountered. The potential academic value of any study must be weighed against the potential consequences, including amplifying harmful content or complicity in illicit activity. Cyberpsychologists must ensure that the risks associated with a study are proportional to the value of the study while strictly adhering to applicable moral guidelines.

Researchers may offer dynamic consent options when obtaining informed consent to allow individuals to provide initial consent and withdraw their consent at different stages throughout the study if desired.[47] In addition to dynamically obtaining informed consent, researchers extend the principle of data minimization to include stripping indirect identifiers (e.g., usernames, timestamps, crypto wallet addresses) where possible. Ethical researchers also generally encrypt collected data, store that data offline, and define data destruction protocols. To maximize safety for involved parties, researchers typically deploy a variety of strategies. For participant safety, researchers may paraphrase participants to decrease likelihood of identification and delay publication of time-sensitive materials. In terms of operational security (OpSec), researchers leverage a variety of technologies and tactics. Identity obfuscating technologies, such as sandboxes, VPNs, and Tor, provide identity-related OpSec. Consulting outside counsel, maintaining a clear chain of custody, and documenting events via detailed field notes are additional ways to procedurally enhance OpSec. In terms of psychological OpSec, researchers may cap daily screen time with disturbing materials, mandate clinical debriefings, and rotate activities with other researchers if possible.

Conclusion

The journey from BBSs to synchronized psychological orchestration reveals a fundamental truth: while technology has evolved exponentially, human psychology remains remarkably constant. What has changed is how the adversary exploits this consistency, leading to the emergence of WAVE from this historical foundation as an operational necessity. The online disinhibition effect that Suler identified as an interesting behavioral curiosity has become the psychological foundation for trillion-dollar cybercrime enterprises. Every major cybersecurity incident now demonstrates WAVE's three core principles: resonance over isolation, adaptation over static targeting, and environmental orchestration over direct manipulation. From romance scams that exploit variable-ratio reinforcement schedules to BEC attacks that weaponize organizational psychology, modern cybercrime succeeds through psychological precision.

Chapter 3 examines the anatomy of cybercrime. We will explore how modern illicit organizations function as psychological engineering firms, complete with research and development divisions that test manipulation techniques, quality assurance processes that refine psychological targeting, and scalable delivery systems that automate synchronized attacks. It explores how WAVE principles manifest in real adversary operations: how ransomware groups use precisely timed communication strategies to maintain psychological pressure; how BEC networks create elaborate social proof systems to establish credibility; how romance scam organizations develop psychological profiles that enable mass customization of emotional manipulation. By understanding the anatomy of these operations through the lens of WAVE, we can move beyond reactive technical defenses toward predictive psychological protection.

Reflection Questions

1 How does online identity shift across platforms?
2 Which psychological theory best explains a recent cyber incident?
3 In what ways does the online disinhibition effect influence both benign and toxic digital behaviors?
4 How does the evolution from Web 1.0 pseudonymity to Web 2.0 real-name policies shape the vulnerabilities that adversaries can exploit using WAVE principles?

Skill Builder Labs

Application Scenario: Conduct a Digital Identity Vulnerability Assessment

Analyze the evolution of digital identity across platforms to identify potential exploitation vectors. Take the following steps:

- Map a target persona's digital footprint across at least three platform types (social media, professional networking, and gaming/forums).
- Document identity consistency and inconsistencies between platforms using Suler's six disinhibition factors.
- Identify potential WAVE exploitation points where psychological vulnerabilities intersect with platform design features.
- Develop a risk assessment that prioritizes the most exploitable identity elements.
- Create countermeasures that address both technical and psychological protection mechanisms.

Mini Research Activity: WAVE Analysis in Cybercrime Cases

Objective

Apply WAVE theory's three core principles (resonance, adaptation, orchestration) to analyze a real cybercrime incident and develop psychological intervention strategies.

Instructions

1 Select and map a recent cybercrime incident.
2 Apply cyberpsychology research methodology.
3 Conduct WAVE principle mapping.
4 Develop intervention framework.

Deliverable

Create a case study demonstrating the application of WAVE principles and actionable recommendations for psychological defense strategies.

References

1. Attrill-Smith, A., Fullwood, C., Keep, M., & Kuss, D. J. (Eds.). (2019). *The Oxford handbook of cyberpsychology*. Oxford University Press.
2. Ruan, B., Yilmaz, Y., Lu, D., Lee, M., & Chan, T. M. (2020). Defining the digital self: A qualitative study to explore the digital component of professional identity in the health professions. *Journal of Medical Internet Research, 22*(9), e21416.
3. Avci, H., Baams, L., & Kretschmer, T. (2024). A systematic review of social media use and adolescent identity development. *Adolescent Research Review,* 10, 1–18.
4. Bartle, R.A. (2009). From MUDs to MMORPGs: The History of Virtual Worlds. In: Hunsinger, J., Klastrup, L., Allen, M. (eds) *International Handbook of Internet Research*. Springer, Dordrecht.
5. Zhang, R., & Wu, Q. (2024). Impact of using virtual avatars in educational videos on user experience. *Scientific Reports, 14*(1), 6592.
6. Kang, H., & Kim, H. K. (2020). My avatar and the affirmed self: Psychological and persuasive implications of avatar customization. *Computers in Human Behavior, 112*, 106446.
7. Turkle, S. (2011). *Life on the screen*. Simon and Schuster.
8. Curtis, P. (2014). Mudding: Social phenomena in text-based virtual realities. In *Culture of the Internet* (pp. 121–142). Psychology Press.

9. Bartle, R. (1996). Hearts, clubs, diamonds, spades: Players who suit MUDs. *Journal of MUD Research*, 1(1). https://www.researchgate.net/profile/Richard-Bartle/publication/247190693_Hearts_clubs_diamonds_spades_Players_who_suit_MUDs/links/540058700cf2194bc29ac4f2/Hearts-clubs-diamonds-spades-Players-who-suit-MUDs.pdf
10. Suler, J. (2004). The online disinhibition effect. *Cyberpsychology & Behavior*, 7(3), 321–326.
11. Syrjämäki, A. H., Ilves, M., Olsson, T., Kiskola, J., Isokoski, P., Rantasila, A., ... & Surakka, V. (2024). Online disinhibition mediates the relationship between emotion regulation difficulties and uncivil communication. *Scientific Reports*, 14(1), 30019.
12. Gosling, S. D., Augustine, A. A., Vazire, S., Holtzman, N., & Gaddis, S. (2011). Manifestations of personality in online social networks: Self-reported Facebook-related behaviors and observable profile information. *Cyberpsychology, Behavior, and Social Networking*, 14(9), 483–488.
13. Primack, B. A., Shensa, A., Sidani, J. E., Whaite, E. O., yi Lin, L., Rosen, D., ... & Miller, E. (2017). Social media use and perceived social isolation among young adults in the US. *American Journal of Preventive Medicine*, 53(1), 1–8.
14. Kaluža, J. (2022). Habitual generation of filter bubbles: Why is algorithmic personalisation problematic for the democratic public sphere? *Journal of the European Institute for Communication and Culture*, 29(3), 267–283.
15. Celis, L. E., Kapoor, S., Salehi, F., & Vishnoi, N. (2019). Controlling polarization in personalization: An algorithmic framework. In *Proceedings of the Conference on Fairness, Accountability, and Transparency* Association for Computing Machinery, New York, NY, USA, 160–169.
16. O'Reilly, C., Mannion, S., Maher, P. J., Smith, E. M., MacCarron, P., & Quayle, M. (2024). Strategic attitude expressions as identity performance and identity creation in interaction. *Communications Psychology*, 2(1), 27.
17. Schöne, B., Kisker, J., Lange, L., Gruber, T., Sylvester, S., & Osinsky, R. (2023). The reality of virtual reality. *Frontiers in Psychology*, 14, 1093014.
18. Trabanelli, S., Akselrod, M., Fellrath, J., Vanoni, G., Bertoni, T., Serino, S., ... & Serino, A. (2025). Neural anticipation of virtual infection triggers an immune response. *Nature Neuroscience*, 28, 1968–1977.
19. Eshuis, L. V., Van Gelderen, M. J., Van Zuiden, M., Nijdam, M. J., Vermetten, E., Olff, M., & Bakker, A. (2021). Efficacy of immersive PTSD treatments: A systematic review of virtual and augmented reality exposure therapy and a meta-analysis of virtual reality exposure therapy. *Journal of Psychiatric Research*, 143, 516–527.
20. Park, M. J., Kim, D. J., Lee, U., Na, E. J., & Jeon, H. J. (2019). A literature overview of Virtual Reality (VR) in treatment of psychiatric disorders: Recent advances and limitations. *Frontiers in Psychiatry*, 10, 505.
21. Phillips, K., Davidson, J. C., Farr, R. R., Burkhardt, C., Caneppele, S., & Aiken, M. P. (2022). Conceptualizing cybercrime: Definitions, typologies and taxonomies. *Forensic Sciences*, 2(2), 379–398.
22. Abrahams, T. O., Farayola, O. A., Kaggwa, S., Uwaoma, P. U., Hassan, A. O., & Dawodu, S. O. (2024). Cybersecurity awareness and education programs: A review of employee engagement and accountability. *Computer Science & IT Research Journal*, 5(1), 100–119.
23. Berris, P. G. (2020). *Cybercrime and the law: Primer on the computer fraud and abuse act and related statutes*. Congressional Research Service.
24. U.S. House of Representatives. (1983). *Counterfeit access device and computer fraud and abuse act of 1983: Hearing before the Subcommittee on Crime*. U.S. Government Printing Office.

25 Crown Prosecution Service. (1990). *Computer Misuse Act 1990*. HMSO.
26 Council of Europe. (2001). *Convention on Cybercrime* (ETS No. 185). Council of Europe Treaty Office.
27 European Union. (2013). *Directive 2013/40/EU on attacks against information systems*. Official Journal of the European Union.
28 Cioban, S., Lazăr, A. R., Bacter, C., & Hatos, A. (2021). Adolescent deviance and cyber-deviance. A systematic literature review. *Frontiers in Psychology, 12*, 748006.
29 McGuire, M., & Dowling, S. (2013). Cyber crime: A review of the evidence. *Summary of Key Findings and Implications. Home Office Research Report, 75*, 1–35.
30 The Crown Prosecution Service. *Cybercrime prosecution guidance*. https://www.cps.gov.uk/legal-guidance/cybercrime-prosecution-guidance
31 Kolias, C., Kambourakis, G., Stavrou, A., & Voas, J. (2017). DDoS in the IoT: Mirai and other botnets. *Computer, 50*(7), 80–84.
32 Rege, A. (2009). What's love got to do with it? Exploring online dating scams and identity fraud. *International Journal of Cyber Criminology, 3*(2), 494–512.
33 Cross, C. (2015). No laughing matter: Blaming the victim of online fraud. *International Review of Victimology, 21*(2), 187–204.
34 Agazzi, A. E. (2020). Business email compromise (BEC) and cyberpsychology. *arXiv preprint arXiv:2007.02415*.
35 Nixon, C. L. (2014). Current perspectives: The impact of cyberbullying on adolescent health. *Adolescent Health, Medicine and Therapeutics, 5*, 143–158.
36 Al-Turif, G. A., & Al-Sanad, H. A. (2023). The repercussions of digital bullying on social media users. *Frontiers in Psychology, 14*, 1280757.
37 Sangari, S., & Dallal, E. (2022). Correcting for reporting delays in cyber incidents. *arXiv preprint arXiv:2201.10348*.
38 Amir, E., Levi, S., & Livne, T. (2018). Do firms underreport information on cyber-attacks? Evidence from capital markets. *Review of Accounting Studies, 23*(3), 1177–1206.
39 Gosling, S. D., Vazire, S., Srivastava, S., & John, O. P. (2004). Should we trust web-based studies? A comparative analysis of six preconceptions about internet questionnaires. *American Psychologist, 59*(2), 93.
40 Kosinski, M., Stillwell, D., & Graepel, T. (2013). Private traits and attributes are predictable from digital records of human behavior. *Proceedings of the National Academy of Sciences, 110*(15), 5802–5805.
41 Kohavi, R. & Thomke, S. (2017). The surprising power of online experiments: Getting the most out of A/B and other controlled tests. *Harvard Business Review, 95*(5), 74–82.
42 Kozinets, R. V. (2020). Netnography today: A call to evolve, embrace, energize, and electrify. In Robert V. Kozinets, Rossella Gambetti *Netnography unlimited* (pp. 3–23). Routledge.
43 Fairclough, N. (2013). *Critical discourse analysis: The critical study of language*. Routledge.
44 Creswell, J. W., & Clark, V. L. P. (2017). *Designing and conducting mixed methods research*. Sage publications.
45 Sugiura, L., Wiles, R., & Pope, C. (2017). Ethical challenges in online research: Public/private perceptions. *Research Ethics, 13*(3–4), 184–199.
46 Thomas, D. R., Pastrana, S., Hutchings, A., Clayton, R., & Beresford, A. R. (2017, November). Ethical issues in research using datasets of illicit origin. In *Proceedings of the 2017 internet measurement conference* Association for Computing Machinery, New York, NY, USA, pp. 445–462.
47 Teare, H. J., Prictor, M., & Kaye, J. (2021). Reflections on dynamic consent in biomedical research: The story so far. *European Journal of Human Genetics, 29*(4), 649–656.

3 Anatomy of Cybercrime

Time to Double Click

The digital world fosters a cybercrime ecosystem full of intricacies facilitated by complex psychological, technical, and social architectures. Unbound by geographical and temporal limitations, cybercrime transcends boundaries limiting crime in the physical world. This transcendence exemplifies one of the foundational concepts of WAVE theory: synchronized orchestration makes harmful actions feel rational. In the digital world, physical boundaries do not exist, anonymity may be manufactured, and targets may be exploited in a matter of seconds across the globe. For example, the adversary may now simultaneously identify targets through automated reconnaissance rather than physical surveillance. This transformation extends beyond simple reach because digital interfaces facilitate psychological distance between the adversary and their target, which reduces the perceived impact and severity of one's actions on the target. This fundamental shift in the crime equation demands a deeper investigation. One must examine the relationship between psychological motivations and digital actions to obtain a comprehensive understanding of cybercrime. The recognition that the anatomy of cybercrime is dynamic must also be made. Cybercrime constantly evolves with technological innovations and societal shifts. Chapter 3 dissects cybercrime's anatomy by examining the classification of cybercrime operations, the technical infrastructure that facilitates the actions, and the human aspects that drive the activities. This analysis provides essential components explored in subsequent chapters.

Classifying Cybercrime

Cybercrime is a broad term encompassing a wide spectrum of illicit activities, including technology-dependent crimes and technology-enabled crimes. The classification of specific operations uncovers underlying patterns in the adaptation of adversary psychology between distinct offenses. The relationship between crime and technology is the cornerstone of cybercrime classification, with distinct psychological and operational profiles belonging to each adaptation.

Technology-Dependent Cybercrime

Technology-dependent cybercrimes are offenses that require technology to be perpetrated (e.g., DDoS, ransomware, and data-wipe attacks). This subset of cybercrime represents the clearest form of forensic cyberpsychology applications, as the illicit act may not exist in the absence of the digital world. DDoS attacks provide an example of technology-dependent crimes that transform the traditional concept of coercion through violence into the digital world. The perpetrators of DDoS attacks often reflect an inclination for immediate impact, similar to perpetrators of vandalism in the physical world. This offense grants the adversary immediate gratification through observation of the chaos inflicted on the target.

The use of botnets, compromised devices belonging to others used by the adversary to generate fake traffic, to orchestrate complex DDoS attacks, reveals a sophisticated understanding of network effects and multiplicative impact. Perpetrators of this form of attack demonstrate an appreciation for exploiting resources beyond one's immediate reach in the furtherance of one's own goals. In 2016, the adversary generated a substantial attack against Dyn, a domain name system (DNS) provider, that disrupted many of the most popular websites across the internet by using the Mirai botnet to flood targets with traffic volumes exceeding 1 terabit per second.[1] DDoS attacks create a complex psychological impact by fostering a sense of uncertainty and helplessness in both the direct target of the attacks, as well as the users of the target's services and demonstrate WAVE's environmental orchestration principle. The adversary creates chaos that serves as psychological cover for secondary attacks. While IT teams scramble to restore services, social engineering campaigns may exploit the urgency and confusion. The technical disruption becomes a psychological weapon, amplifying the effectiveness of human-targeted attacks launched simultaneously.

Ransomware is a digital manifestation of extortion tactics observed in the physical world and represents a nuanced application of technological and psychological manipulations. Motivational complexities of ransomware operations extend far beyond financial gain, often incorporating a desire for power and control. Take, for example, the nature of this type of attack. The adversary weaponizes the target's own data against it. An effort that fosters a sense of helplessness in targets echoes psychological dynamics observed in traditional hostage situations. One key example of the scale and potential impact of ransomware operations is the WannaCry ransomware operation, which in 2017, infected over 300,000 computers across 150 countries and created a sense of urgency in targets by incorporating countdown timers.[2] This operation achieved widespread impact as a result of the deployment of these psychological tactics, such as pressuring targets into hastened decision-making by applying arbitrary time limits.[3] Ransomware operators in the early 2020s (e.g., Conti, Darkside) demonstrated a sophisticated understanding of target psychology through complex manipulation strategies designed to exploit cognitive processes in targets (e.g., personalized negotiations, proof-of-life demonstrations).[4]

One of the most psychologically extreme forms of technology-dependent cybercrime occurs when the adversary aims to destroy a target's data in what is known as a data-wipe attack. These attacks illustrate the prioritization of inflicting maximum harm on a target over self-interest, which indicates the adversary may be driven by ideological or personal means. Perpetrators of data-wipe attacks aim to inflict irreversible harm and permanent damage to a target, reflecting a deeper psychological pathology than is evidenced in ransomware attacks. NotPetya was an infamous data-wipe attack initially disguised as ransomware providing targets false hope for recovery through demand for payment, only to permanently destroy a target's data, regardless of payment outcome.[5,6]

Technology-Enabled Cybercrime

When traditional illicit behaviors are adapted to the digital world, the reach, persistence, and impact of these crimes are amplified to an extent rarely observed in the physical world. These types of offenses are classified as technology-enabled cybercrimes, such as digital fraud, cyberbullying and digital harassment, and sextortion. WAVE reveals why technology-enabled crimes often prove more psychologically devastating than their technology-dependent counterparts. These attacks succeed by weaponizing trust mechanisms that evolved for face-to-face interaction against digital environments designed to exploit them. Digital fraud involves the adversary leveraging traditional deception techniques in the digital world to generate an impact that exceeds what is possible in the physical world. This is often facilitated through online means of communication (e.g., social media platforms) to improve the speed and scale of the scheme. The speed at which digital fraud may occur is exemplified by considering the Twitter Hack of 2020, where the adversary compromised the verified accounts of several prominent individuals to solicit cryptocurrency payments and absconded with over $100,000 USD within a few hours.[7]

Romance scams are a sophisticated variation of traditional confidence scams, exploiting digital communication to facilitate long-term psychological manipulation of a target in a variation of digital fraud. The adversary exploits a digital relationship with the target for financial gain. The evidence indicates that the average survivor in 2022 lost $4,400 to a romance scam, illustrating that the digital world is structured in a way that enables the exploitation of targets using cultivated personas to obtain emotional investments from the target, and gradually building this investment to become financial in nature to bleed the target dry.[8] This may occur over a period of months or years, further highlighting the impact of these schemes on targets. The visceral term for long-term psychological manipulation by the adversary through a scheme combining romance scam tactics with investment fraud concepts is pig butchering scams. While the name for this scam is debated in various circles for many reasons, such as the connotation for targets and the name being the one created by the adversary, the graphic nature of the name is important to underscore the impact of the scam on targets and survivors, and that is why it will be used in this book. When perpetrating a pig butchering scam, the adversary builds long-term relationships with targets that eventually lead to the investment of a target's funds into websites controlled by the adversary.[9] The websites often appear as cryptocurrency platforms where targets set up accounts that they believe the invested funds remain within their control. In actuality, the money is sent by the target to the adversary via a cryptocurrency ATM, and the target is only provided with the illusion of control of the funds within the website. To further the scheme, the adversary generally provides charts and statements to the target indicating significant returns. The target often only recognizes potential issues when they attempt to withdraw funds from the account, which additionally leads to reloading scams where the adversary attempts to drain additional funds from the target. Pig butchering scams represent eminent societal threats with losses exceeding $75 billion USD since 2020.[10] The unfortunate reality of pig butchering scams also includes the indication that the perpetrators of these types of scams are oftentimes survivors themselves. In many cases, individuals often answer fraudulent job ads and are enslaved, trafficked, and forced into labor camps (i.e., scam compounds), often in Southeast Asia (e.g., Cambodia, Myanmar), where these individuals are forced to perpetrate the pig butchering scams under severe physical and psychological threats.[11]

Evidence linking these scam compounds to transnational organized crime groups also underscores the scope of this issue. As these compounds traditionally perpetrated pig butchering scams, reports indicate a shift into sextortion scams.[12] Sextortion scams combine traditional extortion with the digital world to facilitate the rapid manipulation and distribution of intimate images of targets, which often include adolescents. The rise in synthetic content expanded this type of crime beyond the requirement of obtaining compromising content from a target, as adversaries are now able to readily generate fraudulent images of targets, which leads to the susceptibility of anyone in the digital world. The sustained increase in sextortion scams underscores a larger insight. The perpetration of cybercrime involves three rudimentary phases where the adversary chooses a target to eventually compromise as a means to execute an objective. These three phases occur to create the cybercrime attack lifecycle, regardless of whether the offense is technology-dependent or technology-enabled.

Cybercrime Attack Lifecycle

The cybercrime attack lifecycle represents the rudimentary, temporal stages of cybercrime offenses. These steps include target selection, target compromise, and objective execution. Understanding cybercrime through the lens of WAVE reveals that successful attacks synchronize psychological manipulation across all three lifecycle phases.

Target Selection

The selection of a target by a perpetrator begins the act of exploitation, regardless of the sophistication level of the attack. In simplified cybercrime attacks, this may involve simply sending unsolicited text messages to a potential target structured to solicit a response, as is a common initial tactic in pig butchering scams. Extensive intelligence gathering combining a variety of technical practices, such as open-source intelligence (OSINT) harvesting, social media analysis, and vulnerability scanning, serves as the initial stage for more sophisticated cybercrime attacks. OSINT harvesting involves collecting information about a potential target that is publicly available online, often through an employer's website, personal social media accounts, professional digital networking accounts, or data aggregators. For instance, the 2016 hack of the Democratic Congressional Campaign Committee (DCCC) and the Democratic National Committee (DNC) allegedly resulted from complex spear-phishing campaigns uniquely targeting specific individuals based on OSINT harvesting efforts, including analyzing interests, communication patterns, and relationships of the target.[13]

By analyzing the social media accounts of potential targets, the adversary may better inform the personalization of an attack to increase the probability of its success, as evidenced in the case of the hacks of the DCCC and DNC. OSINT harvesting focused specifically on social media intelligence (SOCMINT) may entail the adversary studying a target's posts, connections, and interests to structure complex social engineering campaigns personalized to the individual. Given the extent to which individuals volunteer personal information online in the name of digital connection, it is unsurprising that unprecedented opportunities exist for the adversary to construct nuanced psychological profiles of many potential targets. This includes identifying individuals employed by the organization that the adversary wishes to target, as was the case in the 2020 hack of social media platform Twitter, now known as X.[14] This hack was initiated through social engineering campaigns targeted at individuals identified via professional networking sites.[15]

In addition to targeting individuals, the adversary may identify vulnerabilities to target an organization through a variety of other methods, such as vulnerability scanning, which is the process of probing the digital infrastructure of an organization to identify potential opportunities for exploitation. Vulnerability scanning combines automated tools and manual analysis to uncover exposed endpoints. To further enhance targeting, the adversary may also examine the revenue size, industry, or incident history of the potential target to prioritize opportunities that offer the greatest possible return on investment. After pinpointing the potential target, such as an organization with servers missing a critical security patch in the midst of a publicly announced merger, the adversary pivots efforts to compromise the target in an effort to shift intelligence into impact.

Target Compromise

The compromise phase of cybercrime involves the careful orchestration of the attack by the adversary. This may include exploiting a technological vulnerability or psychological one. Although the initial access technique largely depends on the desired aim of the target, social engineering remains one of the most common attack vectors, with reports indicating that incidents involving social engineering vary between over half to nearly all incidents originating from social engineering campaigns.[16–18] By leveraging curated intelligence about the target cultivated during the target selection phase, the adversary crafts messages that bypass technical filtering mechanisms while also circumventing cognitive response patterns through personalization, timing, authority, and urgency. In the context of technology-dependent crimes, the adversary may leverage credential harvesting tactics (e.g., fake login pages impersonating legitimate authentication portals) to entice targets to provide their credentials to the adversary through domain spoofing and design mimicry. Once inside a compromised account, the adversary may aim to obtain escalated privileges to allow for more impact. For example, the adversary may target help-desk personnel and executives in social engineering campaigns after researching organizational procedures to elevate system access. This route is often less involved than attempting to technically escalate a user's privileges. Observing communication patterns and organizational relationships after initially obtaining access to an account allows the adversary to time a potential attack to inflict maximum damage. On an individual level, for example, the adversary may dwell within a compromised account until the right moment to execute a well-timed attack. This could include monitoring email traffic for closing-day emails from a title company to replace legitimate wire instructions with fraudulent instructions when it is clear the target is purchasing a home. Once the adversary's tactics shift from breaking in to cashing out, the offense reaches the objective execution phase.

Objective Execution

As the adversary moves to accomplish the objective of the attack, the next steps vary greatly depending on the type of offense and the goal of the adversary (e.g., financially motivated, ideologically motivated). The adversary may attempt to exfiltrate valuable data from targets to resell data in darknet marketplaces, as confidential data are often worth something to the adversary when sold in these illicit forums. The Equifax breach in 2017 is an example of the adversary exploiting significant dwell time to maximize impact of an attack. The adversary maintained access for several months and exfiltrated the personal information of over 147 million individuals.[19] Once illicit funds are acquired, the adversary may commit follow-on offenses (e.g., money laundering). To conceal ill-gotten gains in crimes involving cryptocurrency, the adversary may conceal the original source of the funds using services like cryptocurrency mixers or peer-to-peer exchanges. For instance, the Lazarus Group, a moniker used to track several subgroups linked to the Democratic People's Republic of Korea (DPRK)(i.e., North Korea), used sophisticated money laundering tactics to move over $620 million in stolen cryptocurrency across multiple mixing services and several cryptocurrency exchanges.[20,21] As reports indicate, illicit funds from the Lazarus Group were later used to fund the DPRK's nuclear missile program.[22] Although a substantial simplification of the cybercrime attack lifecycle, the cybercrime attack lifecycle provides a framework for understanding the nature of cybercrime incidents as a key first step in building out the integrative approach of WAVE theory. To enhance understanding, one must consider the actors and roles that comprise the complex world of cybercrime, given that the psychological factors influencing involvement differ across participant roles.

Human Components of the Cybercrime Ecosystem

The dynamics of manipulation in cybercrime may only be fully understood when analyzed as parts of a singular mechanism rather than in isolation, which is the traditional approach to reviewing cybercrime. Although participants in the cybercrime ecosystem assume specific roles in incidents with different psychological factors incorporated into their actions based on the assumed role and the extent to which the role was assumed (e.g., involuntarily, voluntarily), an important principle in the unifying nature of WAVE theory is that all roles (e.g., the adversary, defenders, targets) within the cybercrime ecosystem are interconnected through the same underlying affective vulnerabilities. By framing actors as interdependent nodes within a broader architecture, WAVE theory provides an approach to integrating insights from across disparate fields into a solitary lens.

The Adversary

In the context of cybercrime, the adversary may act as a front-line executor (e.g., technical architect, operator, affiliate) or back-end facilitator (e.g., money mule, infrastructure provider). Technical architects develop malware, exploit kits, and other tools enabling attacks. Although generative artificial intelligence (GenAI) reduces the need for advanced coding skills, the adversary still often exhibits thrill-seeking tendencies, as well as the desire to establish status (i.e., satisfy the need to belong). Cybercrime-as-a-service (CaaS), a model where the adversary resells goods (e.g., ransomware, exploit kits) to other individuals who are often less technically sophisticated, provides a mechanism for further psychological distancing by the adversary, even beyond what is already available in the digital world. This democratization of cybercrime highlights complex networks where social recognition and status on darknet forums drive continuous innovation.[23]

The adversary may also take on the role of operator (i.e., managing resources for large-scale cybercrime campaigns). Operators often exhibit a psychological profile with significant leadership ability. For example, internal communications of the Conti ransomware operation, which were leaked in 2022, revealed the use of organizational hierarchies and standard operating procedures.[24] Additionally, affiliates (i.e., the individuals who rely on tools and infrastructure provided by other individuals to execute attacks in exchange for a portion of the profits obtained from the attack) represent the final role of the front-line executor branch of the adversary, as observed in Ransomware-as-a-Service (RaaS) enterprises. By lowering technical barriers and dispersing risk, the CaaS model attracts wider participation, contributing, at least in part, to the surge in cybercrime.

Cybercrime organizations use complex structures to support expansive operations, including participants exploited as part of a scheme (e.g., money mules, technology service providers). Money mules, who are often unwitting participants of money laundering schemes recruited through a variety of deceptive techniques, generally believe they are providing legitimate services in exchange for legitimate funds.[25] By deploying carefully crafted narratives to deceive money mules (e.g., employment fraud schemes, romance scams), the adversary provides a plausible explanation to the target for the financial transactions in which the target participates. Money mule networks, which are typically constructed around the wide-scale exploitation of vulnerable populations (e.g., immigrants, students, individuals who are economically disadvantaged), typically aim to foster confusion in targets about the legality of the actions in which they are taking as a means to further complicate the distinguishment from law enforcement between willing and unwitting participation in the illicit activities.[26] Technology service providers (e.g., VPN providers, domain registrars, hosting providers) represent another key component of the cybercrime ecosystem's back-end. Hosting providers, for instance, may support phishing sites while maintaining psychological distance in the form of plausible deniability (e.g., complex terms of service agreements and liability shields shifting responsibility onto customers).[27] Since many hosting providers operate in jurisdictions with limited oversight, holding them often proves difficult. Mixing services (i.e., programs used to obfuscate the source of funds on the blockchain) illustrate another variation of back-end facilitators. Tornado Cash, which processed over $7 billion in cryptocurrency transactions in 2022, provides a prominent example, as much of the total was linked to ransomware and other illicit activities.[28]

Defenders

Defenders in the cybercrime ecosystem (e.g., practitioners, researchers, regulators, law enforcement agencies (LEAs)) work to prevent, detect, mitigate, and punish cybercrime. Importantly, these roles often carry psychological challenges (e.g., hypervigilance, burnout, decision fatigue) as a result of consistent threat exposure.[29] Defenders also face unique dynamics when attempting to overcome threats, such as the juxtaposition between the need for information sharing across organizations to facilitate collective defense versus the pursuit of competitive advantage.[30] Influencers (e.g., insurers, regulators) represent a subset of defenders who indirectly shape the cybercrime ecosystem. By tying coverage to security posture, insurers influence organizational cost-benefit calculations and incentivize cybersecurity investments, which also introduced new dynamics (e.g., adversary exploitation of coverage patterns).[31,32] Regulators also influence cybercrime by enacting compliance requirements and taking enforcement actions that raise baseline security standards across industries. Balancing the often competing interests of multiple stakeholders while adapting conventional policies and procedures to rapidly improving technological capabilities makes the regulator's role challenging, particularly when considered in the global context where conflicting regulations and multiple jurisdictions increase the complexity. LEAs directly impact the cybersecurity threat landscape by investigating and disrupting the adversary's operations. This often entails international coordination on efforts, though jurisdictional boundaries and legal complexities may limit optimization. Ultimately, cybercrime materializes at the intersection of the adversary and defenders in the form of the people and organizations exploited.

Targets

Targets may fall into two broad buckets, individuals or organizations, each comprised of varying profiles and differing vulnerabilities. Individual target vulnerability patterns reflect complex interactions between demographic characteristics, technological competence, and psychological factors to create differential vulnerability across populations. For example, age-related vulnerability patterns demonstrate non-linear relationships where both older adults and younger individuals face elevated risks through different mechanisms. Adults aged 65 years or older experience higher rates of investment, romance, and impersonation scams (e.g., tech support fraud).[33] On the opposite end of the spectrum, individuals aged 20–29 years old reported losing money to fraud (e.g., social media scams, gaming fraud, employment scams) more often than older individuals.[34] Regardless of the age of the target and the type of cybercrime, researchers uncovered proven associations between personality traits and susceptibility. For example, a correlation between confidence in one's abilities using technology and one's vulnerability to online fraud was identified with intermediate users exhibiting higher vulnerability than novices or experts.[35] This essentially amounts to a digital literacy knowledge trough where individuals in the middle prove to exhibit higher susceptibility likely stemming from less guidance and more risk-taking as a result of the confidence. Additional research on personality traits suggests that individuals exhibiting high scores in openness to experience, extraversion, and agreeableness are more susceptible to social engineering campaigns.[36] This is likely attributable to the tendency of these individuals to engage with strangers, disclose personal details, and comply with demands from perceived authority figures. Moreover, financial fragility proves correlated with scam susceptibility across all demographic groups.[37] Given that financial fragility may lower resistance to normally unaccepted risks, the adversary may deliberately target these individuals for cybercrime schemes aimed at exploiting individuals experiencing economic hardship (e.g., employment, investment, advanced-fee, and loan scams). Cybercrime exploiting social cognition (e.g., need for connection) also increases due to social isolation.[38]

While demographic and personality characteristics heighten susceptibility to scams in individuals, organizations face parallel vulnerabilities (e.g., structural weaknesses, decision-making processes). In fact, a disproportionate amount of cybercrime targets small and medium-sized businesses (SMBs) as a result of limited resources to dedicate to cybersecurity despite valuable financial assets and data, often to a detrimental effect with the evidence indicating that 43% of cybercrime attacks target SMBs, and, if successfully exploited by the adversary, 60% of SMBs close within six months of the attack.[39] The value to the adversary also may be a factor of the industry sector in which the business operates.

Healthcare organizations experience frequent targeting, as compared to peers, given the valuable personal health information (PHI) stored within systems, the criticality of incident response (i.e., a ransomware attack on a hospital actually results in life-and-death decisions), and a historical lack of technology investments across the industry.[40] Open network architectures designed to facilitate collaboration across academia pose a unique threat to educational institutions. Given that these risks are often compounded by tight security budgets and a population largely dependent on students who may lack proper incentives for secure behavior, it is unsurprising that the educational institutions are regularly targeted by the adversary.[41] Nation-state actors also routinely target critical infrastructure operators (e.g., telecommunications, utilities).[42] Although an understanding of the human factors in cybersecurity is important to establishing a baseline understanding, it is essential to incorporate perspectives from the broader contextual factors shaping adversary behavior.

Contextual Factors Driving Adversary Behavior

Context always matters, and the main environmental factors influencing cybercrime participation include economic conditions, opportunity structures, and social norms, which foster differential adversarial involvement across populations and regions. Economic disparity represents a significant driver of global cybercrime activity in a variety of ways (e.g., weakened moral opposition to illegal actions stemming from a lack of legitimate alternatives, rendering the option to perpetrate cybercrime more appealing than it otherwise might be).[43] Ideological justification may also stem from social resentment of characterizing an out-group targeted by cybercrime efforts as a deserving target as a result of perceived privilege.[44] Additionally, the adversary may exploit individuals in affluent regions to facilitate arbitrage opportunities and cause participating in cybercrime to become an attractive option for individuals (i.e., income from illegal opportunities far exceed income available from local lawful opportunities) with evidence showing an association between cybercrime engagement and local unemployment rates and economic inequality indicators.[45,46]

Economic conditions, in turn, lead to situations where individuals possess technical capabilities that exceed available legitimate employment opportunities (i.e., digital skills-opportunity gap), particularly in regions with limited technology sector development, which may encourage technically skilled individuals to pursue illicit applications of their capabilities when legitimate applications are unavailable or inadequately compensated.[47] Cybercrime patterns also correlate with political and regulatory environments as a result of varying legal system effectiveness levels and appetites for international collaboration. The adversary may reduce the risk of prosecution by exploiting variations in regulations and law enforcement capabilities. Nations with weak cybercrime legislation, inadequate resources for law enforcement, and a lack of desire for international cooperation often become hubs for adversary activity, regardless of the nationality of the adversary or the location of their targets.[48] Successful cybercrime organizations often demonstrate a sophisticated understanding of international legal and investigative procedures, enabling strategic geographic positioning to manage resulting legal risks. Economic sanctions and international trade isolation may further foster conditions that increase the appeal of cybercrime as a motivator for illicit activities to fund national efforts (e.g., the Lazarus Group).[49] The lucrative nature of cybercrime activities may exacerbate corruption, generating a self-reinforcing environment where prosecution risks are mitigated through bribery or political protection.[50] Political instability additionally fosters conditions ripe for exploitation by cybercrime groups since poor governance may diminish law enforcement and institutional efficacy, such as in societies emerging from conflict, where cybercrime may increase due to social and economic displacement.[51]

Cultural elements also shape adversary behavior by influencing social norms regarding the use of technology and the stigmatization, or normalization, of various forms of illicit behavior. For example, representations of the adversary in popular culture typically rotate between narratives emphasizing target harm and glamorized depictions highlighting adversary prowess and achievement. Depending on the structure of the current narrative, these stories may influence adversary recruitment and policy decisions through society's perception of cybercrime impact and the efficacy of prevention strategies.[52] A popular narrative in mainstream media portrayals includes the depiction of the hacker hero, a technically sophisticated rebel fighting against oppressive institutions. This image serves to legitimize unlawful actions through social rationalization and desensitization. Films, TV shows, and books depicting the adversary as a relatable protagonist may also unintentionally promote cybercrime while downplaying the impact on targets and survivors. Additionally, fear cycle dynamics in cybercrime coverage may foster public anxiety that exceeds actual risk levels while potentially inspiring copycat behavior through detailed attack descriptions and capability discussions. Media coverage that emphasizes successful illicit operations while minimizing defensive capabilities may encourage participation while undermining public confidence in cybersecurity.[53] Cultural perceptions of authority, compliance, and the appropriate balance between individual and collective responsibility further shape adversary participation patterns and target behaviors, resulting in significant variations in cybercrime patterns across different cultures.[54] An essential component of effective national prevention strategies and international collaborative efforts is understanding these differentiating factors across cultures, which stem from the societal perceptions, media portrayals, and cultural norms of the adversary. This multifaceted examination of the anatomy of cybercrime reveals that effective cybercrime prevention requires a holistic understanding of how these interconnected elements synchronize to create vulnerabilities that transcend traditional security approaches.

Conclusion

Jane Doe's 12-second mistake from Chapter 1 perfectly illustrates WAVE theory. The attack succeeded through the synchronized orchestration of trust manipulation, authority exploitation, and cognitive overload. This scenario illustrates that modern cybercrime schemes reflect psychological engineering more than social engineering. Romance scams create emotional resonance while gradually introducing financial elements. Ransomware groups synchronize technical disruption with psychological pressure. When conducting business-email-compromise attacks, the adversary time their strikes to organizational rhythms that maximize compliance probability.

Modern cybercrime succeeds because the adversary masterfully blends technology and psychology. They orchestrate attacks that synchronize technical capabilities with psychological manipulation to create cognitive states where protective mechanisms cannot function. Each attack type demonstrates different aspects of the underlying principle that behavioral resonance is achieved by the adversary through synchronized psychological orchestration. Chapter 4 explores how the convergence of psychology and technology fundamentally altered human cognition, social interaction, and decision-making. We examine how interface design principles manipulate attention and emotion, how algorithmic systems shape belief formation, and how the architecture of digital environments creates psychological states that the adversary exploits, all of which point toward a new paradigm where psychological understanding becomes the foundation for digital defense.

Reflection Questions

1 How do psychological manipulation techniques vary across different cybercrime categories, and what implications does this have for defensive strategy development?
2 What role does organizational culture play in determining susceptibility to social engineering attacks, and how can culture be modified to reduce risk exposure?
3 Which infrastructure element remains most underestimated in defense planning, and what psychological biases might contribute to this systematic oversight in security planning and resource allocation?
4 How might generative AI tooling reshape traditional actor roles over the next five years, and what implications does this have for current threat modeling and defensive strategies?

Skill Builder Labs

Application Scenario: Map a Recent Ransomware Incident to Each Lifecycle Stage

Analyze a recent high-profile ransomware incident by taking the following steps:

- Select and map a recent incident.
- Identify technical and psychological factors that enabled adversary success at each stage.
- Evaluate how different defensive interventions might have disrupted the attack progression.
- Consider how organizational decision-making and culture influenced both attack success and response effectiveness.
- Define the long-term impacts beyond immediate technical damage (e.g., trust erosion, operational changes, industry-wide shifts).
- Document lessons learned for improving defensive strategies across all lifecycle stages.

Mini Research Activity: Analyze Phishing Emails

Objective

Assess email security using psychological vulnerability factors identified in this chapter.

Instructions

1. Review recent email interactions for psychological manipulation attempts (e.g., authority impersonation, urgency creation, and social proof exploitation).
2. Consider how emotional states, work pressure, and social relationships may affect susceptibility to the different phishing approaches.
3. Develop protocols for verification procedures when emails request sensitive information.

Deliverable

Generate a threat intelligence report analyzing recent phishing emails through the application of WAVE theory to user vulnerability, including insights into WAVE-informed defense recommendations.

References

1. Bansal, A., & Mahapatra, S. (2017, October). A comparative analysis of machine learning techniques for botnet detection. In *Proceedings of the 10th international conference on security of information and networks*. Association for Computing Machinery, New York, NY, USA, pp. 91–98.
2. Turner, A. B., McCombie, S., & Uhlmann, A. J. (2019). A target-centric intelligence approach to WannaCry 2.0. *Journal of Money Laundering Control*, 22(4), 646–665.
3. Wheeler, T., & Alderdice, J. L. (2022). Cyber collateral: Wannacry & the impact of cyberattacks on the mental health of critical infrastructure defenders. *Changing Character of War Centre (CCW)*. https://static1.squarespace.com/static/55faab67e4b0914105347194/t/633d5be5aeb3a41a99505e10/1664965606071/The+impact+of+cyberattacks+on+critical+infrastructure+defenders.pdf
4. Wade, M. (2021). Digital hostages: Leveraging ransomware attacks in cyberspace. *Business Horizons*, 64(6), 787–797.
5. Fayi, S. Y. A. (2018). What Petya/NotPetya ransomware is and what its remidiations are. In *Information technology-new generations: 15th international conference on information technology* (pp. 93–100). Springer International Publishing.
6. Greenberg, A. (2018). The untold story of NotPetya, the most devastating cyberattack in history. Wired, August, 22.
7. Rahalkar, C. (2023). A diamond model analysis on Twitter's Biggest Hack. *arXiv preprint arXiv:2306.15878*.
8. U.S. Federal Trade Commission. (2023). Romance scammers' favorite lies exposed. FTC Consumer Protection Data Spotlight.
9. Oak, R., & Shafiq, Z. (2025). "Hello, is this Anna?": Unpacking the lifecycle of pig-butchering scams. *arXiv preprint arXiv:2503.20821*.

10. Griffin, J. M., & Mei, K. (2024). How do crypto flows finance slavery? The economics of pig butchering. *The Economics of Pig Butchering*.
11. Franceschini, I., Li, L., & Bo, M. (2025). *Scam: Inside Southeast Asia's cybercrime compounds*. Verso Books.
12. International Justice Mission (2025). *A potential nexus between forced scamming and the financially-motivated sextortion of children*.
13. U.S. Department of Justice. (2018). *United States of America v. Viktor Borisovich Netyksho, et al.: Indictment*.
14. X. (2020). *An update on our security incident*.
15. U.S. Department of Justice. (2020). *United States v. Mason Sheppard: Criminal complaint*.
16. Verizon. (2025). *2025 Data breach investigations report*. Verizon Business.
17. splunk (2024). *What are social engineering attacks? A detailed explanation*.
18. PurpleSec. (2022). *Cyber security statistics the ultimate list of stats data, & trends for 2022*.
19. The 115th Congress, U.S. House of Representatives, Committee on Oversight and Government Reform, Majority Staff Report. (2018). *The Equifax data breach*.
20. Mitre. (2017). The Lazarus Group. *The Mitre Att&ck Framework, Group G0032*.
21. Federal Bureau of Investigation. (2022). *FBI statement on attribution of the Ronin Bridge hack to North Korea*.
22. U.S. Department of the Treasury. (2019). *Treasury sanctions North Korean state-sponsored malicious cyber groups*.
23. Pete, I., Hughes, J., Chua, Y. T., & Bada, M. (2020, September). A social network analysis and comparison of six dark web forums. In *2020 IEEE European symposium on security and privacy workshops* (pp. 484–493). IEEE.
24. Paternoster, C., Nazzari, M., Jofre, M., & Uberti, T. E. (2025). Inside the leak: Exploring the structure of the Conti ransomware group. *Global Crime*, *26*(2), 148–171.
25. Kingston, S., Cooper, E., Sales, T., & Harding, N. (2025). Money mules: A research-informed evidence based and lived experience driven approach. We fight fraud [White Paper].
26. Abdul Rani, M. I., Syed Mustapha Nazri, S. N. F., & Zolkaflil, S. (2024). A systematic literature review of money mule: Its roles, recruitment and awareness. *Journal of Financial Crime*, *31*(2), 347–361.
27. Communications Act of 1934, 47 U.S.C. § 230 et seq. (2018).
28. U.S. Department of Treasury. (2022). *U.S. treasury sanctions notorious virtual currency mixer Tornado Cash*.
29. Arora, S., & Hastings, J. D. (2024). A survey-based quantitative analysis of stress factors and their impacts among cybersecurity professionals. *arXiv preprint arXiv:2409.12047*.
30. Sedenberg, E. M., & Dempsey, J. X. (2018). Cybersecurity information sharing governance structures: An ecosystem of diversity, trust, and tradeoffs. *arXiv preprint arXiv:1805.12266*.
31. Huang, L., & Cornell, K. (2025). Cyber protection strategies: Balancing insurance and security. In *Proceedings of the 19th International Conference on Cyber Warfare and Security*, 20(1). Academic Conferences and publishing limited.
32. Mott, G., Turner, S., Nurse, J. R., MacColl, J., Sullivan, J., Cartwright, A., & Cartwright, E. (2023). Between a rock and a hard (ening) place: Cyber insurance in the ransomware era. *Computers & Security*, *128*, 103162.
33. U.S. Federal Trade Commission. (2024). *Protecting older consumers 2023–2024*.
34. U.S. Federal Trade Commission. (2024). *Consumer sentinel network data book*.

35 Balakrishnan, V., Ahhmed, U., & Basheer, F. (2025). Personal, environmental and behavioral predictors associated with online fraud victimization among adults. *PLoS One, 20*(1), e0317232.
36 López-Aguilar, P., Urruela, C., Batista, E., Machin, J., & Solanas, A. (2025). Phishing vulnerability and personality traits: Insights from a systematic review. *Computers in Human Behavior Reports, 20*, 100784.
37 Zhao, J., & Tomm, B. (2018). Psychological Responses to Scarcity. *Oxford Research Encyclopedia of Psychology*. Oxford University Press.
38 Lieberz, J. (2023). *Loneliness: Cognitive factors and neurobiological mechanisms*. Rheinische Friedrich-Wilhelms-Universitaet Bonn.
39 Verizon. (2019). *2019 Data breach investigations report*. Verizon Business.
40 Cartwright, A. J. (2023). The elephant in the room: cybersecurity in healthcare. *Journal of Clinical Monitoring and Computing, 37*(5), 1123–1132.
41 Ulven, J. B., & Wangen, G. (2021). A systematic review of cybersecurity risks in higher education. *Future Internet, 13*(2), 39.
42 Val, O. O., Kolade, T. M., Gbadebo, M. O., Selesi-Aina, O., Olateju, O. O., & Olaniyi, O. O. (2024). Strengthening cybersecurity measures for the defense of critical infrastructure in the United States. *Asian Journal of Research in Computer Science, 17*(11), 25–45.
43 Paquet-Clouston, M., & García, S. (2023). On the dynamics behind profit-driven cybercrime: From contextual factors to perceived group structures, and the workforce at the periphery. *Global Crime, 24*(2), 122–144.
44 Taylor, M., Fritsch, E., & Liederbach, J. (2019). *Digital crime and digital terrorism* (3rd ed.). Prentice Hall.
45 Akinyetun, T. S. (2021). Poverty, cybercrime and national security in Nigeria. *Journal of Contemporary Sociological Issues, 1*(2), 86–109.
46 Kigerl, A. (2012). Routine activity theory and the determinants of high cybercrime countries. *Social Science Computer Review, 30*(4), 470–486.
47 Chen, S., Hao, M., Ding, F., Jiang, D., Dong, J., Zhang, S., … & Gao, C. (2023). Exploring the global geography of cybercrime and its driving forces. *Humanities and Social Sciences Communications, 10*(1), 1–10.
48 Peters, A., & Jordan, A. (2020). Countering the cyber enforcement gap: Strengthening global capacity on cybercrime. *Journal of National Security Law and Policy, 10*, 487–524.
49 Park, J. (2021). The Lazarus Group: The cybercrime syndicate financing the North Korea state. *Harvard International Review, 42*(2), 34–39.
50 Richards, N. U., & Eboibi, F. E. (2021). African governments and the influence of corruption on the proliferation of cybercrime in Africa: Wherein lies the rule of law? *International Review of Law, Computers & Technology, 35*(2), 131–161.
51 Lyeonov, S., Vasylieva, T., & Filatova, H. *Financial fraud and cybercrime in wartime: An overview of the scientific landscape and insights from countries*. The Academic Research and Publishing UG (i. G.), Hamburg, Germany.
52 Holt, T., Bossler, A., & Seigfried-Spellar, K. (2017). *Cybercrime and digital forensics: An introduction* (2nd ed.). Routledge.
53 Wall, D. S. (2008). Cybercrime and the culture of fear: Social science fiction (s) and the production of knowledge about cybercrime. *Information, Communication & Society, 11*(6), 861–884.
54 Newman, G. R., & Wolfgang, M. E. (2017). *Comparative deviance: Perception and law in six cultures*. Routledge.

4 Convergence of Technology and Psychology

Interface Psychology

An intricate dance between individuals and their devices plays out multiple times each day. The adversary learned the steps to this dance, allowing for the weaponization of the structure of the applications upon which many aspects of our lives rely. User interface design facilitates technology's influence over individuals, while psychological needs constrain the technological solutions viable for implementation, which is a relationship essential for forensic cyberpsychology and the development of defenses that leverage WAVE theory principles.

Interface design, at the most basic level, represents applied psychology. For example, Jakob Nielsen's usability heuristics continue to influence interface designs despite dramatic changes in technology capabilities and user expectations.[1] The adversary exploits these same concepts as a means to bypass defenses. Cognitive overload attacks involve the deliberate violation of usability principles to manifest feelings of overwhelm in a target as a way to induce poor decisions. Websites impersonating financial institutions may present excessive security warnings, complex verification steps, and urgent countdown timers to bombard a target's information processing capabilities. When presented in tandem, these modalities push a target to comply with demands perceived as reasonable to escape the situation.

Cognitive load theory provides frameworks for understanding how interface complexity affects user performance and decision-making quality.[2] The cognitive system possesses limited processing capacity, with research indicating that most people can effectively manage only about seven inputs at once, give or take two.[3] Interface design can either support the user's brain through clear information architecture or overwhelm it through complexity. Poor interface design creates extraneous cognitive load that consumes mental resources needed for primary task completion and security decision-making.[4] Poorly designed security features often fail by exceeding human cognitive capacity for frequent decision-making. Users face constant permission dialogs that quickly become meaningless due to repetition and lack of meaningful context, leading to automatic approval behavior (e.g., habituation, decision fatigue) that defeats the security purpose.[5] Cognitive load theory supports forensic investigations by facilitating the reconstruction of mental states of targets before and during cybercrime attacks. This analysis identifies reasons why sophisticated users may fall for more apparent cybercrime schemes at various times, including when the target is stressed or multi-tasking.

Designing for Aesthetic Bias

Despite decades of being told otherwise, individuals are stubbornly visual creatures reliant on appearance-based judgments in decisions. This holds true to the evaluation of systems, as well. Interfaces perceived as more attractive are interpreted as more usable, regardless of the actual usability of the underlying interface.[6] This is a concept that is often exploited by the adversary through the creation of visually sophisticated social engineering websites geared toward exploiting the aesthetic bias in a target. For example, pig butchering scams (i.e., sophisticated investment frauds) use websites with real-time charts and visually complex interfaces to trigger perceived legitimacy in the target, including listing fictionalized returns personalized to the target. In a legitimate business context, Apple's interface design philosophy demonstrates how emotional design can build user loyalty while creating psychological barriers to switching platforms.[7] The Apple ecosystem succeeds partly through emotional attachment that pushes users to accept functional limitations or higher costs in exchange for aesthetic satisfaction and identity expression. The phenomenon represents a masterclass in psychological persuasion disguised as design excellence, considering that green messages (i.e., messages from an Android to an iPhone) literally became a status symbol and alleged dating criterion.

Security interface design often neglects emotional factors while focusing exclusively on functional requirements or the overuse of color psychology principles (e.g., green = good, red = bad).[8] While the red warning screens used by many security products may create appropriate urgency for genuine threats, they may also contribute to security fatigue when overused.[9] The psychology of fear-based design creates compliance through anxiety rather than understanding, producing brittle behavioral change that fails under stress. The adversary often exploits security fatigue by timing attacks during high-stress periods for targets, such as immediately following the public announcement of mergers or around filing deadlines (e.g., tax filing deadlines, the end of a target's fiscal year). Trust indicators in interface design exploit psychological shortcuts about credibility and safety through visual cues, including professional appearance, authority symbols, and social proof elements.[10] These same cues may be exploited by malicious adversaries who understand how visual design influences user trust decisions. In fact, researchers uncovered that targets often trust the adversary's interface more than the legitimate pages that were redesigned with new security features due to targets assessing the new, legitimate pages as less professional.[11]

Accessibility and Inclusive UX

Inclusive design principles prove essential for cybersecurity effectiveness because security measures that exclude or disadvantage certain user populations create systematic vulnerabilities that affect entire systems rather than just individual users.[12] In the context of forensic cyberpsychology, accessibility features, or the lack thereof, generate predictable patterns for the adversary to target. The adversary may target a user with a disability who is reliant on insecure workarounds stemming from a lack of accessibility and inclusive design by technology providers. For example, business email compromise and related social engineering campaigns increasingly exploit fatigue during multi-step verification (e.g., repeated MFA prompts). Research shows these workflows are disproportionately challenging for users who have disabilities, such as dyslexia which causes difficulties memorizing one-time passcodes and leads users to abandon multi-,step authentication processes.[13]

The 2017 Equifax breach provides an example of how accessibility failures create security vulnerabilities for entire populations.[14] Successful navigation of the platform to identify available credit monitoring tools required sophisticated knowledge that many impacted targets lacked, which prevented those individuals from accessing protective services after the compromise of their personal information, leaving them vulnerable to follow-on attacks.

Cognitive Impacts of Technology Use

Digital technology fundamentally changed human memory techniques via transactive memory, which is the tendency to rely on external information sources rather than internal memory.[15] While not an inherently positive or negative transformation, this adaptation signifies a transformation in how humans process information. Digital amnesia describes how readily available information storage reduces motivation for remembering information that can be easily retrieved from external sources.[16] For example, individuals are less likely to remember phone numbers, addresses, or factual information that they expect to be able to search for when needed. Navigation abilities provide another concrete example of how external memory systems affect human cognitive capabilities.[17] When individuals heavily rely on GPS, basic navigation skills begin to deteriorate, such as using landmarks and maps to get around when GPS is unavailable. This was evidenced in 2017 when 100 drivers in Colorado followed their GPS down the same dead-end road demonstrating irrational behavior via an overreliance on technology and social proof.[18]

The extended mind thesis suggests that external information storage and processing tools become integrated into human cognitive systems, making the distinction between internal and external cognition less meaningful.[19] From the WAVE perspective, this integration facilitates a critical vulnerability. The adversary effectively manipulates a target's cognitive processing via the exploitation of extended cognition tools. Cognitive dependency on external systems makes interface design an important security consideration given that these external tools function as an extension of human neural processing. Design approaches that support human memory capabilities while leveraging external information storage can optimize the benefits of transactive memory systems while minimizing dependency risks and retrieval failures.[20] These principles reveal how the adversary manipulates memory retrieval systems to facilitate deception. Recognition-based interface design leverages human memory strengths by presenting information that users recognize rather than requiring the recall of complex information from memory, such as menu-based interfaces versus command-line interfaces. The adversary exploits these recognition patterns through the creation of interfaces that mimic familiar systems as a means to trigger automatic responses before a target consciously analyzes the situation.

When viewed through the lens of forensic cyberpsychology, current research identifies cognitive vulnerabilities associated with excessive technology usage. In fact, neuroimaging studies identify quantifiable shifts in brain function linked to excessive use of digital technology.[21] Additional evidence indicates that frequent internet users exhibit a reduction in gray matter density in regions of the brain associated with executive functioning (e.g., attention control, impulse regulation), which are cognitive systems critical to resisting social engineering campaigns.[22] Attention regulation research indicates that frequent technology use may affect the brain's ability to maintain sustained focus on a single task. Individuals operate in a state of continuous partial attention due to demands to remain aware of multiple information streams at all times, which leads to the inability to fully focus on any single source.[23] The adversary exploits this phenomenon by timing attacks to coincide with times in which targets are likely monitoring multiple information streams.[24] Romance scammers initiate contact during social media browsing sessions when targets are in pattern-matching mode rather than analytical mode. Business email compromise attacks arrive during busy email processing periods when executives are rapidly triaging messages rather than carefully evaluating each one.[25]

Key Cognitive Biases in Interface Design

The adversary maximizes compliance with attacks through the application of psychological principles exploiting cognitive biases and heuristics.[26] Systematic biases and cognitive shortcuts influence the decisions that individuals make in both the digital and physical worlds, according to behavioral economics.[27] Default options wield disproportionate influence over user choices because people tend to stick with pre-selected options rather than actively choosing alternatives, even when changing the default would better serve their interests.[28] Researchers call this cognitive tendency the status quo bias.[29] By structuring attacks where compliance becomes the path of least resistance, the adversary weaponizes this default bias. This approach proves effective because targets face cognitive effort requirements for decision-making, experience loss aversion that makes changes feel risky, and encounter implicit endorsement effects where defaults suggest recommended choices.[30] Consider how the adversary might spoof an email from a trusted vendor recommending a security update download with multiple options available to the target. The system pre-selects the immediate download option for the user, which actually downloads the malware payload onto the target's machine. Through the WAVE lens, this attack succeeds when the adversary weaponizes familiar system interfaces and automatic acceptance behaviors. Consequently, malicious interface designs synchronize with cognitive processing to elicit harmful decisions in targets that feel psychologically normal by bypassing conscious decision-making processes.

Moving beyond default manipulation, the adversary also exploits how presentation affects decision-making. The presentation of identical choices in terms of gains and losses (i.e., the framing effect) provides another powerful tool for influencing user decisions.[31] For instance, individuals show a higher likelihood to purchase a program presented as capable of preventing 99% of threats over one marketed as having a 1% failure rate. Although these statistical representations signify the same outcome, presenting the positive aspect leads to a more favorable interpretation of the efficacy of the program. Through fraudulent account recovery pages that warn users to act immediately or leave their accounts at risk, the adversary exploits the framing effect in interface design, often featuring large flashing countdown timers. This pushes targets to engage with the adversary's campaign by creating artificial urgency and fear of loss. Related to framing effects, anchoring bias affects how users evaluate options by over-weighting the first information they receive.[30] Price anchoring in software sales creates situations where users perceive expensive security software as higher quality than less expensive alternatives, regardless of actual effectiveness. Free security software may be perceived as low quality due to anchoring effects, even when independent testing demonstrates superior performance. By establishing credibility markers early in a social engineering campaign (e.g., sophisticated branding, professional layouts, authoritative language), the adversary influences target perception and shapes how subsequent requests receive evaluation.

Finally, confirmation bias leads users to seek information that supports their existing beliefs while avoiding information that challenges their assumptions.[32] This creates significant challenges for security awareness training, as information conflicting with users' self-assessed vulnerability levels often faces rejection. Conversely, information confirming users' sense of security receives uncritical acceptance. Social engineering campaigns leverage a target's tendency to dismiss warning signs that contradict the initial assessment of an attack as a legitimate interaction. This explains how sophisticated targets still fall victim to the adversary's manipulation despite readily apparent red flags. Once the adversary establishes initial credibility in the target's mind, the target will unconsciously filter subsequent information to maintain their initial positive assessment, even when clear indicators suggest malicious intent. These cognitive biases provide the foundation for understanding how the adversary translates psychological vulnerabilities into manipulative interface design strategies. While cognitive biases reveal the mental shortcuts that make users vulnerable, dark patterns represent the systematic implementation of these vulnerabilities through deliberately deceptive user interface design. The adversary leverages dark patterns as the practical application of cognitive bias exploitation, transforming abstract psychological principles into tangible design elements that manipulate user behavior at the interface level.

Weaponized Interface Design

Dark Patterns

Dark patterns (e.g., confirmshaming, roach motels, privacy suckering, bait and switch) represent intentional design choices that trick users into unintended actions or decisions.[33] This includes design features that steer, deceive, or manipulate users into making choices that are not in their best interests.[34] By leveraging dark patterns, the adversary transforms abstract psychological vulnerabilities into concrete manipulation tools that exploit user decision-making processes. Confirmshaming also exploits social psychology principles about self-image and social desirability by presenting decline options with emotionally manipulative language that makes targets feel guilty for refusing offers.[35] Through the WAVE lens, confirmshaming succeeds because it synchronizes with human needs for social acceptance while bypassing rational decision-making processes. Roach motels create situations where users easily enter commitments that later prove difficult or impossible to exit.[36] Entities exploit procrastination tendencies and cognitive effort avoidance by designing complex cancellation procedures. Free trial subscriptions exemplify this pattern, leveraging status quo bias to lure individuals into maintaining subscriptions. Forensic analysis reveals how these patterns create long-term victim relationships that extend beyond initial compromise. The practice of manipulating users into sharing more personal information than they may intend to through complex privacy settings or regularly updating privacy policies without clear user notification is known as Privacy Zuckering.[37] This practice exploits human tendency to maintain existing settings rather than actively managing privacy controls. Privacy Zuckering demonstrates how interface design functions as an information-gathering tool for subsequent targeting and social engineering campaigns. Bait and switch techniques present users with apparent choices that lead to different outcomes than expected.[38] In practice, the adversary creates fake download buttons in ads run on legitimate software download sites to install malware on target devices, a practice exploiting user assumptions based on design patterns.

Attention Engineering

Modern interface design deliberately fragments human attention through sophisticated psychological manipulation masquerading as user engagement.[39] The adversary leverages these same attention-capture mechanisms, exploiting cognitive states already weakened by commercial technology platforms. Notification systems exploit psychological principles about variable reward schedules that create compulsive checking behaviors through operant conditioning.[40] Research shows that typical smartphone users receive about 100 daily notifications, creating cognitive load that exceeds human processing capacity.[41] This volume creates situations where users develop maladaptive coping strategies, including notification dismissal without reading, batch processing that delays critical responses, or notification disabling that may cause them to miss important security information. Unpredictable notification timing mirrors the psychological mechanisms found in gambling addiction, where uncertainty about when rewards will arrive creates stronger behavioral conditioning than predictable reward schedules.[42] Social media platforms deliberately implement variable-ratio reinforcement schedules, encouraging repeated checking for new content through the same operant conditioning principles that establish habitual engagement patterns in casino environments. The adversary weaponizes these conditioned responses by timing social engineering campaigns to arrive during periods of high notification activity, when targets operate in rapid-response mode rather than analytical evaluation mode.

Constant interruptions from application notifications prevent individuals from reaching states of focus needed for in-depth problem-solving and security analysis. Task-switching research indicates that individuals require approximately 20 minutes to fully refocus attention on a primary task following interruption.[43] In modern workplace environments characterized by continuous email, instant messaging, phone calls, and meeting notifications, workers remain trapped in states of cognitive fragmentation that the adversary systematically exploits. Continuous partial attention (i.e., hyper attention) describes the cognitive state where individuals simultaneously maintain surface-level awareness of multiple information streams without achieving deep focus on any single area.[44] This attention pattern makes users particularly vulnerable to social engineering because surface-level processing relies more heavily on heuristic shortcuts and pattern matching rather than analytical evaluation. For instance, romance scammers initiate contact when targets operate in pattern-matching mode (i.e., during social media browsing), while business email compromise attacks often arrive during busy email processing periods when employees may triage messages without careful evaluation. The adversary optimizes attack timing to exploit fragmented attention states due to an understanding that cognitive load reduces analytical thinking and increases reliance on automatic responses.[45] When taken in tandem, the nuanced lens of WAVE theory highlights the importance of understanding the relationship between attention engineering and security vulnerability, given that a strain on cognitive resources often results in a miscalculation of trustworthiness.

Trust Calibration in Human-Technology Interaction

Modern cybersecurity is about more than simply having the right software. It is also about how well humans and technology collaborate. The problem with this approach is that humans often develop unhealthy relationships with automated systems by either trusting them too much or too little (i.e., a miscalibration of trust). These trust dynamics represent a critical area of study for forensic cyberpsychology as the adversary exploits human tendencies toward excessive technological reliance. An overreliance on automated systems while failing to continuously monitor their performance (i.e., automation bias) often leads to the inability to detect automation errors.[46] The phenomenon emerges from fundamental limitations in human cognitive capacity. Individuals cannot effectively monitor multiple complex systems at the same time leading to the development of mental models that assume reliable system performance that does not require active oversight (i.e., automation complacency).[47] For instance, security automation creates particular risks when users develop excessive trust in automated threat detection systems. High false positive rates drive individuals to dismiss legitimate alerts (i.e., alert fatigue) while low false positive rates create overconfidence in the system's capability, leading to users ignoring subtle indicators of system failures.[48] The aviation industry provides a distinct example of the consequences of automation bias. There are numerous accounts of pilots relying on automated systems to the point that the pilots failed to recognize critical flight problems until intervention became impossible. Similarly, drivers using automotive automation features may develop overconfidence in the capabilities of the system, resulting in accidents. These failures also demonstrate how marketing around innovative technologies may lead users to place inappropriate trust in systems without understanding the extent of their limitations. Through the lens of WAVE theory, automation bias and automation complacency represent vulnerabilities for adversaries to exploit through impersonation and mimicry (e.g., MFA bombing). This approach leverages users' conditioned trust responses to bypass conscious security evaluation. Advanced persistent threat (APT) campaigns increasingly incorporate trust miscalibration techniques given that APTs often aim to establish a long-term presence in a target's system. An objective that may be accomplished by overwhelming targets with false alerts to reduce vigilance (i.e., alert fatigue). In other words, these APT campaigns succeed by weaponizing automation bias and automation complacency in targets.

In light of this evidence, it is clear that effective automation requires transparency mechanisms that support informed trust decisions rather than blind compliance. Explainable AI systems (i.e., systems that provide reasoning for automated recommendations) enable better trust calibration than black box systems.[49] Risk assessment frameworks also support user decisions when verification becomes necessary by considering the consequences of automation errors relative to verification costs. For example, organizations may prohibit automation of high-consequence decisions while allowing minimal human supervision for the automation of low-consequence processes. Sampling strategies enable users to verify automation performance periodically without checking every automated decision, although optimal sampling rates depend on error consequences and automation reliability. Domain expertise additionally affects a user's ability to verify automated recommendations, with research showing that experts identify automation errors at a higher frequency due to a nuanced understanding of design parameters.[50] It is important to note that evidence also exists supporting that expertise may create overconfidence, leading to inadequate verification (e.g., users assume their knowledge compensates for automation limitations).[51]

Regulatory Frameworks

The regulatory landscape for addressing manipulative interface design remains fragmented, with different jurisdictions pursuing varying approaches to balance consumer protection with innovation incentives. The European Union's Digital Services Act establishes comprehensive requirements for platforms to assess and mitigate risks from their systems, including explicit consideration of risks from addictive design features and psychological manipulation.[52] This regulation creates precedent for holding platforms accountable for psychological harms caused by interface design choices, representing a fundamental shift toward recognizing digital psychological manipulation as a form of consumer harm warranting regulatory intervention. In the United States, the California Privacy Rights Act (CPRA) includes specific provisions addressing dark patterns in privacy choice interfaces by requiring the presentation of privacy controls in neutral language without manipulation and prohibiting the use of any dark patterns.[53] These regulatory approaches recognize that privacy effectiveness depends on interface design, enabling user choice rather than manufactured consent tantamount to psychological manipulation. Multiple enforcement actions against companies using dark patterns in subscription services, advertising, and privacy controls were previously brought by the Federal Trade Commission and established legal precedent that certain design practices constitute unfair or deceptive trade practices, regardless of user consent to terms of service, which signaled a willingness to expand protections to user experience.[54]

Despite these efforts, global technology platforms create enforcement challenges when companies operate across multiple jurisdictions with varying consumer protection standards and cultural attitudes toward psychological manipulation. Regulatory arbitrage allows companies to structure operations in jurisdictions with less restrictive standards while serving users in more protective regulatory environments. International cooperation agreements establishing common standards for acceptable design practices may prove essential for effective regulation of psychological manipulation in technology. Without coordinated approaches, regulatory fragmentation may create incentives for companies to optimize for the least restrictive jurisdictions while globally undermining consumer protection. Class-action litigation additionally achieved relative success in establishing that manipulative interface design may constitute breach of contract, violation of consumer protection laws, or other actionable claim, even when users technically agree to terms of service. The gaps discussed in this section clearly demonstrate the need for a shift from reactive enforcement of violations toward a more proactive approach in fostering appropriate interface designs. In the context of cybercrime, this patchwork of regulations underscores the need for application designs incorporating safety within the digital interface itself.

Frictionless and Ethical Design in Cybersecurity

The evidence indicates that effective cybersecurity design must account for limitations while supporting user agency and well-being. This requires a fundamental shift away from security approaches that increase cognitive burden (e.g., security fatigue). Security fatigue occurs when users become overwhelmed by security decision-making demands, which leads to poor security choices. This phenomenon reflects both cognitive limitations in human decision-making capacity and poor security system design that requires excessive user effort. In other words, repeated security prompts create decision fatigue that leads to degraded security decision-making and fosters counterproductive situations where additional security features reduce overall security effectiveness.[55] Password requirements are an often-cited example of how security measures may undermine their own objectives through user fatigue. Complex password requirements incentivize users to reuse the same password across multiple accounts. Users may also store passwords in plain view (e.g., sticky notes on their computer) to circumvent these controls. When users are required to regularly update their passwords, they often default to predictable password creation patterns designed solely to meet technical requirements rather than provide actual security.[56] Frictionless security design describes the attempt to provide protection without requiring user effort or decision-making (e.g., automatic software updates, background scanning, single sign-on systems). One example includes risk-based authentication systems that adjust security requirements based on contextual factors (e.g., location, device characteristics, user behavior patterns) to allow organizations to require additional authentication only when risk indicators suggest potential compromise. Additionally, progressive security disclosure provides users with security information precisely when needed for decision-making rather than overwhelming them with continuous security messaging. This just-in-time approach to security guidance provides relevant information without creating cognitive overload.

Another approach to mitigating cybersecurity issues stemming from user interface design is incorporating ethical design principles that extend beyond immediate business objectives. By placing user agency as a primary design consideration and creating interfaces to facilitate genuine user-driven decisions rather than manufactured compliance, this approach provides transparency in information framing and policy explanation to support informed consent. Privacy by design principles provide an example of integrating privacy throughout the entire product development cycle rather than being treated as a compliance afterthought (e.g., data minimization practices, default privacy-focused settings, transparent explanations of data collection and usage).[57] Ethical design approaches prove essential for cybersecurity because privacy violations often provide targeting information to the adversary beyond which targets may be aware (i.e., individuals may not realize the adversary has access to data prior to the weaponization of that data against them). Treating accessibility as a security feature also ensures accommodations for diverse user needs (e.g., MFA systems that accommodate individuals with disabilities), which strengthens overall system security by improving security program efficacy through discouraging the need for workarounds that lack security.[58] Moreover, algorithmic transparency enables better collaboration between humans and technology by providing clear explanations of system limitations, leading to enhanced user decision-making and trust calibration. In summary, directly embedding security considerations into digital environments through ethical and accessible practices serves the overall posture of cybersecurity for entities via supportive interfaces.

Conclusion

The convergence of technology and psychology constitutes the battleground of modern cybercrime. This chapter demonstrated how the adversary weaponizes the psychological principles embedded within user interfaces. Through the lens of WAVE, it is clear that successful attacks supplement technical sophistication with psychological synchronization. The evidence indicates that traditional cybersecurity approaches often fail due to designs reliant on external mitigations instead of considering cognitive implications. Perhaps most critically, the boundary between legitimate persuasive design and malicious manipulation increasingly blurs. Variable reward schedules, confirmation bias exploitation, and status quo bias manipulation serve both commercial applications and the adversary with equal effectiveness. This convergence creates a landscape where users cannot reliably distinguish between helpful technology and predatory systems. As we examine the broader duality of technological innovation in Chapter 5, the foundations established in this chapter provide an understanding of the complex reality individuals face in the digital world. The same technological capabilities that create unprecedented opportunities also serve as new ways for the adversary to manipulate targets. Through the continued application of WAVE principles, Chapter 5 explores how technological innovation poses both benefits and threats to humanity, including the importance of understanding this duality as an essential component of resilient defenses in an increasingly connected world.

Reflection Questions

1 How can the adversary exploit UX factors (e.g., cognitive load, aesthetic bias, dark patterns) to manipulate targets?
2 What does healthy skepticism look like in practice?
3 What specific design choices demonstrate respect for user agency while maintaining security effectiveness?
4 How might psychological adaptations (e.g., attention span, memory, decision-making) create vulnerabilities that the adversary may exploit?

Skill Builder Labs

Application Scenario: Evaluate Trust in an Autonomous Vehicle Dashboard

Examine an autonomous vehicle interface.

- Assess how design choices might affect appropriate trust calibration.
- Evaluate whether system confidence indicators provide meaningful information about actual system capabilities and limitations.
- Analyze the clarity and accessibility of manual override controls.
- Review the tone and content of safety communications.
- Consider how different user populations might interpret interface cues differently based on their technical knowledge, driving experience, or trust propensities.

Mini Research Activity: Track Notification Interactions for 48 Hours

Objective

Enhance understanding of how digital interruptions affect attention and behavior patterns.

Instructions

1. Document digital notifications for a two-day period.
2. Record the frequency, timing, and sources of notifications received.
3. Notate any emotional and behavioral responses to different types of alerts.
4. Track how notifications interrupt ongoing activities.
5. Identify how long it took to return to previous tasks after addressing notifications.
6. Analyze patterns in notification responses.
7. Consider how notification timing affects willingness to engage.
8. Evaluate current notification management strategies.
9. Identify opportunities for more intentional notification control.

Deliverable

Generate a digital attention audit report of notification patterns and impact, including a personalized notification management strategy to reduce cognitive vulnerabilities.

References

1. Nielsen, J. (1994). *Usability engineering.* Morgan Kaufmann.
2. Sweller, J. (1988). Cognitive load during problem solving: Effects on learning. *Cognitive Science, 12*(2), 257–285.
3. Miller, G. A. (1956). The magical number seven, plus or minus two: Some limits on our capacity for processing information. *Psychological Review, 63*(2), 81–97.
4. Chandler, P., & Sweller, J. (1991). Cognitive load theory and the format of instruction. *Cognition and Instruction, 8*(4), 293–332.
5. Wijesekera, P., Baokar, A., Hosseini, A., Egelman, S., Wagner, D., & Beznosov, K. (2015). Android permissions remystified: A field study on contextual integrity. In *24th USENIX Security Symposium (USENIX Security 15)* (pp. 499–514). USENIX. Washington, D.C.
6. Tractinsky, N., Katz, A. S., & Ikar, D. (2000). What is beautiful is usable. *Interacting with Computers, 13*(2), 127–145.
7. Cant, M. C., Machado, R., & Seaborne, H. C. (2014). Brand advocates–An Apple phenomenon? An exploratory study on brand advocacy amongst Apple consumers. *Journal of Corporate Ownership & Control, 11*(2), 535–541.
8. Elliot, A. J., & Maier, M. A. (2014). Color psychology: Effects of perceiving color on psychological functioning in humans. *Annual Review of Psychology, 65*, 95–120.
9. Stanton, B., Theofanos, M. F., Prettyman, S. S., & Furman, S. (2016). Security fatigue. *IT Professional, 18*(5), 26–32.

10 Fogg, B. J. (2003). Prominence-interpretation theory: Explaining how people assess credibility online. CHI '03 Extended Abstracts on Human Factors in Computing Systems, 722–723.
11 Dhamija, R., Tygar, J. D., & Hearst, M. (2006, April). Why phishing works. In *Proceedings of the SIGCHI conference on Human Factors in computing systems*. Association for Computing Machinery, New York, NY, USA, pp. 581–590.
12 Renaud, K., & Coles-Kemp, L. (2022). Accessible and inclusive cyber security: A nuanced and complex challenge. *SN Computer Science, 3*, 346.
13 Erinola, A., Buckmann, A., Friedauer, J., Yardım, A., & Sasse, M. A. (2023, July). "As Usual, I Needed Assistance of a Seeing Person": Experiences and challenges of people with disabilities and authentication methods. In *2023 IEEE European symposium on security and privacy workshops* (pp. 575–593). IEEE.
14 U.S. House of Representatives, Committee on Oversight and Government Reform. (2018). *The Equifax data breach: Majority staff report*.
15 Wegner, D. M. (1987). Transactive memory: A contemporary analysis of the group mind. In B. Mullen & G. R. Goethals (Eds.), *Theories of group behavior* (pp. 185–208). Springer.
16 Sparrow, B., Liu, J., & Wegner, D. M. (2011). Google effects on memory: Cognitive consequences of having information at our fingertips. *Science, 333*(6043), 776–778.
17 Ishikawa, T., Fujiwara, H., Imai, O., & Okabe, A. (2008). Wayfinding with a GPS-based mobile navigation system: A comparison with maps and direct experience. *Journal of Environmental Psychology, 28*(1), 74–82.
18 Lopez, M. (2019). *From detour to disaster: Google Maps got dozens of Colorado drivers in a mud mess on Sunday*. Denver7.
19 Clark, A., & Chalmers, D. (1998). The extended mind. *Analysis, 58*(1), 7–19.
20 Risko, E. F., & Gilbert, S. J. (2016). Cognitive offloading. *Trends in Cognitive Sciences, 20*(9), 676–688.
21 Kühn, S., & Gallinat, J. (2015). Brains online: Structural and functional correlates of habitual Internet use. *Addiction Biology, 20*(2), 415–422.
22 Lin, F., Zhou, Y., Du, Y., Qin, L., Zhao, Z., Xu, J., & Lei, H. (2012). Abnormal white matter integrity in adolescents with internet addiction disorder: A tract-based spatial statistics study. *PLoS One, 7*(1), e30253.
23 Loh, K. K., & Kanai, R. (2014). Higher media multi-tasking activity is associated with smaller gray-matter density in the anterior cingulate cortex. *Plos one, 9*(9), e106698.
24 Lyu, C., Gao, S., & Zhang, Q. (2025). The impact of time pressure and type of fraud on susceptibility to online fraud. *Frontiers in Psychology, 16*, 1508363.
25 Zhuo, S., Biddle, R., Betts, L., Arachchilage, N. A. G., Koh, Y. S., Russello, G., & Lottridge, D. (2024). The impact of workload on phishing susceptibility: An experiment. In *Symposium on usable security and privacy*. https://www.ndss-symposium.org/wp-content/uploads/usec2024-24-paper.pdf
26 Cialdini, R. B., & Goldstein, N. J. (2004). Social influence: Compliance and conformity. *Annual Review of Psychology, 55*, 591–621
27 Tversky, A., & Kahneman, D. (1974). Judgment under uncertainty: Heuristics and biases. *Science, 185*(4157), 1124–1131.
28 Jachimowicz, J. M., Duncan, S., Weber, E. U., & Johnson, E. J. (2019). When and why defaults influence decisions: A meta-analysis of default effects. *Behavioural Public Policy, 3*(2), 159–186.
29 Samuelson, W., & Zeckhauser, R. (1988). Status quo bias in decision making. *Journal of Risk and Uncertainty, 1*(1), 7–59.

30 Kahneman, D., Knetsch, J. L., & Thaler, R. H. (1991). Anomalies: The endowment effect, loss aversion, and status quo bias. *Journal of Economic Perspectives, 5*(1), 193–206.
31 Tversky, A., & Kahneman, D. (1981). The framing of decisions and the psychology of choice. *Science, 211*(4481), 453–458.
32 Nickerson, R. S. (1998). Confirmation bias: A ubiquitous phenomenon in many guises. *Review of General Psychology, 2*(2), 175–220.
33 Brignull, H. (2010). *Dark patterns: Dirty tricks designers use to make people do stuff.* Harry Brignull's 90 Percent of Everything blog.
34 Federal Trade Commission. (2022). *Bringing dark patterns to light: An FTC workshop.* FTC.
35 Mathur, A., Acar, G., Friedman, M. J., Lucherini, E., Mayer, J., Chetty, M., & Narayanan, A. (2019). Dark patterns at scale: Findings from a crawl of 11K shopping websites. *Proceedings of the ACM on Human-Computer Interaction, 3*(CSCW), 1–32.
36 Sheil, A., Acar, G., Schraffenberger, H., Gellert, R., & Malone, D. (2024, May). Staying at the roach motel: Cross-country analysis of manipulative subscription and cancellation flows. In *Proceedings of the 2024 CHI conference on human factors in computing systems.* Association for Computing Machinery, New York, NY, USA, Article 298, 1–24.
37 Jones, T. (2010). *Facebook's evil interfaces.* Electronic Frontier Foundation.
38 Luguri, J., & Strahilevitz, L. J. (2021). Shining a light on dark patterns. *Journal of Legal Analysis, 13*(1), 43–109.
39 Sharek, D., Swofford, C., & Wogalter, M. (2008). Failure to recognize fake internet popup warning messages. In *Proceedings of the Human Factors and Ergonomics Society Annual Meeting, 52*(6), 557–560.
40 Stothart, C., Mitchum, A., & Yehnert, C. (2015). The attentional cost of receiving a cell phone notification. *Journal of Experimental Psychology: Human Perception and Performance, 41*(4), 893.
41 Mehrotra, A., Pejovic, V., Vermeulen, J., Hendley, R., & Musolesi, M. (2016, May). My phone and me: Understanding people's receptivity to mobile notifications. In *Proceedings of the 2016 CHI conference on human factors in computing systems.* Association for Computing Machinery, New York, NY, USA, pp. 1021–1032.
42 Clark, L., & Zack, M. (2023). Engineered highs: Reward variability and frequency as potential prerequisites of behavioural addiction. *Addictive Behaviors, 140*, 107626.
43 Mark, G., Gudith, D., & Klocke, U. (2008). The cost of interrupted work: More speed and stress. In *Proceedings of the SIGCHI conference on human factors in computing systems.* Association for Computing Machinery, New York, NY, USA, pp. 107–110.
44 Hayles, N. K. (2007). Hyper and deep attention: The generational divide in cognitive modes. *Profession,* 187–199. Modern Language Association.
45 Wright, R. T., & Marett, K. (2010). The influence of experiential and dispositional factors in phishing: An empirical investigation of the deceived. *Journal of Management Information Systems, 27*(1), 273–303.
46 Romeo, G., & Conti, D. (2025). Exploring automation bias in human–AI collaboration: A review and implications for explainable AI. *AI & Society,* 1–20. https://link.springer.com/article/10.1007/s00146-025-02422-7#citeas
47 Singh, I. L., Molloy, R., & Parasuraman, R. (1993). Automation-induced" complacency": Development of the complacency-potential rating scale. *The International Journal of Aviation Psychology, 3*(2), 111–122.
48 Böhme, R., & Köpsell, S. (2010, April). Trained to accept? A field experiment on consent dialogs. In *Proceedings of the SIGCHI conference on human factors in computing systems.* Association for Computing Machinery, New York, NY, USA, pp. 2403–2406.

49 Minh, D., Wang, H. X., Li, Y. F., & Nguyen, T. N. (2022). Explainable artificial intelligence: a comprehensive review. *Artificial Intelligence Review, 55*(5), 3503–3568.
50 Bruder, C., & Hasse, C. (2019). Differences between experts and novices in the monitoring of automated systems. *International Journal of Industrial Ergonomics, 72*, 1–11.
51 Dror, I. E., Pascual-Leone, A., Ramachandran, V., Cole, J., Della Sala, S., & Manly, T. (2011). The paradox of human expertise: Why experts get it wrong. In Narinder Kapur *The paradoxical brain* (pp. 177–188). Cambridge University Press.
52 European Commission, Regulation (EU) 2022/2065 of the European Parliament and of the Council of 19 October 2022 on a Single Market for Digital Services and amending Directive 2000/31/EC (Digital Services Act).
53 California Privacy Rights Act, CA Civil Code § 1798.185(a)(19).
54 U.S. Federal Trade Commission. (2022). Bringing dark patterns to light: Staff Report.
55 Stanton, B., Theofanos, M. F., Prettyman, S. S., & Furman, S. (2016). Security fatigue. *It Professional, 18*(5), 26–32.
56 U.K. National Cyber Security Centre. *Guidance: Password administration for system owners.*
57 Schaar, P. (2010). Privacy by design. *Identity in the Information Society, 3*(2), 267–274.
58 Furnell, S., Helkala, K., & Woods, N. (2022). Accessible authentication: Assessing the applicability for users with disabilities. *Computers & Security, 113*, 102561.

5 The Duality of Technological Innovation

The Prometheus Paradox

In November 2020, DeepMind announced a breakthrough made by the AlphaFold 2 system. Researchers found the AI system was capable of accelerating the treatment of diseases through the informing of drug research.[1] AI-enabled protein-design tools capable of generating novel proteins also raise concerns around the exploitation of the technology by the adversary, including engineering novel bioweapons.[2] By representing the duality of technological innovation and exemplifying a fundamental concept in the unifying WAVE theory, this example outlines the ideas explored throughout this chapter. Technology advancements expand human potential while generating new threat vectors for the adversary.

As the myth goes, Prometheus stole fire from the gods to gift it to the mortals with the understanding that it may be used to both forge tools of construction and weapons of destruction. Advancements in technology continue to unlock human potential in ways that would have been interpreted as magic by previous generations. Yet, there is a clearly observable consequence, albeit oftentimes unintended, for every glamourous iteration birthed in Silicon Valley. Technology and innovation are not the culprit, however. No, the ingenuity required to identify and weaponize technological innovations remains a uniquely human trait, at least at present.

Connected Minds, Distributed Solutions

The COVID-19 pandemic offered humanity an impromptu stress test of global digital collaboration. Within weeks, researchers were sharing genetic sequences across continents faster than they could share coffee with colleagues down the hall.[3] This unprecedented speed of knowledge transfer probably saved millions of lives while also demonstrating how fragile our scientific infrastructure becomes when Twitter feuds start influencing the peer review processes. The Human Genome Project stands as perhaps the most successful international collaboration in scientific history, completed ahead of schedule and under budget.[4] Of course, this feat required scientists to overcome their natural territorial instincts, a challenge that proved more difficult than mapping human DNA itself. The project's success hinged on carefully negotiated agreements. This is a practice science has long attempted to balance, the norm of openness with the equally powerful impulse to secure recognition for one's contributions.[5]

While the Human Genome Project demonstrated what elite scientific institutions could achieve through coordinated effort, the internet was simultaneously enabling a more anarchic approach to knowledge creation that would challenge the very notion of expertise itself. Wikipedia, for example, represents either the greatest experiment in democratic knowledge creation or convincing evidence that humanity's collective wisdom may be distilled into endless arguments about whether hot dogs are sandwiches.[6] The notion of collective intelligence, on which Wikipedia was founded, continues to come full circle as debates surrounding the censorship of truth in the age of disinformation enter the mainstream, once again. The ability for millions to contribute to what is deemed true in a world that ventures beyond that concept via synthetic content and institutional distrust makes Wikipedia a unique concept.[7] Open-source software development represents another important version of global knowledge networks with systems and programs, such as Linux, Apache, and Python, powering applications from smartphones to spaceships.[8] Unfortunately, the prevalence of supply chain attacks targeting projects maintained by what essentially equates to volunteers reveals a picture resembling a magnificent skyscraper built on a foundation laid by someone who does it on the weekends for fun.[9] The same digital infrastructure that enabled researchers to collaborate across continents and Wikipedia editors to debate sandwich taxonomy also played out in millions of home offices around the world.

Remote work technology reached sudden maturity in March 2020 as knowledge workers around the globe discovered that the term work from home was tantamount to the notion of live at work.[10] While the coffee may have been worse, the transition revealed both the liberating potential of location-independent collaboration and the dystopian reality of being perpetually available to colleagues. The digital innovation of virtual meeting software gave way to virtual meeting fatigue, a term used to capture the notion that virtual meetings overrun the workday of millions of Americans each day. This phenomenon underscores the notion that staring at video feeds of oneself each day for eight hours straight while trying to stay engaged with a monotone presenter is not the most efficient approach to productivity.[11] In fact, organizations that rely more on asynchronous communication (e.g., email) report higher levels of productivity and lower levels of burnout.[12] The remote work revolution represented just one facet of a broader transformation in how human intelligence could be harnessed across geographic boundaries (e.g., citizen-scientists making astronomical discoveries).

Beyond the arguments in Wikipedia forums, examples of crowdsourced innovation provide hope for the future of humanity (e.g., Galaxy Zoo, Foldit), as well as the potential pitfalls. In the early 2000s, Galaxy Zoo pioneered the concept of citizen-science by providing volunteers with the opportunity to classify astronomical images.[13] As it turned out, individuals excelled at this complex pattern recognition program. Volunteers beat automated systems and generated legitimate scientific discoveries through a crowdsourced approach. The success of Galaxy Zoo underscores the importance of using AI as a supplement to natural intelligence, rather than as a direct replacement.

Foldit presented a gamified approach to the complex notion of protein folding through presenting a competitive puzzle game.[14] The gamification of science drove sustained motivation in participants that created scientific breakthroughs in record amounts of time. One such example was when a team of non-scientists uncovered the structure of a key AIDS-related enzyme in a few weeks, which was a problem that stumped experts for over a decade. The successes of Galaxy Zoo and Foldit represent the positive aspects of citizen-science as an approach to leverage untapped resources through user engagement and community dynamics. The evidence provided by these programs supports the concept of democratization of scientific challenges to facilitate breakthroughs, while also raising questions concerning why scientific institutions excluded public participation in science for so long.

Mind the Gap: Digital Divides and Cultural Paradoxes

The Promethean fire of digital connectivity illuminates the most stark contradictions of technological progress. Even after decades of technological advancements and policy efforts, the digital divide remains evident in the United States. In fact, the Federal Communications Commission stated that 24 million Americans lack access to fixed broadband connectivity, which is roughly 7% of the country's population, in a report issued in March 2024 relying on data from 2022.[15] However, technological innovations democratized access to information in unexpected ways. In Kenya, for example, M-Pesa turned mobile phones into banking systems, offering financial services access to populations that were previously unbanked.[16] The success of this and similar efforts illustrates how technological advancements may meet genuine social demands by aligning public interests with business models.

This duality extends to deeper questions around inclusion and cultural preservation. Women encounter obstacles (e.g., cultural limitations, financial challenges, safety concerns) that restrict participation in digital economies, while harassment predominantly targeting women and marginalized groups reveals how technology amplifies rather than supplants existing social dynamics.[17,18] The myth of the internet as a utopian destination collides with the reality that digital spaces often mirror and magnify offline inequalities. Another indicator of the duality of technological innovation, with the same advancements aimed at solving a problem being the underlying cause of that problem, is the Rosetta Project, which involved using digital resources to preserve endangered languages before they vanished.[19] While the effort is important and commendable, it is important to note that the project also serves to highlight the role of globalization and digital communication in hastening language extinction. Tangentially related to this principle is the concept of social media platforms as a means to maintain cultural connections and facilitate the sharing of traditional knowledge in Indigenous communities across geographical distances.[20] Several platforms contain groups and videos teaching traditional crafts, languages, and practices that might otherwise be lost to cultural assimilation. While important, it is an unfortunate reality that the same global technology platforms that preserve local cultural traditions simultaneously threaten them through persistent cultural homogenization pressures.[21] These cultural and social transformations are inseparable from the economic forces that drive them. The same technologies that create digital divides and cultural paradoxes also serve as the primary engines of modern economic growth by generating unprecedented wealth opportunities and restructuring entire industries.

Economic Drivers of Technological Innovation

Remarkable increases in productivity gains while simultaneously removing the need for humans to complete dangerous and monotonous tasks are key realizations of automation in manufacturing.[22] Another example that revolutionized agriculture is tractors guided by GPS rather than humans, which allowed for more efficient resource optimization and reductions in environmental impact.[23] Contemporary farmers may also use algorithms to facilitate more accurate planting, fertilization, and harvesting in ways that would not be possible when solely relying on traditional methods.[24] These innovations highlight the transformational nature of technology as a means to satisfy human needs through thoughtful deployment, rather than solely in the pursuit of efficiency for its own sake. The difficulty, therefore, lies in making certain that productivity improvements provide an advantage to workers and communities, in addition to shareholders. To that end, evidence shows that healthcare automation produces mixed results. For instance, electronic health records improved data management while creating new administrative burdens and security concerns.[25] In another manifestation, diagnostic imaging analysis achieved superhuman accuracy in some domains while introducing new forms of algorithmic bias in others. The IBM Watson oncology system, for example, serves as a cautionary tale about overselling AI capabilities to healthcare providers desperate for technological solutions to systemic problems.[26] Perhaps even more damning is the finding that oncologist skills may atrophy as a result of reliance on AI-enhanced diagnostic tools.[27]

Beyond automation, digital platforms democratized entrepreneurship and economic freedom by reducing traditional barriers to market entry, although research shows they replaced those hurdles with new forms of platform dependency (e.g., e-commerce platforms enable global reach for small businesses while simultaneously using marketplace data to identify and compete with successful sellers).[28] Additionally, the gig economy promises flexibility and independence while delivering precarious employment with algorithmic management.[29] For example, Uber drivers enjoy the freedom to set their own schedules while earning below minimum wage and bearing all business risks that traditional employers would absorb.[30] More broadly, the digital platform model socializes risks while privatizing profits, creating wealth for platform owners while leaving users to navigate the vagaries (e.g., deplatforming). The asymmetric power relationship between platforms and businesses reveals the illusion of independence in platform-mediated markets and illustrates the fundamental mechanism of WAVE theory. Technological advancements expand human potential while also creating new vectors for exploitation. The gig economy that promises flexibility delivers anxiety. The platforms that enable entrepreneurship create dependency. The automation that increases productivity displaces workers. Given that economic disruption stemming from technological innovation serves as both motivation and opportunity for manipulation, it is essential to investigate the negative implications associated with new technological iterations and advancements.

Dark Side of Innovation

Every technological breakthrough carries within it the seeds of unintended applications, as if innovation itself operates according to Murphy's Law dressed in venture capital clothing. The same AI systems used to decode proteins to advance modern science may be exploited to engineer bioweapons. The platforms that democratize knowledge creation provide avenues for disinformation warfare. As such, this paradoxical nature exemplifies a key component of WAVE theory, which is the idea that advancements in human capability generate new exploitation opportunities.

Macro-Level Evidence: Cyberwarfare and Disinformation

Stuxnet signaled the beginning of cyberwarfare by demonstrating that software may be capable of damaging targets as comprehensively as bombs.[31] The coordinated attacks by Russia against the power grid of Ukraine shifted infrastructure operations into military targets by circumventing traditional laws of war.[32] The SolarWinds supply chain attack weaponized trust itself, demonstrating how adversaries could exploit the collaborative networks that define modern innovation.[33] Beyond these historical innovations lies the potential future of warfare as autonomous weapons development proceeds with the inexorable logic of military competition despite humanitarian concerns. On the positive side, arguments include the idea that this technology promises reduced military casualties through precision targeting. Arguments from detractors include the raising of existential questions about machines making life-and-death decisions without sufficient human oversight. For example, predictive defense systems may trigger conflicts through algorithmic misinterpretation, conducting warfare at machine speed beyond human decision-making thresholds. To put it another way, the same collaborative intelligence that enables citizen-science may become a threat if mediated through autonomous systems designed for weapons that are not adequately supervised.

Deepfake technology represents another manifestation of the weaponization of human trust since it enables synthetic media to exploit the psychological foundations of interpersonal relationships.[34] In the geopolitical context, deepfakes threaten democratic discourse by enhancing the liar's dividend (i.e., the notion of dismissing authentic evidence as a fabricated narrative).[35] Moreover, information warfare evolved from crude propaganda to sophisticated narrative manipulation that exploits social media algorithms and human psychology.[36] Election interference operations achieve strategic objectives through relatively modest investments in targeted content and algorithmic amplification with success demonstrating how understanding platform dynamics and cognitive biases enables small actors to influence political outcomes in major democracies. Put another way, the same platforms that enable democratic participation also provide vectors for foreign interference and create security dilemmas pitting openness against security in ways that democratic theory continues to fail to resolve. Thus, the same social media algorithms that connect communities and democratize information become instruments for psychological manipulation when weaponized by the adversary, a clear application of WAVE theory. Beyond the revelations around the negative repercussions of innovation in terms of cyberwarfare and misinformation at the nation-state level, the rise of the surveillance economy, and subsequent dissipation of anonymity, demonstrates the adverse potential for innovation at the organizational and individual level.

Meso- and Micro-Level Evidence: The Surveillance Economy and Anonymity Collapse

Surveillance capitalism (i.e., the practice of collecting and selling large quantities of user data) transformed human experiences into raw material for behavioral prediction products creating the equivalent of an industry based on psychological extraction. Data brokers (i.e., the companies that buy and sell user data) maintain comprehensive surveillance operations that exceed the capabilities of many totalitarian regimes while maintaining the veneer of commercial service.[37] Location tracking through smartphone applications provides a clear example of this concept where users trade convenience for privacy, although opaqueness around the voluntary nature of the exchange stems from complex terms of service. The extent of collected data generated an economy based on human attention with advertisers competing for a user's eyeballs. Real-time bidding systems auction access to individual users within milliseconds of data point collection to create markets for human consciousness that operate faster than conscious thought.[38] The psychological manipulation involved makes traditional advertising seem refreshingly honest by comparison. Internet of Things (IoT) devices (i.e., the various devices connected to the internet as a means to simplify the life of an individual) represent a key component of the surveillance economy. The reality of the proliferation of these devices is that smart gadgets made living rooms into platforms for data gathering through continuously active microphones and sensors.[39] The convenience of voice interfaces also provides a tradeoff as it relates to the surveillance capabilities provided by these devices that normalize monitoring of individuals under the guise of customer service. IoT devices frequently emphasize convenience at the expense of security, resulting in weaknesses that facilitate adversary access to door locks, thermostats, and kitchen appliances. For example, the Mirai botnet showcased the potential weaponization of hacked IoT devices to facilitate distributed attacks, underscoring the inherent tradeoff between convenience and security of these devices.[40]

As a result of the surveillance economy, anonymous data proves to be an oxymoron in practice, as researchers repeatedly demonstrate how supposedly anonymized datasets can be reidentified through correlation with other information sources.[41] One incident involving a popular streaming platform evidenced this lesson when researchers reidentified users from anonymous movie ratings by correlating viewing patterns with public reviews from an online content website.[42] The psychological impact extends beyond mere privacy violation as individuals modify their behavior when they realize their activities may be traced back to them. Furthermore, facial recognition technology enables identification of individuals in public spaces through increasingly sophisticated algorithms that can recognize faces despite masks, sunglasses, and deliberate attempts at disguise. The technology's widespread deployment despite documented bias problems creates a chilling effect on public behavior, particularly among marginalized communities who experience higher error rates. Research also shows that the knowledge of being constantly identifiable transforms public spaces into panopticons where individuals self-censor to create the psychological preconditions for broader social control.[43,44] Additionally, evidence indicates that social network analysis may reveal personal relationships, political affiliations, and behavioral patterns through analysis of communication metadata. Leaked materials from the U.S. National Security Agency (NSA), for example, demonstrated how just metadata may provide more invasive surveillance than traditional wiretapping while evading legal protections designed for content surveillance.[45] As such, the distinction between metadata and content becomes meaningless when algorithmic analysis infers private information from communication patterns. The resulting psychological toll associated with knowing that online activity may be traced back to an individual facilitates a form of anticipatory conformity where people change behavior due to the anticipation of observation, rather than to obfuscate deviant acts. Thus, the collapse of anonymity resulting from the surveillance economy fosters psychological vulnerabilities that enable manipulation by more than just the adversary. In alignment with a central tenet of WAVE theory, technologies designed to improve services transform into instruments for exploitation by the adversary.

Psychological Ramifications

The transition from surveillance to manipulation represents a natural evolution in the weaponization of human vulnerability. Variable-ratio reinforcement schedules embedded in social media notifications create psychological dependency by exploiting fundamental elements of human psychology via operant conditioning.[46] Infinite scroll designs exemplify this concept by eliminating natural stopping points in digital content consumption and complicating conscious decisions regarding content consumption.[47] When viewed through the lens of WAVE theory, these notions represent the idea that technologies designed to enhance connection in theory actually foster loneliness and self-isolation in practice. Screen dependency among adolescents reached levels that concern many mental health professionals with some teenagers reportedly spending over eight hours daily on smartphones.[48,49] Digital detox emerged as a practice to manage screen dependency, which implies that healthy technology use requires deliberate effort and the inherent mismatch between human psychology and technology design priorities that favor engagement over well-being.

Algorithmic biases provide another manifestation of psychological harm stemming from technological innovation. Research shows hiring algorithms penalized women and minorities when trained on historical data.[50] While criminal justice algorithms used for bail, sentencing, and parole decisions also allegedly perpetuate racial disparities, recommendation algorithms on social media platforms additionally fragment shared foundations of truth needed for healthy democratic discourse, feeding amplified political polarization through limited exposure to diverse perspectives.[51,52] Forums dedicated to conspiracy theories illustrate how online communities can create alternate reality bubbles that isolate individuals from mainstream society while potentially inspiring real-world violence and self-isolation.[53,54] Research shows that fear-based media coverage amplified by social media algorithms creates anxiety disorders and unrealistic risk perceptions, influencing personal and political decisions.[55] Additionally, social media comparison culture encourages users to evaluate their lives against curated presentations of others' experiences, creating unrealistic expectations and reduced life satisfaction.[56] When each of these findings is viewed as a component of the broader WAVE theory, these psychological ramifications reveal the potential manipulation as technologies designed to improve life facilitate psychological harm. The challenge, therefore, lies in crafting responses to protect human welfare without stifling technological progress.

Ethical & Regulatory Challenges

Governance Frameworks

Governing technology's dual nature requires navigating between innovation and protection, a dynamic that also proves important to forensic cyberpsychology by shaping the nature of the threats that society faces. The unfortunate reality is that regulatory intervention itself reproduces the Prometheus Paradox by introducing vulnerabilities and unintended consequences. Multi-stakeholder governance sounds wonderfully democratic until participants discover that stakeholder often means anyone with enough money to hire lobbyists. Internet governance through ICANN demonstrates how technical expertise can coexist with political accountability, though the organization's effectiveness depends on voluntary cooperation that becomes strained when economic or political interests diverge.[57] The Internet Governance Forum also provides a platform for dialog that enables all stakeholders to express their views while ensuring that none of them has binding authority to implement solutions. Another timely example relates to AI governance initiatives, which multiply like academic conferences, all while generating ethical frameworks that compete for attention while avoiding binding commitments. This proliferation creates opportunities for the exploitation of cognitive overload, where the sheer volume of competing standards prevents meaningful evaluation. Corporate ethics boards, which represent well-intentioned attempts to integrate moral considerations into business decision-making, provide another example of multi-stakeholder governance. Unfortunately, their effectiveness depends on authority and independence that companies are reluctant to provide. This fosters the concept of moral licensing (i.e., the tendency to engage in deviant behavior after establishing ethical credentials). Regulatory sandboxes attempt to balance innovation with protection by creating controlled environments for testing new technologies under relaxed regulatory requirements. From a WAVE theory perspective, these arrangements often provide competitive advantages to selected participants while creating regulatory gaps that adversaries may exploit. Similarly, adaptive regulation promises flexible frameworks that evolve with technological change while maintaining accountability for outcomes. In practice, adaptive regulation often favors the regulated entities rather than public interests, particularly when industry expertise exceeds regulatory knowledge. The development of algorithmic auditing frameworks provides another manifestation of this notion via calls for transparency for automated decision-making systems, which unfortunately often fail at the enforcement stage of implementation due to the proprietary nature of algorithms.

Ethical Frameworks

In addition to these more modern approaches to regulatory frameworks (e.g., multi-stakeholder, sandboxes, adaptive), technology ethics became a growth industry, leading to consultants, academic programs, and corporate positions aimed at providing the appearance of moral seriousness. Ethics-by-design in the context of AI provides an example of this approach by promising to integrate moral considerations into innovations from the beginning.[58] In practice, the implementation of ethics-by-design often reduces production to compliance checklists designed to satisfy lawyers more than to address psychological vulnerabilities. To a similar end, ethics review boards proliferate throughout technology companies and create well-paying employment opportunities for philosophers. Amazingly, these company-funded ethical review boards typically generate guidance that coincides with business interests. To a similar end, AI liability frameworks attempt to establish accountability for algorithmic harm while addressing the challenge of tracing responsibility through complex sociotechnical systems. Proposed approaches range from strict liability (i.e., making developers responsible for all algorithmic outcomes) to negligence standards (i.e., requiring proof of unreasonable care). The diversity of proposals reflects fundamental disagreements about whether AI systems should be regulated like products, services, or something entirely new. Algorithmic transparency requirements mandate disclosure of AI system operation for decisions affecting individual rights. The implementation of these requirements faces sustained resistance from companies claiming trade secret protections. Interestingly, the potential adoption of professional licensing standards for AI developers and programmers illustrates an approach to refine ethical obligations of the profession in a manner similar to fields such as doctors and engineers, although industries generally resist professional regulations that limit flexibility and increase legal liability. Further support for the concept of AI developer or programmer licensing includes the callout that most jurisdictions require licensure for hairdressers and barbers.

Environmental, Social, and Governance (ESG) reporting expanded to include cybersecurity factors as some investors prioritize social impact. ESG measurement for technology companies faces the challenge of quantifying intangible harms (e.g., psychological manipulation, social fragmentation, democratic erosion). Technology-focused ESG reporting often emphasizes easily measured factors (e.g., energy consumption, employee diversity) while downplaying harder-to-quantify impacts (e.g., algorithmic bias, mental health impact).[59] As a result, ESG reporting often manifests as reporting aimed at satisfying investor demand for responsibility while avoiding accountability for the harms. In addition to ESG reporting, algorithmic transparency reports provide information about automated decision-making.[60] These reports often include sophisticated, technical jargon, leading to questions about the definition of transparency as it relates to explainability. Many dissenters argue that transparency without plain-language disclosure generates an illusion of accountability that may actually impede genuine oversight by satisfying demands for disclosure while preventing effective scrutiny. Similarly, content moderation transparency reports document platform policy enforcement while revealing the nature of content moderation decisions that affect millions of users each day, which often appear arbitrary as a result of absent context.[61] These reports demonstrate the challenge of moderating content at a global scale while highlighting how platform policies become de facto speech regulation if appropriate oversight is not incorporated. In terms of WAVE theory, transparency without enforcement creates symbolic accountability that enables continued psychological manipulation through systems perpetuating technocratic governance.

Legal Frameworks

The GDPR represents Europe's attempt to restore individual control over personal data while creating compliance burdens that favor large technology companies capable of absorbing regulatory costs.[62] GDPR's global impact reflects regulatory ambitions and the difficulty of maintaining different privacy practices across jurisdictions. While the regulation improved privacy awareness and generated impressive fine revenue for European regulators, it fails to address the fundamental psychological manipulation enabled by data collection. In the United States, the CCPA provides Californians with data ownership rights that most other Americans lack.[63] The CCPA demonstrates both the potential for subnational privacy regulation and the complexity associated with privacy rights varying by geography rather than principle. In response to the GDPR and CCPA, many companies provide minimum compliance rather than maximum protection, which suggests privacy legislation requires further examination to foster the desired outcome.

Privacy law compliance additionally proves challenging when data processing involves complex technical systems that lawyers struggle to understand and technologists struggle to explain. Legal requirements for informed consent essentially become meaningless when privacy policies require graduate-level reading skills and data processing occurs through ever-changing algorithmic systems. The gap between legal theory and technical reality fosters compliance theater rather than genuine privacy protection. Furthermore, cross-border data transfers create jurisdictional nightmares, benefiting technology companies capable of exploiting regulatory arbitrage. Data localization requirements were enacted in some countries to combat this issue. However, these policies create compliance costs while potentially undermining privacy protection by forcing data storage in countries with weaker legal protections. In essence, the fragmentation of global data governance creates opportunities for regulatory shopping that benefit sophisticated actors while disadvantaging consumers and smaller companies. International technology governance faces similar fundamental challenges as cybercrime prosecution, given that digital platforms operate globally while legal authority remains territorially bounded. Platform liability varies dramatically across jurisdictions and creates compliance challenges for companies and protection gaps for users. For instance, some countries provide broad immunity to platforms for user-generated content, while others impose strict liability for illegal material on a platform. This bifurcation often culminates in a platform required to choose between over-censorship and legal risk, which provides avenues for exploitation by the adversary. Therefore, the evidence clearly supports that the fundamental issue across all regulatory approaches is that they attempt to govern technological systems rather than focusing on the psychological vulnerabilities these systems exploit. Effective governance necessitates a deep understanding of how human psychology interacts with algorithmic systems. A concept highlighting the importance of incorporating psychological principles from WAVE theory into future regulatory approaches to avoid missing the core mechanisms that enable the weaponization of technology to manipulate cognitive vulnerabilities.

Conclusion

The fire of technological capability, once stolen from the realm of impossibility, burns according to its own logic. It forges tools of unprecedented human flourishing and weapons of unprecedented destruction. The evidence presented throughout this chapter reveals the fundamental truth that technological innovation cannot be stopped. Every breakthrough that expands human potential, from AlphaFold's protein folding capabilities to the collaborative networks that advanced astronomical research, also creates new vectors for exploitation. This duality constitutes the core mechanism through which technology becomes weaponized against cognitive vulnerability. Remote collaboration platforms that connect global scientific communities also enable sophisticated psychological manipulation. Digital platforms that democratize entrepreneurship create new forms of economic dependency ripe for exploitation. Surveillance technologies that promise security transform privacy into a luxury good while creating psychological conditions for broader social control. The pattern repeats…Each solution generates new problems, each connection creates new vulnerabilities, and each enhancement of human capability opens new avenues for its weaponization.

It is evident that traditional approaches to technology will continue to prove inadequate until the incorporation of forensic cyberpsychology principles occurs. The cyclical nature of history continues to prove that regulatory frameworks focusing on technical specifications miss the psychological dimensions through which technology becomes truly dangerous, given that the exploitation of technological vulnerabilities extends far beyond corporate boardrooms. Forensic cyberpsychology offers tools for analyzing how technological systems interact with psychology and enables more nuanced assessments of both benefits and risks. By extension, WAVE theory provides a framework for anticipating how beneficial technologies might be weaponized to support proactive mitigation rather than awaiting a reactive response. To build on this understanding and identify practical applications of WAVE theory, Chapter 6 explores how cybercrime evolved from simple computer intrusions perpetrated by a lone wolf into sophisticated attacks orchestrated by transnational crime syndicates.

Reflection Questions

1 Which innovation has yielded the most ambiguous societal impact? What factors determine whether its benefits outweigh its harms?
2 How can privacy rights be preserved without stifling beneficial data uses that depend on large-scale information collection?
3 Where does corporate responsibility end and regulation begin when addressing technology-related harms?
4 What metrics should reporting include to identify potential psychological harm? How could these impacts be reliably measured?

Skill Builder Labs

Application Scenario: Prometheus Analysis

Select a new technological advancement with which you are familiar and do the following:

- Identify specific benefits that the technology provides.
- For each benefit identified, identify how the technology may be weaponized against human psychological vulnerabilities.
- Write a brief synopsis applying WAVE theory to the scenario.

Mini Research Activity: Comparing AI ethics Governance Models

Objective

Analyze efficacy and challenges of AI governance frameworks.

Instructions

1 Select 3–4 AI governance frameworks.
2 Compare the scope of the model (e.g., covered applications, requirements, emerging technology coverage).

3 Describe any enforcement mechanisms (e.g., monitoring, penalties, compliance verification).
4 Explain stakeholder participation methodologies (e.g., affected communities, power balances, democratic input).
5 Identify likely outcomes (e.g., behavioral changes, unintended consequences).
6 Evaluate implementation feasibility and adaptability.
7 Outline lessons for improving AI governance effectiveness.

Deliverable

Produce a comparative governance analysis report evaluating multiple AI governance frameworks, including evidence-based recommendations for enhancement.

References

1. Jumper, J., Evans, R., Pritzel, A., Green, T., Figurnov, M., Ronneberger, O., ... & Hassabis, D. (2021). Highly accurate protein structure prediction with AlphaFold. *Nature*, *596*(7873), 583–589.
2. Hunter, P. (2024). Security challenges by AI-assisted protein design: The ability to design proteins in silico could pose a new threat for biosecurity and biosafety. *EMBO Reports*, *25*(5), 2168–2171.
3. Research Consulting Limited. (2022). *Intelligent open science: A case study of viral genomic data sharing during the COVID-19 pandemic* (Prepared for the UK Government). Research Consulting Limited.
4. National Human Genome Research Institute. (2020). *An overview of the Human Genome Project*. National Institutes of Health.
5. Resnik, D. B. (2006). Openness versus secrecy in scientific research. *Episteme*, *2*(3), 135–147.
6. Shi, F., Teplitskiy, M., Duede, E., & Evans, J. A. (2019). The wisdom of polarized crowds. *Nature Human Behaviour*, *3*(4), 329–336.
7. Giles, J. (2005). Internet encyclopaedias go head to head. *Nature*, *438*(7070), 900–901.
8. NASA. (n.d.). *NASA open source software*.
9. Ohm, M., Plate, H., Sykosch, A., & Meier, M. (2020). Backstabber's knife collection: A review of open source software supply chain attacks. In *International conference on detection of intrusions and malware, and vulnerability assessment* (pp. 23–43). Springer International Publishing.
10. Barrero, J. M., Bloom, N., & Davis, S. J. (2021). Why working from home will stick. *National Bureau of Economic Research Working Paper* 28731.
11. Bailenson, J. N. (2021). Nonverbal overload: A theoretical argument for the causes of Zoom fatigue. *Technology, Mind, and Behavior*, *2*(1), 1–6.
12. Jhala, M., & Menon, R. (2021). Examining the impact of an asynchronous communication platform versus existing communication methods: An observational study. *BMJ Innovations*, *7*(1), 68–74.
13. Lintott, C. J., et al. (2008). Galaxy Zoo: Morphologies derived from visual inspection of galaxies from the Sloan Digital Sky Survey. *Monthly Notices of the Royal Astronomical Society*, *389*(3), 1179–1189.
14. Cooper, S., et al. (2010). Predicting protein structures with a multiplayer online game. *Nature*, *466*(7307), 756–760.
15. U.S. Federal Communications Commission. (2024). *2024 Section 706 Report*.

16 Lauzon, C. (2025). Fintech in Un-Banked Populations of the World. *SSRN 5187117*.
17 Raihan, M. M., Subroto, S., Chowdhury, N., Koch, K., Ruttan, E., & Turin, T. C. (2025). Dimensions and barriers for digital (in) equity and digital divide: A systematic integrative review. *Digital Transformation and Society*, *4*(2), 111–127.
18 Henry, N., & Powell, A. (2018). Technology-facilitated sexual violence: A literature review of empirical research. *Trauma, Violence, & Abuse*, *19*(2), 195–208.
19 Mason, J. M. (2003). Collaborative project: The Rosetta Project-ALL Language Archive. *NSF Award Number 0333727. Directorate for STEM Education*, *3*(333727), 33727.
20 Botangen, K. A., Vodanovich, S., & Yu, J. (2018). Preservation of indigenous culture among indigenous migrants through social media: The Igorot peoples. *arXiv preprint arXiv:1802.09685*.
21 Balogun, S. K., & Aruoture, E. (2024). Cultural homogenization vs. cultural diversity: Social media's double-edged sword in the age of globalization. *African Journal of Social and Behavioural Sciences*, *14*(4), 1491–1512.
22 Lowe, B. D., Hayden, M., Albers, J., & Naber, S. (2023). Case studies of robots and automation as health/safety interventions in small manufacturing enterprises. *Human Factors and Ergonomics in Manufacturing & Service Industries*, *33*(1), 69–103.
23 Stentz, A., Dima, C., Wellington, C., Herman, H., & Stager, D. (2002). A system for semi-autonomous tractor operations. *Autonomous Robots*, *13*(1), 87–104.
24 Jha, K., Doshi, A., Patel, P., & Shah, M. (2019). A comprehensive review on automation in agriculture using artificial intelligence. *Artificial Intelligence in Agriculture*, *2*, 1–12.
25 Penchala, R., & Parimala, V. K. (2025). Perspective chapter: Securing the future of digital healthcare with EHR systems for modern cyber threats. In *Electronic health records-issues and challenges in healthcare systems*. IntechOpen.
26 Strickland, E. (2019). IBM Watson, heal thyself: How IBM overpromised and underdelivered on AI health care. *IEEE Spectrum*, *56*(4), 24–31.
27 Natali, C., Marconi, L., Dias Duran, L. D., & Cabitza, F. (2025). AI-induced deskilling in medicine: A mixed-method review and research agenda for healthcare and beyond. *Artificial Intelligence Review*, *58*(11), 1–40.
28 Cutolo, D., & Kenney, M. (2021). Platform-dependent entrepreneurs: Power asymmetries, risks, and strategies in the platform economy. *Academy of Management Perspectives*, *35*(4), 584–605.
29 Rosenblat, A., & Stark, L. (2016). Algorithmic labor and information asymmetries: A case study of Uber's drivers. *International Journal of Communication*, *10*, 27.
30 Dubal, V. (2019). An Uber ambivalence: Employee status, worker perspectives, & regulation in the gig economy. *UC Hastings Research Paper*, (381).
31 Collins, S., & McCombie, S. (2012). Stuxnet: the emergence of a new cyber weapon and its implications. *Journal of Policing, Intelligence and Counter Terrorism*, *7*(1), 80–91.
32 Limnéll, J. (2015). The exploitation of cyber domain as part of warfare: Russo-Ukrainian war. *International Journal of Cyber-Security and Digital Forensics*, *4*(4), 521–532.
33 Datta, P. (2022). Hannibal at the gates: Cyberwarfare & the Solarwinds sunburst hack. *Journal of Information Technology Teaching Cases*, *12*(2), 115–120.
34 Popa, C., Pallath, R., Cunningham, L., Tahiri, H., Kesavarajah, A., & Wu, T. (2025). Deepfake technology unveiled: The commoditization of AI and its impact on digital trust. *arXiv preprint arXiv:2506.07363*.
35 Schiff, K. J., Schiff, D. S., & Bueno, N. (2022). The liar's dividend: Can politicians use deepfakes and fake news to evade accountability. *American Political Science Review*, *100*(1), 1–20.

36 Prier, J. (2020). Commanding the trend: Social media as information warfare. In *Information warfare in the age of cyber conflict* (pp. 88–113). Edited By Christopher Whyte, A. Trevor Thrall, Brian M. Mazanec Routledge.
37 Crain, M. (2018). The limits of transparency: Data brokers and commodification. *New Media & Society*, *20*(1), 88–104.
38 Ou, W., Chen, B., Dai, X., Zhang, W., Liu, W., Tang, R., & Yu, Y. (2023). A survey on bid optimization in real-time bidding display advertising. *ACM Transactions on Knowledge Discovery from Data*, *18*(3), 1–31.
39 Gray, S. (2016). Always on: privacy implications of microphone-enabled devices. Future of Privacy Forum, Washington, D.C.
40 Kambourakis, G., Kolias, C., & Stavrou, A. (2017, October). The mirai botnet and the iot zombie armies. In *MILCOM 2017–2017 IEEE military communications conference* (pp. 267–272). IEEE.
41 Ji, S., Li, W., Srivatsa, M., & Beyah, R. (2016). Structural data de-anonymization: Theory and practice. *IEEE/ACM Transactions on Networking*, *24*(6), 3523–3536.
42 Narayanan, A., & Shmatikov, V. (2006). How to break anonymity of the Netflix prize dataset. *arXiv preprint cs/0610105*.
43 Foucault, M. (2012). *Discipline and punish: The birth of the prison*. Vintage.
44 Lyon, D. (Ed.). (2006). *Theorizing surveillance*. Routledge.
45 Miller, S., & Walsh, P. (2016). The NSA leaks, Edward Snowden, and the ethics and accountability of intelligence collection. In *Ethics and the future of spying* (pp. 193–204). Edited By Jai Galliott, Warren Reed Routledge.
46 Alter, A. (2017). *Irresistible: The rise of addictive technology and the business of keeping us hooked*. Penguin Press.
47 Montag, C., Lachmann, B., Herrlich, M., & Zweig, K. (2019). Addictive features of social media/messenger platforms and freemium games against the background of psychological and economic theories. *International Journal of Environmental Research and Public Health*, *16*(14), 2612.
48 Twenge, J. M., & Campbell, W. K. (2018). Associations between screen time and lower psychological well-being among children and adolescents: Evidence from a population-based study. *Preventive Medicine Reports*, *12*, 271–283.
49 Rideout, V., & Robb, M. B. (2021). *The common sense census: Media use by tweens and teens*. Common Sense Media.
50 Bolukbasi, T., Chang, K.-W., Zou, J. Y., Saligrama, V., & Kalai, A. (2016). Man is to computer programmer as woman is to homemaker? Debiasing word embeddings. *Advances in Neural Information Processing Systems*, *29*, 4349–4357.
51 Pariser, E. (2011). *The filter bubble: What the internet is hiding from you*. Penguin Press.
52 Sunstein, C. R. (2017). *#Republic: Divided democracy in the age of social media*. Princeton University Press.
53 Douglas, K. M., Sutton, R. M., & Cichocka, A. (2017). The psychology of conspiracy theories. *Current Directions in Psychological Science*, *26*(6), 538–542.
54 Zannettou, S., Caulfield, T., De Cristofaro, E., Kourtelris, N., Leontiadis, I., Sirivianos, M., … & Blackburn, J. (2017, November). The web centipede: Understanding how web communities influence each other through the lens of mainstream and alternative news sources. In *Proceedings of the 2017 internet measurement conference*. Association for Computing Machinery, New York, NY, USA, 405–417.
55 Bail, C. A. (2021). *Breaking the social media prism: How to make our platforms less polarizing*. Princeton University Press.

56 McCarthy, P. A., & Morina, N. (2020). Exploring the association of social comparison with depression and anxiety: A systematic review and meta-analysis. *Clinical Psychology & Psychotherapy, 27*(5), 640–671.
57 Brey, P., & Dainow, B. (2024). Ethics by design for artificial intelligence. *AI and Ethics, 4*(4), 1265–1277.
58 Brey, P., & Dainow, B. (2024). Ethics by design for artificial intelligence. *AI and Ethics, 4*(4), 1265–1277.
59 Homavazir, Z., Madan, S., Verma, S., Gambhir, V., & Homavazir, M. (2025). Governance for the digital age: ESG-driven framework for ethical and inclusive innovation. *Advances in Consumer Research, 2*(3). 257–264.
60 Luria, M. (2023, June). Co-design perspectives on algorithm transparency reporting: Guidelines and prototypes. In *Proceedings of the 2023 ACM conference on fairness, accountability, and transparency*. Association for Computing Machinery, New York, NY, USA, 1076–1087.
61 Urman, A., & Makhortykh, M. (2023). How transparent are transparency reports? Comparative analysis of transparency reporting across online platforms. *Telecommunications Policy, 47*(3), 102477.
62 European Commission, Regulation (EU) 2016/679 of the European Parliament and of the Council of 27 April 2016 on the protection of natural persons with regard to the processing of personal data and on the free movement of such data, and repealing Directive 95/46/EC (General Data Protection Regulation, GDPR).
63 California Consumer Privacy Act. (2018). Cal. Civ. Code § 1798.100 et seq.

6 Evolution and Transformation of Cybercrime

Proto-Hacks (1960s–1980s)

Each shiny new technology arrives with promises of human betterment, only to be immediately weaponized by individuals who view laws merely as suggestions. The reactionary posture of cybersecurity programs leads to executives fighting tomorrow's wars with yesterday's strategies. The numbers support this analogy with reported cybercrime losses reaching $16.6 billion in 2024, marking a 33% jump from 2023.[1] For context, that figure roughly equals the revenue attributable to sales of Ozempic, the diabetes drug that transformed Novo Nordisk into a pharmaceutical giant and one of the most valuable companies in Europe, in 2024.[2] While medical researchers spent decades perfecting molecular GLP-1 based interventions through rigorous testing, the adversary also perfected psychological manipulations through trial and error on live targets. No clinical trials. No ethical oversight. No safety protocols. Instead, relentless experimentation on human cognitive vulnerabilities at an industrial scale. When viewed through the lens of WAVE theory, cybercrime evolution follows a clear pattern. Each technological breakthrough that enhances human capability creates new vectors for psychological manipulation. What appears as cybercrime evolution actually reveals the adversary's growing sophistication through orchestrating behavioral resonance across multiple cognitive systems. This chapter traces that evolution from the early days of the internet marked by curiosity-driven exploration to contemporary applications marked by industrial-scale operations.

Cybercrime began almost as soon as computers themselves existed, which should surprise exactly no one familiar with human nature. During the mainframe era, computing resources were expensive and access was limited. Unauthorized use represented both technical achievement and psychological transgression rolled into one intellectually satisfying package. The Massachusetts Institute of Technology Compatible Time-Sharing System experienced some of the first documented intrusions when students discovered they could access other users' files.[3] These curious kids found arbitrary system boundaries less compelling than system administrators intended. The university environment, designed to encourage intellectual exploration, inadvertently became a laboratory for the first generation of unauthorized access techniques. Beyond the laboratory, phone phreaking emerged when John Draper discovered that toy whistles from cereal boxes could manipulate telephone switching systems.[4] Captain Crunch, as Draper was known, demonstrated principles fundamental to WAVE theory. Technical capability (e.g., frequency generation) synchronized with social manipulation (e.g., exploiting trust in telecommunications infrastructure) was combined by Captain Crunch to create behavioral resonance. Kevin Mitnick also refined social engineering during this period by establishing patterns that the adversary still leverages decades later, which proves cognitive vulnerabilities remain constant across technological generations.[5] Mitnick's genius lay in understanding how human psychology may be manipulated to bypass technical controls. These early hackers demonstrated motivations centered on intellectual satisfaction rather than solely on financial gain and documenting a hacker ethos that emphasized technical excellence and information freedom. Although the determination as to whether these boundaries held depends on one's personal definition of harm, this era of hacking established a framework that generations of hackers continue to leverage to this day while supporting the establishment of hacking communities and culture.

In the late 1970s, BBSs created the first communities where tactics, techniques, and procedures (TTPs) might be shared among geographically dispersed individuals.[6] These gathering places fostered a culture viewing information as inherently free while treating the security of systems as puzzles begging for solutions. Bulletin board culture developed hierarchies based on technical knowledge and system compromises. Status came from demonstrating capabilities rather than accumulating wealth, creating incentive structures that encouraged innovation and risk-taking. This cultural structure reflected the status hierarchies modern hackers exhibit on Darknet forums, highlighting the importance of integrating timeless social psychology insights into shifting technological programs. The hacker ethic also emphasized computer access for learning, information freedom, authority decentralization, and evaluation based on technical merit. These principles provided justification for unauthorized access while attempting to maintain boundaries around destruction. In practice, this framework rationalized adversary actions rather than constraining them. The Chaos Computer Club (CCC), established in 1981, originally represented European hacker culture by combining technical skill with activism. Known for prominent showcases of vulnerabilities (e.g., the BTX hack), the CCC championed digital rights while demonstrating the use of technical skills for reasons beyond financial incentive.[7] This marked the beginning of ideologically motivated hackers. Additionally, hacker publications (e.g., 2600: *The Hacker Quarterly (THQ)*) provided venues for sharing technical information among security enthusiasts.[8] *THQ*, and similar publications, fostered tension between the need to share information as a means to enhance collective cybersecurity postures without facilitating adversary activity, a discourse that still persists in cybersecurity communities over 50 years later.

The CFAA of 1986 represented the first federal legislation targeting cybercrime.[9] The CFAA's scope showed limited foresight regarding technological innovation, a problem that persists today. More fundamentally, the CFAA embodied the conflict between security research and unlawful conduct that remains at the forefront of conversations in this space. Prosecutors argued for strict liability, while researchers asserted that vulnerability testing was essential for discovering flaws before the adversary. The first conviction by a jury of a felony under the CFAA was Robert Morris for releasing what was termed the Morris Worm. The Morris Worm infected approximately 10% of internet-connected computers at the time and demonstrated how network connectivity amplifies attacks beyond anything possible with isolated systems. Morris, who was allegedly conducting cybersecurity research at the time the worm was released in November 1988, denied any intent to cause damages that were ultimately estimated between $5 and $12 million at the time.[10] The Morris Worm incident provided two powerful insights. These included how automated propagation may create effects exceeding creator intentions, a lesson that needs repeating with each technological wave (e.g., contemporary debates surrounding artificial intelligence exploitation), as well as potential limitations around prosecuting the CFAA (e.g., resource limitations, jurisdictional complications, knowledge gaps). As was the case in United States v. Morris, early prosecutions under the CFAA concentrated on incidents with financial losses or government system involvement. These factors combined to create a boon in adversary operations lasting decades, during which the adversary learned to exploit legal gaps while perfecting psychological manipulation techniques.

Globalization (1990s–2010s)

The transition from isolated systems to networked environments transformed the scale of cybercrime operations. The early internet's design prioritized connectivity and functionality over security, a decision that seemed reasonable to everyone, right up until everyone included people with questionable intentions and sophisticated psychological manipulation capabilities. Early web applications lacked security protections because developers focused on functionality rather than security. Development prioritized time-to-market over security considerations, establishing technical debt that persisted for decades. This approach also supported the notion that humans prefer not to learn from history when quarterly earnings were at stake. Meanwhile, the adversary learned to exploit this shortsightedness through psychological manipulation. For example, e-commerce development created new targets for the adversary as businesses began processing transactions and storing customer data without protection. Early e-commerce sites transmitted sensitive data without encryption while storing information in accessible databases.[11] The assumption that obscurity provided security proved catastrophically wrong as the adversary developed automated tools for discovering and exploiting web applications while refining social engineering techniques to bypass human verification protocols. Many early hackers demonstrated exploratory motivations rather than predatory ones, although this changed as commercial internet value became apparent to both targets and the adversary.

The rise of financially motivated hackers stems, in part, from the initial democratization of hacking tools, which enabled individuals with limited technical skills (i.e., script kiddies) to conduct attacks previously requiring programming knowledge.[12] Automated tools provided user-friendly interfaces that transformed point-and-click into point-and-pwn. Tools like Back Orifice and NetBus enabled remote control through simple installation procedures.[13] Automated vulnerability scanners identified exploitable systems without requiring deep technical knowledge of underlying vulnerabilities. Tool availability transformed cybercrime from a specialized technical activity to something accessible to anyone with basic computer skills and motivation to commit illicit acts. Script kiddie culture emerged as individuals with limited programming skills used existing tools for status within online communities rather than financial gain. The adversary also adapted these tools for financial opportunities, leading to the initial commercialization of adversary activities. This evolution necessitated forensic cyberpsychology to evolve to address the shift from ego-driven demonstrations to financially motivated attacks. For example, the warez scene created organized communities focused on software piracy.[14] Warez communities facilitated complex techniques for bypassing copyright protections, distributing software, and anonymizing file-sharing networks. These communities established organizational models and technical approaches that influenced later adversary operations, proving that pirates may be surprisingly organized when properly motivated.

The shift to an adversary that is financially motivated may be attributable to the spread of hacking techniques via online tutorials reducing technical abilities required for attack execution. Websites and forums provided step-by-step instructions for common attack methods while building communities supporting continued learning and technique development. Educational infrastructure supporting legitimate computer learning simultaneously enabled illicit skill development, an unintended consequence that educational institutions never adequately addressed. DDoS attack tools also enabled unsophisticated attackers to disrupt websites. High-profile attacks against Yahoo, Amazon, and other early websites demonstrated how illicit activities may affect mainstream internet users while generating media attention.[15] These attacks revealed how the adversary began to orchestrate psychological pressure campaigns through technical disruption and established templates for synchronized attacks targeting both technical infrastructure and human decision-making processes.

At this time, the adversary began conducting online auction fraud on early e-commerce platforms (e.g., eBay).[16] These schemes demonstrated how digital marketplaces may be exploited through fake listings, non-delivery, and identity manipulation that is difficult to detect or prosecute across jurisdictional boundaries.[17] Internet commerce anonymity and reach created environments where traditional trust mechanisms proved inadequate as the adversary exploited cognitive biases (e.g., optimism bias, confirmation bias) to manipulate targets. The introduction of credit cards led to credit card fraud, which evolved to exploit weaknesses in early e-commerce systems that transmitted or stored payment information without encryption or access controls. The adversary developed automated tools for testing stolen credit card numbers while e-commerce sites lacked fraud detection systems.[18] While online fraud economics enabled profitable operations even with low success rates, the global nature of internet commerce further complicated fraud investigation and prosecution because illicit activities may involve targets, perpetrators, and infrastructure in multiple countries with different legal systems and enforcement capabilities. These jurisdictional complications created safe havens where the adversary could operate with reduced prosecution risk while perfecting psychological manipulation techniques across cultural boundaries. The psychological tactics developed during these early instances of e-commerce fraud continue to influence contemporary social engineering attacks, such as exploiting psychology rather than technical vulnerabilities. As the dust began to settle from the burst of the dot-com bubble, the early 2000s ushered in a new era of the internet where it shifted from a speculative venture to a piece of foundational infrastructure.

Professionalization and Industrialization (2010s–2020s)

The early 2000s witnessed cybercrime industrialization through large-scale automated systems generating revenue by executing bulk illicit activities. These organizations demonstrated how technological automation may achieve economies of scale to make previously unprofitable illicit activities economically viable while simultaneously perfecting psychological manipulation techniques at unprecedented scale. For instance, the Storm worm (i.e., Peacomm) demonstrated how malware may create networks of compromised computers for the adversary to manipulate as a means to generate revenue through spam distribution, pharmaceutical sales, and rental services for other threat actors.[19] At its peak, the Storm worm controlled millions of infected computers worldwide, and the botnet's resilience against takedown efforts revealed how a distributed architecture insulated illicit operations from law enforcement disruption at the time.[20]

In addition to botnets, spam campaigns grew in popularity during this period as spam economics revealed how bulk email distribution may generate profits even with extremely low response rates. Low costs and minimal prosecution risk made spam attractive for the adversary who discovered that response rates as low as 0.01% may generate profits when applied to millions of email addresses, proving that sufficient scale may make any terrible business model profitable.[21] The adversary also began to develop specialized business models (e.g., sector-specific targeting efforts, affiliate models) mimicking legitimate businesses while conducting illicit activities. The Rustock botnet, for example, specialized in pharmaceutical spam distribution and accounted for nearly half of all spam messages across the globe at its peak.[22] Operation b107 dismantled Rustock in 2011, demonstrating how coordinated efforts may disrupt adversary operations while also revealing the scale of illicit enterprises achieved at this time.[23] In response to the rise of coordinated takedown efforts from defenders, Botnet-as-a-Service models emerged as the adversary developed platforms enabling other threat actors to rent access to compromised computer networks.[24] These models reduced barriers to entry for illicit activities while improving operational efficiency, which demonstrated the capability of the adversary to industrialize psychological manipulation at scale. The next iteration of Botnet-as-a-Service models was the emergence of CaaS models. CaaS transformed individualized activities into organized enterprises. This professionalization enabled individuals with complementary skills to collaborate, as well as facilitate the proliferation of complex tools. The rise of the banking Trojan known as ZeuS, including a variant built on a peer-to-peer infrastructure (i.e., Gameover ZeuS), exemplified another step toward this service model with operators providing individuals with the source code for sophisticated malware capable of stealing banking credentials and establishing affiliate programs.[25,26]

The growth of underground forums on darknets led to the development of reputation systems, escrow services, and quality assurance mechanisms to enable the adversary to remain anonymous while establishing business relationships with reduced fraud risk. These marketplaces operated with customer reviews, vendor ratings, and dispute resolution processes paralleling legitimate e-commerce platforms.[27] These illicit forums and marketplaces further facilitated adversary specialization by supporting individual focus on specific aspects of the cybercrime ecosystem (e.g., malware development, money laundering, survivor identification, technical infrastructure management). This division of labor improved operational efficiency while reducing technical knowledge required for individual participation. As cybercrime became industrialized, established organizations developed advantages through economies of scale, technical expertise, and operational experience that new entrants could not easily replicate. Quality control and customer service became crucial elements of operations as illicit organizations competed for customers in underground markets. These illicit service providers offered guarantees, technical support, and regular updates to maintain customer satisfaction and ensure continued revenue streams.[28] While the irony of the adversary providing better customer service than many legitimate businesses was not lost on security researchers, it demonstrates how the adversary may apply business principles to psychological manipulation systematization.

As CaaS models proved profitable and darknet marketplaces continued to rise in popularity with the adversary, ransomware evolved from individual adversary activities to large-scale organized operations demonstrating how cybercrime may achieve industrial scale through business model innovation. CryptoLocker in 2013, for instance, established a technical foundation for ransomware through effective encryption, payment collection systems, and target communication enabling the reliable monetization of computer compromise while maintaining operational security.[29] As cryptocurrency grew in popularity for both illicit and mainstream purposes, ransomware operators leveraged adoption to obtain pseudo-anonymous payment collection capabilities. The ability of cryptocurrency to facilitate nearly instantaneous cross-border transactions with minimal verification, if any, required across the globe created an environment conducive to the economics of ransomware, which contributed, at least in part, to the exponential growth of this form of cybercrime over the same period. Due to this profitability explosion, RaaS models emerged as the adversary identified opportunities to essentially license ransomware to other members of the adversary (i.e., Ransomware affiliates). RaaS models allowed ransomware developers to scale operations through the development of platforms and profit-sharing arrangements with affiliates who may lack the ability to perpetrate ransomware attacks without the support offered by the ransomware operators. A prominent early example of the RaaS model was the Conti ransomware operation (Conti). Internal documentation revealed that Conti managed hundreds of affiliates while maintaining operational security against law enforcement investigation, proving how illicit organizations could systematize psychological manipulation through business process management.[30]

Critical infrastructure attacks demonstrated how ransomware may affect essential services (e.g., hospitals). A prominent example of the manifestation of physical world consequences stemming from ransomware attacks includes the first known death caused by a ransomware attack in 2019 when the adversary attacked a hospital in Germany.[31] The attack disrupted operations at the target hospital causing ambulances to be rerouted to other locations, which contributed to the death of an individual who died in transit when the individual was rerouted as a result of the ransomware attack. Reports indicate that several hospitals experience patient safety incidents during ransomware attacks. Ransomware attacks on critical infrastructure demonstrate that the adversary learned to weaponize societal dependencies on digital infrastructure through carefully timed attacks that maximized psychological pressure through service disruption. Beyond ransomware attacks, the evolution of cybercrime reflects adoption of emerging technologies including artificial intelligence, IoT devices, and quantum computing capabilities, which all create new attack vectors and opportunities for the adversary. As indicated throughout history, each technological advancement spawns new exploits by the adversary that manipulate new capabilities faster than defensive countermeasures can be developed to mitigate them.

As the pandemic of fear caused by ransomware continued to spread, technical improvements (e.g., faster encryption algorithms, better evasion techniques, improved persistence mechanisms) made recovery from a ransomware attack more difficult while reducing detection risks. The adversary additionally optimized psychological pressure through technical capability enhancement. While traditional ransomware focused solely on data encryption to extort payment for decryption keys, the evolution of ransomware led to data theft and threats of public exposure with the goal of creating additional payment pressure even if a target possessed appropriate backups to enable data recovery. This double extortion model increased payment rates from targets while demonstrating adversary innovation techniques that simultaneously exploited multiple psychological pressure points. Next, ransomware attacks evolved to include triple extortion methodology, which added threats against the original target's customers, partners, and stakeholders whose data had been stolen during the attack. This explosion and evolution of cybercrime to a global threat led to increased efforts by defenders to collaborate across borders.

Cross-Border Policing and MLAT Limits

International cybercrime investigations revealed limitations in traditional law enforcement approaches relying on territorial jurisdiction and bilateral cooperation agreements. The internet's nature enabled the adversary to conduct operations involving multiple countries while exploiting differences in legal systems and enforcement capabilities, while also creating psychological distance from consequences to enable moral disengagement.

The Council of Europe Convention on Cybercrime (i.e., Budapest Convention) represented the first international treaty addressing cybercrime cooperation, though effectiveness was limited by small number of participating countries and implementation variations.[32] Many countries with significant threat actor operations declined participation, while others implemented the treaty with limitations, reducing practical effectiveness and creating jurisdictional arbitrage opportunities that the adversary exploited through careful infrastructure placement. Jurisdictional arbitrage enabled the adversary to locate operations in countries with weak cybercrime laws, limited law enforcement capabilities, or political unwillingness to cooperate with international investigations. Some countries became known as safe havens for threat actor operations, which created geographic advantages that adversaries may exploit through careful infrastructure placement. In the United States, Mutual Legal Assistance Treaty (MLAT) procedures proved inadequate for cybercrime investigations requiring rapid response to preserve digital evidence and disrupt ongoing threat actor operations.[33] The issue stems from the fact that traditional diplomatic channels operated on timescales measured in months, while digital evidence may be destroyed in minutes, and threat actor operations may relocate to new jurisdictions within hours. Attribution problems further complicated international cybercrime investigations because technical evidence often revealed attack infrastructure rather than perpetrators. The adversary used compromised computers, proxy services, and identity theft to obscure locations and identities while conducting operations appearing to simultaneously originate from multiple countries. As a result, entities grew to understand the importance of collaboration across sectors (e.g., private sector participants), given that most attack infrastructure was owned and operated by private companies rather than government entities. Within the context of the backdrop provided through the historical analysis of cybercrime, it is also important to review milestone breaches that represented additional key shifts in the threat landscape.

Significant Incidents: Theory in Reality

Watershed incidents in cybercrime (e.g., Stuxnet, Target, Equifax) demonstrated how theory applies to catastrophic real-world consequences. These digital disasters provided expensive and invaluable lessons about technical and human vulnerabilities.

Stuxnet and State Operations

Stuxnet represented a paradigm shift in cyber operations, demonstrating how software may be weaponized to cause physical destruction in air-gapped industrial environments. Discovered in 2010, this attack combined multiple zero-day exploits with intelligence about industrial control systems to achieve precision in targeting

Iran's nuclear enrichment facilities.[34] Through the WAVE lens, the Stuxnet operation demonstrated state-level psychological warfare where technical sophistication served broader strategic objectives related to undermining confidence in critical infrastructure protection. Stuxnet's complexity revealed resources and expertise available to state-sponsored adversaries who could afford custom exploit development for specific targets rather than relying on broadly applicable attack techniques. The malware included four zero-day exploits, stolen digital certificates, and detailed knowledge of Siemens industrial control systems, suggesting extensive intelligence collection and development resources. The delivery mechanism combined multiple vectors, including infected USB devices, network propagation, and supply chain compromise, to maximize the probability of reaching air-gapped systems. Stuxnet demonstrated how the adversary may bridge gaps between internet-connected systems and isolated industrial networks through careful planning and resource investment, while the psychological impact created uncertainty about critical infrastructure protection that extended far beyond the immediate target. The malware's design included concealment techniques that hid its presence from system administrators and security software while maintaining access to compromised systems. Stuxnet operated undetected for months while conducting reconnaissance and preparation activities prior to executing its payload against specific industrial equipment. Attribution analysis revealed circumstantial evidence suggesting joint U.S.-Israeli development as part of Operation Olympic Games.[35] Technical sophistication and specific targeting suggested nation-state capabilities, while geopolitical context provided motives for disrupting Iran's nuclear program through non-military means in an operation that served to establish precedent for leveraging cyber operations to achieve strategic objectives while maintaining plausible deniability that conventional attacks may not provide. The international response to Stuxnet revealed the absence of frameworks for addressing state-sponsored cyberattacks and highlighted the need for new legal mechanisms to manage conflicts in the digital world. Existing international law provided limited guidance for addressing cyber operations causing physical damage while operating below traditional thresholds for armed conflict. Contemporary research on cyber conflicts shows the lines between state-sponsored, financially-motivated, and ideological adversaries continuing to blur, including examples of illicit organizations providing services to nation-states or state-sponsored groups conducting illicit activities for funding.[36]

Target and Equifax Data Breaches

The 2013 breach of the Target Corporation demonstrated how the adversary may exploit trusted business relationships and credential management weaknesses to achieve compromises affecting millions of consumers. The attack began through compromise of a heating and air conditioning contractor that maintained network access to Target systems for remote monitoring and maintenance.[37] This exemplifies principles from WAVE theory, where the adversary weaponized trust relationships within a network while exploiting organizational psychology that treated vendor access as routine rather than risky. Credential theft from the HVAC contractor provided the adversary with network access, which enabled lateral movement within Target's environment without triggering security alerts designed to detect external intrusion attempts. The adversary leveraged this access to escalate privileges and establish a persistent presence within Target's network infrastructure over several months. The Target breach affected over 40 million credit and debit card accounts plus personal information for approximately 70 million customers, which created one of history's largest retail data breaches. Consumer confidence in retail payment systems declined, while credit monitoring services experienced unprecedented demand from affected individuals seeking identity theft protection, illustrating how data breaches may create cascading impacts affecting entire market sectors.

And yet, credit monitoring services are not immune to incidents. For example, the Equifax breach of 2017 resulted from the failure to apply available security patches to a public-facing web application processing consumer credit information. The Apache Struts vulnerability enabling the breach was disclosed with patches available months before the attack, indicating Equifax failed to implement the update across its systems prior to exploitation.[38] This incident highlights how patch management failures create vulnerabilities, regardless of available security controls. The Equifax breach exposed personal information for approximately 147 million consumers, including Social Security numbers, birth dates, addresses, and credit information, enabling comprehensive identity theft. The scope of the breach meant nearly half the U.S. population had potentially compromising personal information stolen from a single incident.

Both breaches involved adversaries maintaining persistent access to compromised systems for extended periods before detection, enabling comprehensive data collection exceeding initial penetration objectives. The attacks demonstrated how modern adversaries operated with patience and sophistication, enabling maximum impact through careful reconnaissance and preparation. The use of legitimate system administration tools and techniques made detection difficult because adversary activities appeared similar to normal system operations. The psychological impact of large-scale data breaches extends beyond financial losses to include long-term emotional and mental health consequences for affected individuals. This demonstrates how the adversary learned to weaponize data breach trauma for follow-on psychological manipulation campaigns. Importantly, class-action litigation resulting from both breaches established legal precedents for corporate liability in data protection while revealing limitations in existing frameworks for addressing consumer harm from data breaches. Settlement amounts failed to provide meaningful compensation to affected individuals while highlighting the inadequacy of existing remedies for privacy violations and creating psychological conditions where survivors felt abandoned by both technical protection and legal recourse. Stock market reactions to both breach announcements demonstrated how cybersecurity incidents may create immediate financial impacts through investor confidence effects exceeding direct breach costs. Target's stock price dropped significantly following the breach disclosure, while Equifax faced even more severe market reactions due to credit information's sensitive nature. Furthermore, consumer behavior changes resulting from these breaches, primarily the Target breach, included the increased use of credit monitoring services, greater skepticism about providing personal information to retailers, and adoption of payment methods like chip cards that improved security when compared to traditional magnetic stripe cards.

Emerging Trends

Offensive and Defensive AI

Artificial intelligence capabilities enable the adversary to automate and scale social engineering attacks while improving the sophistication and personalization beyond what the adversary was capable of manually achieving in the past. Large Language Models (LLMs), for example, enable the automated generation of phishing emails, social media posts, and other content customized for specific targets while maintaining linguistic quality exceeding historical communications from the adversary. This iteration demonstrates how the adversary learned to weaponize content generation for psychological manipulation and leverage known red flags of cybercrime against targets as organizations scrambled to update published materials, noting that typographical errors were a key indicator of a social engineering campaign, a statement that no longer holds true as a result of LLMs. AI-powered social engineering campaigns may be capable of analyzing target social media profiles, professional networks, and publicly available information to create content referencing specific relationships, interests, and current events relevant to specific targets and enabling precise psychological manipulation at scale. Additional generative AI tactics (e.g., deepfakes) demonstrate a consistent and exponential increase driven by adoption of technology by the adversary. Deepfake technology enables the creation of synthetic audio or video content, which may be exploited to impersonate trusted individuals to perpetrate social engineering attacks against a target. The adversary also demonstrated capabilities to use deepfakes to bypass traditional verification methods relying on photo, voice, or video identification. Reports indicate this may include using deepfake images of identity documentation to circumvent new account creation controls or leverage public media to compromise accounts or transactions via the authentication stage of the transaction process, such as using AI-generated videos to impersonate executives as a means to authorize fraudulent wire transfers worth hundreds of millions of dollars.[39] The success of these types of attacks continues to demonstrate that the weaponization of a target's trust in sensory evidence through technical manipulation of communication channels previously considered reliable, indicating the need for a fundamental shift in understanding of the meaning of truth in the digital world, where seeing is no longer believing.

BEC attacks leveraged AI capabilities to improve email spoofing sophistication while also analyzing organizational communication patterns to identify optimal timing and content for fraudulent requests. AI analysis of leaked email datasets or structured reconnaissance of a target's processes enables the adversary to maximize the likelihood of success by making fraudulent requests more convincing through the weaponization of psychology. The psychological impact of AI-enhanced social engineering reportedly creates anxiety among potential targets who question their ability to identify artificial content, while the adversary leverages this uncertainty through campaigns designed to blur the boundaries between authentic and synthetic communication. Furthermore, machine learning techniques enable automated vulnerability discovery by analyzing software systems to identify exploitable weaknesses. These capabilities threaten to shif the advantage toward the adversary who may discover and exploit vulnerabilities before defensive patches may be deployed. For instance, AI-powered fuzzing tools generate test inputs designed to trigger software failures while learning from previous results to improve effectiveness of the attacks. These tools continuously operate without human supervision while testing millions of potential attack vectors against target applications and systems, which enables the adversary to industrialize vulnerability discovery through persistent probing. LLMs tuned for adversary usage (e.g., DarkBERT, FraudGPT) are growing in popularity on cybercrime forums.[40] These models do not adhere to the guardrails implemented in traditional LLMs made available to the public and are instead geared for use by the adversary (e.g., generate exploit code and social engineering scripts). Thus, the democratization of exploit development through offensive AI tools exemplifies the enablement of individuals with limited programming skills to perpetrate attacks. Offensive AI capabilities may also enable attacks targeted at defensive AI systems, including generating inputs designed to cause misclassification or system failures. These attacks may potentially blind security monitoring systems while enabling adversaries to operate undetected within protected environments.

Defensive AI applications include automated threat detection, incident response, and vulnerability management operating at machine speed to counter AI-powered attacks. Integration of AI capabilities into security operations creates requirements for new skills and organizational structures to effectively leverage automated systems while maintaining human oversight and decision-making authority. Security teams must develop capabilities for managing AI systems while understanding limitations and potential failure modes. Behavioral analysis powered by machine learning identifies suspicious activities deviating from normal patterns while adapting to evolving attack techniques without requiring manual rule updates. These systems can potentially detect zero-day attacks and advanced persistent threats evading traditional signature-based detection methods. This AI arms race between offensive and defensive applications creates concerns about escalating capabilities that may exceed human understanding in the near future, such as autonomous systems developing attack techniques that human analysts cannot readily comprehend at the time.

IoT and Edge Threats

IoT device proliferation created attack surfaces consisting of billions of connected devices with varying security capabilities and update mechanisms. The Mirai botnet demonstrated how poorly secured IoT devices may be compromised at scale to create distributed attack platforms (i.e., botnets) while revealing fundamental security weaknesses in consumer IoT devices.[41] This rarely included technically sophisticated methodologies, with the adversary often using compromise campaigns targeting default credentials and unpatched vulnerabilities. The persistence of default credentials in IoT devices reflected manufacturing practices and consumer behaviors prioritizing convenience over security. Additionally, firmware update mechanisms for IoT devices often proved inadequate for addressing security vulnerabilities, with many devices lacking update capabilities. The absence of reliable update mechanisms meant security vulnerabilities may persist indefinitely across deployed device populations, which enables the adversary to maintain persistent access to compromised devices for extended campaigns. Limited processing power and memory in IoT devices created tradeoffs between functionality and security, which the adversary learned to exploit through attacks specifically designed for resource-limited environments. This problem was further exacerbated by IoT integration into critical infrastructure systems. In these instances, cybersecurity incidents may directly endanger human life through compromise (e.g., medical devices, transportation systems), which makes these types of IoT attacks distinct from traditional cybersecurity incidents primarily affecting data and business operations. The rise of smart city implementations relying on IoT systems for traffic management and emergency services creates complex interdependencies where the adversary may disrupt essential municipal services to endanger public safety.

The diversity of IoT device types and manufacturers creates a fragmented security landscape where vulnerability disclosure and defensive coordination prove challenging. Unlike traditional computing platforms with established security ecosystems, IoT environments often lack centralized mechanisms for managing security across heterogeneous device populations. Additionally, supply chain security for IoT devices revealed risks from compromised components to malicious firmware installation during manufacturing processes. Given the global nature of IoT supply chains, opportunities for the adversary to introduce backdoors into devices during production while complicating efforts to verify device integrity abound. Attempts to develop IoT security standards aim to address the fundamental security weaknesses of IoT devices through the establishment of baselines for industry guidelines and regulatory requirements. Unfortunately, the voluntary nature of these efforts limits their overall effectiveness. Compounding this issue is the economics of IoT device manufacturing, which requires device makers to balance the expenses associated with long-term security support and update requirements against device revenues. This conflict creates risks that persist throughout the device lifecycle. The implementation of zero-trust architecture principles applied to IoT environments assumes all devices are potentially compromised and requires network segmentation, device authentication, and continuous monitoring often exceeding traditional network security capabilities. To be effective, device identity and authentication systems are required to scale to support billions of connected devices while providing cryptographic assurance of device legitimacy and integrity, which requires new approaches to certificate management, key distribution, and identity verification. The distribution of computing capabilities to edge locations further complicates security management while creating new targets for adversaries. Edge computing architectures processing IoT data locally additionally create distributed attack surfaces. In these environments, security controls need to be implemented across numerous edge locations with varying physical security and network connectivity.

Quantum-Era Risks

Quantum computing development threatens to undermine current cryptographic systems protecting digital communications, financial transactions, and sensitive data storage. The prospect of quantum computers capable of breaking widely used encryption algorithms creates a future threat requiring immediate preparation despite uncertain timelines for quantum cryptanalytic capabilities. The harvest now, decrypt later (HNDL) threat model assumes the adversary may collect encrypted data today with intention of decrypting it once quantum computing capabilities become available.[42] This approach enables retroactive compromise of currently secure communications. For instance, the Rivest-Shamir-Adleman (RSA) algorithm and elliptic curve cryptography protect most internet communications today. These forms of cryptography are vulnerable to quantum attacks in the future (e.g., Shor's Algorithm).[43] While symmetric encryption algorithms (e.g., AES) are less vulnerable to quantum attacks, these algorithms still require increased key sizes to maintain equivalent security against quantum adversaries using Grover's algorithm.[44] To combat this emerging threat, NIST identified novel, post-quantum cryptography (PQC) algorithms.[45] The potential also exists for hostile nation-states with quantum research programs to achieve cryptanalytic capabilities before their availability becomes publicly known to create periods of time where quantum attacks succeed while defensive preparations remain incomplete.

When considering PQC implementations, legacy system integration challenges arise because post-quantum cryptography may prove incompatible with existing hardware, software, and protocols designed around current cryptographic algorithms necessitating that organizations plan for expensive infrastructure upgrades while managing compatibility requirements during transition periods. Performance implications of PQC implementation include increased computational requirements, larger message sizes, and slower cryptographic operations affecting system performance and user experience illustrating the potential tradeoffs between quantum resistance and operational requirements. Furthermore, PQC migrations require industry-wide coordination to ensure interoperability and security during transition periods when different organizations may operate at various stages of implementation. Network effects of cryptographic systems mean partial adoption may create security and compatibility problems across entire industries. Compounding this uncertainty is the fact that estimates for cryptographically relevant quantum computers range from a year to several decades to never. This creates uncertainty around the appropriate investment timelines for post-quantum cryptography adoption. Organizations face the psychological burden of investing in protection against threats that may never materialize while managing operational requirements that demand immediate attention. Through the WAVE lens, this uncertainty becomes a weapon the adversary exploits by manipulating resource allocation decisions and creating decision paralysis through temporal pressure.

Conclusion

From Captain Crunch's cereal box whistles to AI-generated deepfakes, the evidence indicates the adversary orchestrates behavioral resonance across multiple cognitive systems with increasing sophistication and precision. WAVE theory illuminates the pattern hiding in plain sight throughout cybercrime history. Each breakthrough that expanded human potential, from bulletin board communities to quantum computing research, created new vectors for psychological manipulation. By understanding how to synchronize technical capabilities with human cognitive vulnerabilities to create states where protective mechanisms fail to function, the adversary proves illicit innovation outpaces defensive adaptation when organizations treat cybersecurity as a technical problem with human elements rather than recognizing it as a human problem with technical amplifiers. As illustrated by the past, the future promises that new attacks will exceed current defensive imagination, which underscores the importance of applying WAVE theory to develop resilient defenses. The battle for cybersecurity ultimately becomes a battle for preserving human psychological autonomy in an age of synchronized manipulation campaigns designed to overwhelm cognitive defenses, which is a key theme examined in Chapter 7 when the psychology driving cybercrime perpetration is explored.

Reflection Questions

1 What ethical frameworks guide defenders in adopting more agile, experimental approaches to cybersecurity without crossing moral boundaries that distinguish legitimate security research from adversarial exploitation?
2 What emerging technologies of today may follow similar trajectories as the ones discussed throughout this chapter?
3 How can organizations leverage WAVE theory to break the cycle of reactive cybersecurity measures?
4 What is the appropriate way for society to balance innovation with security without stifling progress?

Skill Builder Labs

Scenario Application: Timeline a Famous Breach and Map Controls to Stop It

Select a major cybersecurity incident from the past decade and take the following steps:

- Create an attack timeline with psychological manipulation points identified.
- Map which current security controls address technical versus human vulnerabilities.

- Analyze how adversaries weaponized trust relationships and cognitive biases, and
- Identify where behavioral resonance enabled attack progression.

Mini Research Activity: Compare Two AI-Phishing Toolkits on Dark-Web Forums

Objective

Understand how AI has transformed social engineering capabilities.

Instructions

1. Research two AI-phishing toolkits available for sale on darknet forums.
2. Compare the features and effectiveness claims of each tool.
3. Analyze pricing models and accessibility to low-skill adversaries.
4. Evaluate detection challenges these tools create for current defenses.
5. Examine how AI capabilities changed social engineering attack sophistication.
6. Propose countermeasures that address AI-generated content identification.

Deliverable

Create a threat intelligence brief with defensive recommendations, including countermeasures.

References

1. U.S. Federal Bureau of Investigation. (2024). *Internet Crime Report.*
2. Novo Nordisk (2025). *Company announcement: Financial report for the period 1 January 2024 to 31 December 2024.*
3. Levy, S. (1984).*Hackers: Heroes of the computer revolution.* Dell Publishing.
4. Draper, J. T., & Fraser, C. W. (2018). *Beyond The Little Blue Box: The biographical adventures of John T Draper (aka Captain Crunch). Notorious' Phone Phreak', legendary internet pioneer and ardent privacy advocate.* Friesen Press.
5. Mitnick, K. D., & Simon, W. L. (2003). *The art of deception: Controlling the human element of security.* John Wiley & Sons.
6. Sterling, B. (2020). *The hacker crackdown: Law and disorder on the electronic frontier.* Open Road Media.
7. Denker, K. (2013). Heroes yet criminals of the German computer revolution. In Alberts, G., Oldenziel, R. (eds) *Hacking Europe: From computer cultures to demoscenes* (pp. 167–187). Springer.
8. Müller, S. D., & Ulrich, F. (2015). The competing values of hackers: The culture profile that spawned the computer revolution. In *Proceedings of the 48th annual Hawaii international conference on system sciences (HICSS 48)* (pp. 3434–3443). IEEE.
9. U.S. Computer Fraud and Abuse Act. (1986). 18 U.S.C. § 1030
10. Nelson, B. (1990). Straining the capacity of the law: The idea of computer crime in the age of the computer worm, 11 computer LJ 299 (1991). *UIC John Marshall Journal of Information Technology & Privacy Law, 11*(2), 299–321.

11. Rubin, A. D., & Geer, D. E. (1998). A survey of Web security. *Computer*, *31*(9), 34–41.
12. Holt, T. J. (2010). Examining the role of technology in the formation of deviant subcultures. *Social Science Computer Review*, *28*(4), 466–481.
13. Larimer, J., & Piccard, P. (1999). Backdoors. *ITNOW*, *41*(5), 32–32.
14. Rehn, A. (2004). The politics of contraband: The honor economies of the warez scene. *The Journal of Socio-Economics*, *33*(3), 359–374.
15. Lau, F., Rubin, S. H., Smith, M. H., & Trajkovic, L. (2000). Distributed denial of service attacks. In *SMC 2000 conference proceedings. 2000 IEEE international conference on systems, man and cybernetics* (vol. 3, pp. 2275–2280). IEEE.
16. Chua, C. E. H., Wareham, J., & Robey, D. (2007). The role of online trading communities in managing internet auction fraud. *MIS Quarterly*, *31*(4). 759–781.
17. Albert, M. R. (2002). E-buyer beware: Why online auction fraud should be regulated. *American Business Law Journal*, *39*(4), 575–644.
18. Chan, P. K., Fan, W., Prodromidis, A. L., & Stolfo, S. J. (2002). Distributed data mining in credit card fraud detection. *IEEE Intelligent Systems and Their Applications*, *14*(6), 67–74.
19. Holz, T., Steiner, M., Dahl, F., Biersack, E. W., & Freiling, F. C. (2008). Measurements and mitigation of peer-to-peer-based botnets: A case study on storm worm. *Leet*, *8*(1), 1–9.
20. Elliott, C. (2010). Botnets: To what extent are they a threat to information security? *Information Security Technical Report*, *15*(3), 79–103.
21. Kanich, C., Kreibich, C., Levchenko, K., Enright, B., Voelker, G. M., Paxson, V., & Savage, S. (2008, October). Spamalytics: An empirical analysis of spam marketing conversion. In *Proceedings of the 15th ACM conference on computer and communications security*. Association for Computing Machinery, New York, NY, USA, 3–14.
22. Thonnard, O., & Dacier, M. (2011). A strategic analysis of spam botnets operations. In *Proceedings of the 8th annual collaboration, electronic messaging, anti-abuse and spam conference*. Association for Computing Machinery, New York, NY, USA, 162–171.
23. Microsoft. (2011). *Taking down botnets: Microsoft and the Rustock botnet*.
24. Chang, W., Wang, A., Mohaisen, A., & Chen, S. (2014). Characterizing botnets-as-a-service. In *Proceedings of the 2014 ACM conference on SIGCOMM*. Association for Computing Machinery, New York, NY, USA, 585–586.
25. Etaher, N., Weir, G. R., & Alazab, M. (2015). From zeus to zitmo: Trends in banking malware. In 2015 IEEE Trustcom/BigDataSE/ISPA (Vol. 1, pp. 1386–1391). IEEE.
26. Manky, D. (2013). Cybercrime as a service: a very modern business. *Computer Fraud & Security*, *2013*(6), 9–13.
27. Krylova, Y. (2019). The Rise of Darknet Markets in the Digital Age: Building Trust and Reputation. In M. Brown Sr. & L. Hersey (Eds.), Returning to Interpersonal Dialogue and Understanding Human Communication in the Digital Age (pp. 1–24). Hershey, PA: IGI Global Scientific Publishing.
28. Brinck, J., Nodeland, B., & Belshaw, S. (2023). The "yelp-ification" of the dark web: An exploration of the use of consumer feedback in dark web markets. *Journal of Contemporary Criminal Justice*, *39*(2), 185–200.
29. Kalaimannan, E., John, S. K., DuBose, T., & Pinto, A. (2017). Influences on ransomware's evolution and predictions for the future challenges. *Journal of Cyber Security Technology*, *1*(1), 23–31.
30. Paternoster, C., Nazzari, M., Jofre, M., & Uberti, T. E. (2025). Inside the leak: Exploring the structure of the Conti ransomware group. *Global Crime*, *26*(2), 148–171.
31. Klick, J., Koch, R., & Brandstetter, T. (2021). Epidemic? The attack surface of German hospitals during the COVID-19 pandemic. In 2021 13th International Conference on Cyber Conflict (CyCon) (pp. 73–94). IEEE.

32. Council of Europe. (2001). *Convention on Cybercrime* (ETS No. 185). Council of Europe Treaty Office.
33. Vermeer, M. J., Woods, D., & Jackson, B. A. (2018). *Identifying law enforcement needs for access to digital evidence in remote data centers*. RAND.
34. Aanonsen, C. E. (2025). Stuxnet, revisited (again): producing the strategic relevance of cyber operations. *Journal of Cyber Policy*, *10*(1), 1–17.
35. Hojnacki, D. (2021). Prescient warnings for a post-stuxnet world. *SAIS Review of International Affairs*, *41*(2), 143–145.
36. Park, J. (2021). THE LAZARUS GROUP. *Harvard International Review*, *42*(2), 34–39.
37. U.S. Senate, Committee on Commerce, Science, and Transportation. (2014). *A kill chain analysis of the 2013 target data breach* [Staff Report].
38. The 115th Congress, U.S. House of Representatives, Committee on Oversight and Government Reform, Majority Staff Report. (2018). *The Equifax data breach*.
39. Beemamol, M. Unmasking the threat: A viewpoint on AI-based deepfake financial crimes. In Shishir Kumar Shandilya, Devangana Sujay, V.B. Gupta *Advancements in cyber crime investigations and modern data analytics* (pp. 123–142). CRC Press.
40. Lin, Z., Cui, J., Liao, X., & Wang, X. (2024). Malla: Demystifying real-world large language model integrated malicious services. In *33rd USENIX Security Symposium (USENIX Security 24)* (pp. 4693–4710). USENIX.
41. Kolias, C., Kambourakis, G., Stavrou, A., & Voas, J. (2017). DDoS in the IoT: Mirai and other botnets. *Computer*, *50*(7), 80–84.
42. Olutimehin, A. T., Joseph, S., Ajayi, A. J., Metibemu, O. C., Balogun, A. Y., & Olaniyi, O. O. (2025). *Future-proofing data: Assessing the feasibility of post-quantum cryptographic algorithms to mitigate 'harvest now, decrypt later' attacks*. SSRN.
43. Bhatia, V., & Ramkumar, K. R. (2020, October). An efficient quantum computing technique for cracking RSA using Shor's algorithm. In *2020 IEEE 5th international conference on computing communication and automation (ICCCA)* (pp. 89–94). IEEE.
44. Belkhir, M., Benkaouha, H., Benkhelifa, E., Meriem, N. K., & Hiba, L. (2024, December). Quantum computing and password security: Applying Grover's Algorithm and QRNG with Qiskit. In *Global congress on emerging technologies (GCET-2024)* (pp. 35–42). IEEE.
45. U.S. National Institute of Standards and Technology, Computer Security Resource Center. (2024). *Announcing approval of three federal information processing standards (FIPS) for post-quantum cryptography*.

7 Psychological Drivers of Perpetrating Cybercrime

From Minecraft to Mayhem

According to public records, Paras Jha, Josiah White, and Dalton Norman did not initially intend to create one of history's most devastating botnets. These three individuals, who were college students at the time, set out in 2016 with the aim to gain a competitive advantage in Minecraft server hosting by knocking their competitors offline. After Jha and White co-founded ProTraf Solutions, LLC, a company that provided DDoS protection services to Minecraft server providers, the individuals began knocking competitors and other websites offline to generate new business for the company.[1] Their Mirai malware, initially designed to knock rival gaming servers offline, eventually infected hundreds of thousands of internet-connected devices worldwide and launched distributed denial-of-service attacks that disrupted major internet services, including social media platforms and e-commerce platforms. The psychological progression demonstrated by the trio illustrates how ordinary individuals may transform into members of the adversary through escalating rationalization. Each step required deeper moral disengagement that reframed increasingly serious crimes as legitimate business competition.

Through the lens of WAVE theory, cybercrime motivation reveals itself as more than individual psychological pathology. The adversary orchestrates behavioral resonance across multiple systems, such as exploiting financial desperation or synchronizing thrill-seeking impulses with moral relativism. These psychological drivers do not operate in isolation. They converge to create the affective vulnerability states that make both perpetration and compliance feel inevitable rather than chosen. The same psychological vulnerabilities that drive threat actor recruitment enable manipulation. The same cognitive biases that justify illegal behavior facilitate social engineering success. The same community dynamics that sustain illicit enterprises inform the psychological pressure tactics deployed against organizations.

In essence, cybercrime motivation distills down into three key pillars (e.g., money, meaning, and mayhem). This chapter dissects how adversaries pursue financial enrichment, ideological satisfaction, or personal gratification through their digital exploits. The analysis reveals that while technology evolves at breakneck speed, human motivations remain refreshingly predictable (i.e., greed trumps altruism and revenge tastes sweeter than forgiveness). This chapter explores how the adversary weaponized the very foundations of human motivation to create psychological manipulation campaigns that threaten the infrastructure of digital society itself.

Financial Drivers

As the saying goes, money makes the world go 'round...Importantly, it typically makes a target's money go 'round to the adversary's account in the context of cybercrime. Financial motivation remains the primary driver of adversary behavior and lures individuals ranging from unemployed teenagers to organized crime syndicates to perpetrate cybercrimes.[2,3] This occasionally involves follow-on attacks, where crimes perpetrated by sophisticated actors are followed by attempts to perpetrate similar crimes by members of the adversary who may or may not have been involved in the original incident. The 2023 collapse of FTX, a cryptocurrency exchange, illustrated this principle. While Sam Bankman-Fried's legal trouble stemmed from allegedly misappropriating billions in customer funds, the incident itself spawned countless phishing campaigns targeting creditors.[4] Within days of the bankruptcy announcement, multiple fraudulent recovery websites designed to harvest credentials from desperate users seeking access to frozen accounts were identified.[5] The speed and success rates of this response by the adversary demonstrate how quickly the adversary capitalizes on incidents. WAVE theory reveals why these opportunistic attacks succeed. Financial desperation creates affective vulnerability states where rational decision-making deteriorates. The adversary synchronizes authority manipulation (e.g., fake recovery sites), scarcity pressure (e.g., limited time to recover funds), and social proof (e.g., testimonials from supposed successful recoveries) to create behavioral resonance that bypasses skeptical analysis in targets, which transforms desperation into compliance. The adversary additionally may exploit sensitive information harvested in the breach to craft sophisticated social engineering campaigns against targets. This is often compounded by delayed, or nonexistent, reporting by the organization impacted by the data breach, which leaves targets defenseless as they are unaware their data may be weaponized against them. The irony of the adversary exploiting a security breach to commit additional security breaches provides an example tantamount to pirates selling life preservers to the survivors of ships they just sank.

This area of cybercrime (i.e., social engineering) is burgeoning with organizations reporting significant year-over-year increases in incidents.[6] Beyond traditional email campaigns, smishing (SMS phishing) and vishing (voice phishing) expanded the attack surface of targets, exposing mobile users to an average of one threat per week. Business-email-compromise represents the aristocracy of email fraud, targeting corporate accounts, often as a means to authorize fraudulent wire transfers. In 2024, BEC incidents drained over $2.77 billion across 21,442 complaints, making it the second-costliest cybercrime category after investment fraud.[7] The psychology underlying BEC success lies in its exploitation of corporate hierarchy and trust relationships. Adversaries impersonate executives or trusted vendors, leveraging urgency and familiarity to convince finance teams to bypass normal verification procedures. In other words, BEC attacks weaponize the very efficiency that modern businesses depend upon to remain in business.

It is well-established that the adversary exploits cognitive biases as part of a social engineering campaign.[8] Exploitation of the scarcity principle drives action by suggesting limited availability. Phishing emails warning of account closure in 24 hours to exploit the fear of loss to override rational caution. The adversary impersonates banks, government agencies, or technical support teams to inherit credibility they never earned and exploit authority bias. Social proof amplifies persuasion by suggesting that others have already taken the desired action. Fake testimonials, inflated user counts, and manufactured urgency (e.g., 100 people are viewing this offer) further the illusion of legitimacy. The psychology of commitment and consistency drives targets to maintain behavior patterns that align with their stated beliefs or previous actions, enabling the adversary to extract escalating concessions through carefully structured interaction sequences through the exploitation of the reciprocity principle. Large-scale emergencies (e.g., national disasters, acts of terror, global pandemics) or public events (e.g., mergers, bankruptcies) also provide fertile ground for these tactics to bloom. Through WAVE theory, these principles become weapons for orchestrating behavioral resonance across multiple cognitive systems, illustrating that manipulation is not isolated to solitary variables. The adversary, unfortunately, discovered that combining these principles creates psychological pressure that overwhelms individual cognitive defenses and facilitates successful manipulation of targets well before the presentation of WAVE theory. Importantly, targets do not consciously choose to be deceived; rather, they feel compelled to act by the orchestrated manipulation of their affective vulnerabilities. The success of these psychological manipulation tactics enabled the industrialization of cybercrime itself, an insidious evolution of the adversary's tactics. What began as isolated adversary activities evolved into sophisticated economies where psychological manipulation techniques became products to be packaged, sold, and scaled across global networks via marketplaces on darknets.

As cybercrime proved financially lucrative, organized crime groups began to ramp up efforts related to cybercrime, as well as individual members of the adversary began to organize into groups based on specializations. Since darknets were initially launched in the late 1990s, illicit marketplaces evolved into sophisticated e-commerce platforms with similarities to traditional businesses (e.g., reputation systems, technical support mechanisms). These platforms demonstrate how cybercrime industrialized beyond individual actors into collaborative enterprises. For instance, the DarkMarket investigation, which culminated in arrests across Europe in 2021 and the seizing of approximately $170 million in cryptocurrency.[9] From a WAVE perspective, these marketplaces and hacker forums exploit fundamental human needs (e.g., community, recognition, achievement) by providing psychological benefits that many participants lack. Forum hierarchies based on technical skill and successful operations create meritocracies where status derives from illicit achievement rather than conventional success metrics that may be missing from the participant's life in the physical world.[10] Moreover, this psychological appeal becomes a recruitment and retention mechanism that traditional law enforcement approaches struggle to counter. Adversary specialization also created distinct professional roles, including initial access brokers who sell network credentials, ransomware developers who create encryption tools, money launderers who convert digital currencies to untraceable assets, and customer service representatives who negotiate with targets. This division of labor enables efficiency gains while reducing individual risk exposure through operational compartmentalization. The Zeus banking Trojan exemplified how illicit enterprises adopt professional business practices (e.g., comprehensive documentation, customer support channels, affiliate recruitment programs) that enabled non-technical threat actors to conduct attacks.[11] Revenue-sharing models provide incentives for continued participation while quality assurance processes ensure reliable illicit tools.[12]

The advent and popularization of cryptocurrencies further revolutionized cybercrime economics by enabling anonymous transactions that circumvent traditional banking mechanisms. Bitcoin adoption by ransomware operators provided payment collection capabilities that enabled instantaneous global operations. Although blockchain analysis techniques increasingly enabled law enforcement to trace cryptocurrency transactions, the adversary adopted more sophisticated money laundering techniques. The 2022 arrest of Ilya Lichtenstein and Heather Morgan for laundering 119,754 bitcoin stolen from the Bitfinex exchange demonstrated how digital forensics may penetrate illicit financial operations even years after the occurrence of initial crimes.[13] Privacy coins (e.g., Monero, Zcash) offer enhanced anonymity features that appeal to threat actors seeking to evade detection. The psychological comfort provided by perceived anonymity enables illicit risk-taking that may not occur if only traditional payment methods were available. Importantly, cryptocurrency exchanges continue to limit illicit access to anonymous cryptocurrency systems through enhanced due diligence and compliance efforts. In response to this evolution from centralized cryptocurrency exchanges, decentralized finance (DeFi) protocols grew in popularity and created new opportunities for innovation by the adversary, such as smart contracts that automate illicit activities while reducing human operational security risks.[14] The popularization of DeFi protocols led to new attack vectors and methodologies, such as flash loan attacks, enabling the adversary to manipulate markets and extract millions of dollars within single blockchain transactions. While financial incentives fostered sophisticated illicit ecosystems, money alone cannot explain the full spectrum of adversary behavior. Beyond profit motives lies a swath of the adversary driven by ideology, political conviction, and the intoxicating belief that their digital weapons serve higher purposes than mere enrichment of themselves.

Ideological Drivers

While the material gain associated with cybercrime attracted professional and organized crime groups, the ability to accomplish ideologically motivated attacks also attracted members of the adversary. The anonymous collective exemplifies how ideological motivation transforms ordinary individuals into the adversary willing to risk legal consequences for abstract principles.[15] The group's origins trace to the imageboard 4chan, where users bonded over shared grievances against perceived injustices (e.g., corporate censorship, government surveillance) with the adoption of Guy Fawkes masks creating a unifying symbol enabling individual actors to subsume personal identity under collective purpose.[16] WAVE theory reveals how hacktivist operations succeed through synchronized ideological manipulation. The adversary weaponizes moral outrage, collective identity, and perceived justice to create behavioral resonance that overrides legal and ethical constraints. Importantly, participants in groups that conduct hacks to accomplish specific social goals (i.e., hacktivists) do not view themselves as threat actors. Rather, the evidence indicates these individuals feel justified by higher moral purposes.[17]

The 2010 Operation Payback campaign demonstrated hacktivism's capacity for coordinated disruption. Following WikiLeaks' release of classified military documents, financial companies like PayPal and Visa ceased processing donations to the organization.[18] Anonymous responded by allegedly conducting DDoS attacks to temporarily cripple these companies' websites. The psychological satisfaction derived from these attacks appeared to outweigh potential legal consequences, suggesting that ideological motivation may override traditional risk-reward calculations in the mind of the adversary. Operation Tunisia and Operation Egypt during the Arab Spring demonstrated how hacktivist operations may also support broader social movements.[19] Anonymous conducted attacks against government websites while additionally providing technical support for circumventing internet censorship. These alleged operations further exemplify moral relativism in the mind of the adversary that reframes illegal activities as necessary resistance against authoritarian oppression.

Beyond attacks driven solely by ideology, some groups blend ideological motivation with personal motivation (e.g., amusement). LulzSec, a subgroup of Anonymous, blended ideological motivation with entertainment-seeking behavior through a series of attacks in 2011.[20] The group's name comes from combining the term lulz, which is internet slang for amusement, and the term security, which reflects the group's fusion of ideological protest with other motivations. Many of LulzSec's purported attacks incorporated elements of trolling into activism, such as allegedly protesting a documentary by hacking the PBS website to post a fake story that Tupac Shukur was alive in New Zealand.[21]

In addition to hacktivist collectives, there also exist nation-state cyber operators. These members of the adversary represent the intersection of professional duty with strategic objectives that transcend traditional deviant motivations. The psychology of these groups involves serving national interests while maintaining operational security that enables plausible deniability. The 2007 cyberattacks against Estonia demonstrate how geopolitical tensions may manifest through coordinated campaigns that blur the lines between state-sponsored operations and volunteer hacktivist activities. In these attacks, Russian-speaking members of the adversary targeted Estonian government, media, and banking websites following disputes over Soviet war memorial relocation.[22] More direct nation-state operations demonstrate even greater sophistication in their psychological frameworks. For example, reports indicate Chinese APT operations blend professional military culture with technical expertise to conduct sustained intelligence collection campaigns through organizational structures resembling traditional military units.[23,24] The SolarWinds supply chain attack of 2020, which was attributed to a group affiliated with the Russian Foreign Intelligence Service, further demonstrated the sophisticated thinking underlying nation-state operations.[25] Rather than directly targeting thousands of organizations, the adversaries compromised a single software vendor whose updates reached approximately 18,000 customers, including several agencies within the U.S. government.[26] The psychological insight driving this approach recognized that organizations trust software updates from legitimate vendors more than unsolicited communications, effectively turning a security mechanism into an attack vector, which demonstrated the long-term perspective of nation-state actors. The Stuxnet worm represents another example of sophisticated nation-state considerations about cyberwarfare as a means to accomplish strategic objectives. Rather than causing widespread disruption, the malware targeted specific industrial control systems in Iran's nuclear program with precision that minimized collateral damage, arguably demonstrating how state actors could rationalize cyberwarfare as an alternative to kinetic military action.[27]

WAVE theory illuminates how ideologically motivated groups orchestrate behavioral resonance in perpetrators by appealing to duty, identity, and purpose. Ideologically motivated groups develop moral justification for illegal activities while maintaining psychological coherence about their actions. In other words, these members of the adversary view themselves as serving the greater good, which enables group leaders to illicit activities that individuals may reject in purely illicit contexts. This often involves portraying targets as corrupt or oppressive institutions that deserve disruption while framing attackers as advocates for justice. The concept of hacktivism itself represents a psychological framing device that combines technical capability with political activism to create identity categories that transcend traditional threat actor labels. Participants may maintain positive self-concepts while engaging in illegal activities by emphasizing political motivations over personal gain.[28] While ideologically motivated members of the adversary justify their actions through the lens of achieving a higher purpose, another category of the adversary operates based on deeply personal drivers that have little to do with politics, patriotism, or social change.

Personal Drivers

Seeking Revenge

In addition to individuals driven by financial gain or ideological conviction, the adversary may consist of individuals driven to satisfy intimate psychological needs (e.g., control, revenge), which may manifest in cyberstalking, cyberbullying, and malicious insiders. In these types of attacks, the adversary seeks to exert power over specific individuals rather than achieve broader notoriety.

Unlike traditional stalking, digital environments provide persistent access to targets while offering perpetrators perceived anonymity and psychological distance. The 2021 case of Matthew Herrick, who endured a three-year digital stalking campaign by an ex-partner, illustrates how technology amplifies obsessive behavior.[29] The perpetrator created fake dating profiles using Herrick's information, directing strangers to his workplace and home while impersonating him. In cases of cyberstalking, digital connectivity is weaponized by the adversary against a personal target, including social media monitoring and GPS tracking, as a means to maintain psychological proximity to targets. In other words, the technological infrastructure designed to connect people becomes weaponized to prevent disconnection.

Cyberbullying reveals how digital environments amplify traditional bullying dynamics through scalability, persistence, and audience amplification. Unlike physical bullying constrained by time and location, cyberbullying follows targets into their homes and operates continuously through social media, messaging platforms, and gaming environments. The 2012 case of Amanda Todd, whose cyberbullying ordeal began with digital exploitation and escalated through coordinated harassment campaigns, demonstrates how an adversary who is personally motivated may orchestrate severe psychological damage to a target.[30] The psychology underlying cyberbullying often involves power dynamics, social dominance needs, and disinhibition effects created by digital mediation. Perpetrators may seek to elevate their social status by diminishing others, express frustration through displaced aggression, or participate in group dynamics that normalize cruel behavior. The perceived anonymity and physical distance provided by digital platforms reduce empathy while amplifying aggressive impulses that might remain controlled in face-to-face interactions.

Malicious insiders demonstrate how workplace grievances transform employees into adversaries against their own organizations. These individuals leverage legitimate access privileges to cause harm, steal data, or sabotage operations based on personal vendettas rather than external recruitment. The 2016 case of Ricky Joe Mitchell exemplifies this psychological profile. After learning of impending termination, Mitchell planted logic bombs in his employer's computer systems designed to delete critical data after his departure.[31] His actions reflected psychological retaliation against perceived unfair treatment. Research indicates that malicious insiders often exhibit specific psychological precursors, including feelings of entitlement, grievance collection, and boundary testing behaviors that escalate over time. These individuals may rationalize their actions as justified responses to workplace injustice while maintaining that their organizations deserve the consequences. The insider's legitimate access becomes a weapon for expressing displaced anger and reasserting control over situations where they felt powerless.

These personally motivated cybercrimes share common psychological characteristics. The adversary prioritizes emotional satisfaction over material gain, targets specific individuals rather than anonymous masses, and often involves escalating patterns of behavior that become compulsive rather than rational. The adversary in these cases frequently knows their target personally, transforming intimate knowledge into weapons for psychological manipulation and perpetrating harm. In addition to these personally motivated cybercrimes against personal targets, there also exist personally motivated members of the adversary who do not necessarily focus on a specific target. Instead, these individuals, who are often driven to satisfy psychological needs such as recognition and stimulation, transform the digital world into a stage to demonstrate superiority via audacious exploits.

Seeking Recognition and Status

The intersection of malignant personality traits with threat actor capability creates individuals who prioritize thrill, recognition, and gratification alongside or above financial gain. These individuals view the digital world as a stage for demonstrating superiority and building personal mythology through increasingly audacious exploits. Sabu, who was the leader of LulzSec group before becoming an FBI informant, exemplifies aspects of this psychological profile.[32] Hector Xavier Monsegur, also known as Sabu, transformed from skilled hacker to threat actor leader to government cooperator revealing the complex motivations underlying high-profile cybercrime activities. His public statements consistently emphasized the lulz derived from successful attacks rather than the pursuit of monetary rewards, which demonstrated how social recognition and intellectual satisfaction may motivate some illicit behavior more than financial incentives.[33] When viewed through the lens of WAVE theory, these types of individuals prove particularly dangerous because they orchestrate behavioral resonance through technical superiority, media attention, and peer recognition. These psychological rewards create feedback loops that escalate attack sophistication and target prominence. Unlike purely financially motivated entities, narcissistic individuals seek psychological validation that drives continued escalation regardless of the associated increasing risks.

Darknet hacking forums may also serve to exasperate this psychological radicalization. Even in the mainstream context, social media platforms amplify narcissistic impulses in individuals by providing immediate feedback through likes, shares, and follower counts. Thus, it is unsurprising that the adversary also derives psychological benefits from adversarial social platforms (e.g., Darknet hacking forums) to broadcast attack claims, share technical achievements, and engage in performative banter that builds personal brands within a digital community.[34,35] The associated psychological satisfaction is derived from both technical accomplishment and public recognition. The psychological dynamic additionally extends to target selection, where the adversary with narcissistic tendencies may prioritize high-profile targets to generate media attention over more financially lucrative targets without the associated potential for further recognition.[36] The preference for worthy opponents reflects a need for validation that mundane illicit activity may not provide (i.e., stealing data from a major corporation generates more ego satisfaction than defrauding individual consumers). Darknet forums additionally create competitive environments where reputation derives from successful attacks, technical innovation, and community contribution.[37] These status systems exploit one's need for recognition and achievement while providing social reinforcement for illicit activities. Given the gaming elements in illicit forums exploit sensation-seeking motivation (e.g., achievement systems, leaderboards, recognition mechanisms) that provide psychological rewards for accomplishments, the gamification of threat actor activity transforms potentially anxiety-provoking illegal behavior into exciting competitive challenges. For example, the platform RankMyHack.com exemplified this dual nature by creating what the website touted as the world's first elite hacker ranking system.[38] Participants submitted proof of website breaches to earn ranking points. The psychological appeal lay in competitive recognition for technical achievement, regardless of the legal implications.

Seeking Sensations

Beyond ego gratification and seeking social status, the adversary may derive personal satisfaction from the thrill of perpetrating attacks, as illustrated by Kevin Mitnick in the 1990s. Mitnick demonstrated how thrill-seeking can override rational risk assessment continuing to pursue increasingly sophisticated targets, including Digital Equipment Corporation and Pacific Bell, despite facing federal prosecution.[39] Mitnick's autobiography further revealed that the intellectual challenge and sense of accomplishment derived from successful intrusions outweighed concerns about legal consequences in a psychological cost-benefit analysis that consistently favored immediate gratification over long-term well-being.[40] This pattern aligns with research indicating that the adversary often exhibit elevated levels of sensation-seeking traits that drive the pursuit of novel, intense, and risky experiences.[41] These psychological characteristics predispose individuals toward activities that provide stimulation and excitement, making cybercrime appealing for psychological rather than purely financial reasons. The progression from curiosity-driven exploration to illicit activity often follows predictable patterns where initial successes create psychological reinforcement that encourages escalation.[42] The teenager who successfully accesses a school computer system may experience psychological rewards that motivate attempts against more challenging and consequential targets. Evidence indicates that sensation-seeking behavior may involve biological factors including dopamine system functioning that influences risk-taking propensity and reward sensitivity.[43] Furthermore, there is evidence that perpetrating cybercrime may be addictive from a behavioral perspective.

Take flow theory, developed by psychologist Mihály Csíkszentmihályi, as an example. Flow theory describes psychological states where challenges perfectly match individual skills, creating experiences of total absorption and heightened satisfaction.[44] Research has identified how threat actors experience flow states during intrusion activities, making the psychological rewards of hacking potentially addictive.[45] A study of 457 participants revealed that flow motivation follows a distinctive pattern with both novice and highly competent individuals experiencing strong flow states while intermediate-level adversaries reported a flow crisis (i.e., reduced satisfaction that motivates either skill development or escalation).[46] This psychological dynamic explains why some individuals transition from ethical hacking to illicit activity given it represents a potential means of utility.[47]

Rationalizing Cybercrime Behavior

In addition to examining the psychological motivations for perpetrating cybercrime, it is important to explore the psychological mechanisms that the adversary may leverage to justify perpetrating illicit acts. While these may vary across underlying motivations, the fundamental concepts are important to understand the initial moral relativism processes that facilitate a foray into cybercrime. Moral disengagement theory explains how individuals override internal moral constraints through cognitive mechanisms that legitimize harmful behavior.[48] Digital environments amplify these processes through anonymity, psychological distance, and reduced empathy for targets who exist only as abstractions rather than real people to the adversary. Hacker communities may develop and reinforce neutralization techniques that provide psychological frameworks for rationalizing activities.[49] Forum analysis reveals how illicit communities systematically reinforce neutralization techniques through peer validation, success stories, and normalization of illegal activities.[50] New participants in hacking forums often learn both technical skills and psychological justification frameworks through community interaction and mentorship.[51] These techniques function as social learning mechanisms that enable new participants to adopt deviant behavior while maintaining psychological coherence.[52]

Denial of injury, where the adversary rationalizes actions (e.g., they can afford the loss, insurance will cover the damages) represents the most common justification mechanism among threat actors.[53,54] Denial of victim similarly involves claiming that targets deserve attack enabling the adversary to maintain that their actions serve justice or appropriate punishment rather than causing unjustified harm.[55,56] An appeal to higher loyalties involves justifying illicit activities as serving important objectives that outweigh legal constraints, which is a tactic commonly leveraged by Hacktivist groups.[57,58] Diffusion of responsibility occurs naturally in distributed threat actor networks where no single actor feels fully accountable for collective damage.[59] Ransomware-as-a-Service platforms exemplify this dynamic by separating technical development from deployment, allowing each participant to minimize their perceived role in causing harm. The psychological distance created by specialization and anonymity enables individuals to participate in serious crimes while maintaining that they are merely providing services rather than directly harming targets. Condemnation of condemners shifts focus from illicit behavior to perceived hypocrisy or corruption among authority figures who enforce laws. The adversary may also rationalize their activities by pointing to corporate data collection practices, government surveillance programs, or law enforcement overreach as justification for their own illegal behavior. The psychological comfort of these neutralization techniques rationalizations allows the adversary to maintain positive self-concepts while engaging in objectively harmful behaviors.

Conclusion

The behavior of the adversary is represented through three key pillars, including financial enrichment, ideological conviction, and personal gratification. These motivations form the psychological foundation upon which the adversary constructs sophisticated manipulation campaigns. Financial motivations demonstrate how economic desperation and opportunistic greed create predictable behavioral patterns. From the teenagers who stumbled into the Mirai botnet to the organized syndicates operating RaaS platforms, money remains the great equalizer that transforms ordinary individuals into members of the adversary. Ideological drivers reveal how moral relativism and collective identity may override legal constraints. Whether Anonymous hacktivists targeting corporate censorship or nation-state operators serving strategic objectives, ideologically motivated individuals demonstrate the dangerous intersection of capability and conviction. Personally motivated individuals transform cybercrime into performance art through narcissistic validation, addictive flow states, and systematic moral disengagement.

When analyzed through WAVE theory, these seemingly disparate motivational categories converge to reveal psychological symmetry between perpetrators and targets. The financial incentive that motivates a teenager to initiate a botnet operation mirrors the financial incentives that facilitate the recruitment of money mules. The authority bias that enables nation-state operators to conduct supply chain attacks parallels the authority bias that fosters compliance with social engineering campaigns. The peer validation that drives forum-based hacking competitions on darknets reflects the social proof mechanisms that make cryptocurrency investment scams successful. As we transition from examining psychological drivers of behavior in the adversary to analyzing the ways in which they deceive targets, the psychological underpinnings examined in this chapter provide the foundation for the concepts explored in Chapter 8, which will provide insights into how the adversary weaponizes psychology.

Reflection Questions

1 How might the three pillars of cybercrime motivation (financial, ideological, and personal) interact or evolve within the same individual over time?
2 How might understanding illicit motivations inform defensive strategies that go beyond technical controls to address human factors?
3 How do the psychological drivers of cybercrime differ from those underlying traditional illicit activities, and what implications does this have for prevention and response strategies?
4 Choose one specific cybercrime case from this chapter and analyze how WAVE theory explains both the perpetrator's initial involvement and their subsequent ability to manipulate targets. What does this symmetry reveal about human psychological vulnerabilities in digital environments?

Skill Builder Labs

Application Scenario: Build a Persona-Based Mitigation Plan for a Ransomware Affiliate

Develop a psychological threat profile for a ransomware affiliate exhibiting strong financial motivation, moderate technical skill, and a high-risk tolerance. Take the following steps:

- Research typical entry vectors employed by this type of adversary (e.g., social engineering).
- Analyze potential ransomware variants (e.g., LockBit) to prioritize monitoring of associated indicators of compromise and threat intelligence feeds.
- Design countermeasures that address the psychological and technical characteristics of this adversary type.
- Coordinate incident response playbooks that assign specific roles for technical containment and legal aspects of an attack.

Mini-Research Activity: Motivation Mapping

Objective

Apply the chapter's theoretical frameworks to analyze a real cybercrime case and identify psychological intervention points.

Instructions

1 Choose one significant cybercrime incident from the past two years.
2 Conduct three-pillar analysis, including primary and secondary motivations.
3 Apply WAVE theory analysis to the incident.
4 Conduct an assessment of potential rationalization concepts.
5 Identify mitigation strategies.

- Recommend three specific intervention strategies that address the underlying motivational drivers rather than just technical capabilities.
- Identify early warning indicators that might have predicted this incident.

Deliverable

Create a case report demonstrating an application of the chapter's frameworks, including specific examples from the chosen case that tie theory to practice.

References

1 Sujatha, R., Prakash, G., & Jhanjhi, N. Z. (Eds.). (2022). *Cyber security applications for industry 4.0*. CRC Press.
2 Goldman, Z. K., & McCoy, D. (2015). Deterring financially motivated cybercrime. *Journal of National Security Law & Policy, 8*, 595.

3. Paquet-Clouston, M., & García, S. (2022). On the motivations and challenges of affiliates involved in cybercrime. *Trends in Organized Crime*, 1–30.
4. Scharfman, J. (2024). *The cryptocurrency and digital asset fraud casebook*, Volume II. Springer Books.
5. Chia, O. (2022). New scam involving fake website targets FTX investors hoping to recover losses. *The Straits Times*.
6. Bethany, M., Galiopoulos, A., Bethany, E., Karkevandi, M. B., Beebe, N., Vishwamitra, N., & Najafirad, P. (2025). Lateral phishing with large language models: A large organization comparative study. *IEEE Access*.
7. U.S. Federal Bureau of Investigation. (2024). *Internet crime report*.
8. Sharma, M., Kumar, M., Gonzalez, C., & Dutt, V. (2022). How the presence of cognitive biases in phishing emails affects human decision-making?. In International Conference on Neural Information Processing (pp. 550–560). Singapore: Springer Nature Singapore.
9. Europol. (2021). *DarkMarket: World's largest illegal dark web marketplace taken down*.
10. Leukfeldt, E. R., Kleemans, E. R., & Stol, W. P. (2017). Cybercriminal networks, social ties and online forums: Social ties versus digital ties within phishing and malware networks. *The British Journal of Criminology*, *57*(3), 704–722.
11. Etaher, N., Weir, G. R., & Alazab, M. (2015, August). From Zeus to Zitmo: Trends in banking malware. In *2015 IEEE Trustcom/BigDataSE/ISPA* (pp. 1386–1391). IEEE.
12. Patsakis, C., Arroyo, D., & Casino, F. (2024). The malware as a service ecosystem. In Gritzalis, D., Choo, KK.R., Patsakis, C. (eds) *Malware: Handbook of prevention and detection* (pp. 371–394). Springer Nature Switzerland.
13. Gray, G. L. (2024). An exploration of the money laundering associated with the Bitfinex Bitcoin Hack. *Journal of Emerging Technologies in Accounting*, *21*(1), 43–57.
14. Adisa, O., Ilugbusi, B. S., Obi, O. C., Awonuga, K. F., Adelekan, O. A., Asuzu, O. F., & Ndubuisi, N. L. (2024). Decentralized Finance (DEFI) in the US economy: A review: Assessing the rise, challenges, and implications of blockchain-driven financial systems. *World Journal of Advanced Research and Reviews*, *21*(1), 2313–2328.
15. Goode, L. (2018). Anonymous and the political ethos of hacktivism. In Jonas Andersson Schwarz, Patrick Burkart *Popular communication, piracy and social change* (pp. 99–112). Routledge.
16. Postmes, T., & Spears, R. (1998). Deindividuation and antinormative behavior: A meta-analysis. *Psychological Bulletin*, *123*(3), 238.
17. Romagna, M., & Leukfeldt, R. E. (2024). Becoming a hacktivist. Examining the motivations and the processes that prompt an individual to engage in hacktivism. *Journal of Crime and Justice*, *47*(4), 511–529.
18. Mansfield-Devine, S. (2011). Anonymous: Serious threat or mere annoyance? *Network Security*, *2011*(1), 4–10.
19. Bellaby, R. W. (2023). Political autonomy, the Arab Spring and anonymous. In *The ethics of hacking* (pp. 53–72). Bristol University Press.
20. Moran, G. (2014). We are anonymous: Inside the hacker world of lulsec, anonymous, and the global cyber insurgency. *Journal of Information Ethics*, *23*(2), 95.
21. Pendergrass, S., & Morris, R. (2012). Hackers gone wild: The 2011 spring break of lulzsec. *Issues in Information Systems*, *13*(1), 133–143.
22. Herzog, S. (2011). Revisiting the Estonian cyber attacks: Digital threats and multinational responses. *Journal of Strategic Security*, *4*(2), 49–60.
23. Mandiant. (2013). *APT1: Exposing one of China's cyber espionage units*. Mandiant Intelligence Center Report.
24. Mandiant. (2019). *APT40: Examining a China-nexus espionage actor*.

25 Liang, L., & Kettunen, M. (2024). *Major Cyber incident: SolarWinds*. European Repository of Cyber Incidents.
26 Solarwinds Corporation. (2020). *Form 8-K Filing: December 14, 2020*.
27 Falliere, N., Murchu, L. O., & Chien, E. (2011). W32.Stuxnet dossier. *White Paper, Symantec Corp., Security Response*, 5(6), 29.
28 Vegh, S. (2013). Classifying forms of online activism: The case of cyberprotests against the World Bank. In McCaughey, M. & Ayers, M. (eds.) Cyberactivism (pp. 71–95). Routledge.
29 Fisher, C., Rogers, M. M., Fontes, L., & Ali, P. (2023). Technology-facilitated abuse. In Ali, P., Rogers, M.M. (eds) *Gender-based violence: A comprehensive guide* (pp. 555–569). Springer International Publishing.
30 Cartwright, B. E. (2016, June). Cyberbullying and cyber law. In *2016 IEEE International Conference on Cybercrime and Computer Forensic (ICCCF)* (pp. 1–7). IEEE.
31 Ring, T. (2015). The enemy within. *Computer Fraud & Security*, 2015(12), 9–14.
32 Schurman, K. (2012). *LulzSec: How a handful of hackers brought The US Government to its knees: 50 days of Lulz*. Hyperink Inc.
33 Sabu. (2011, June 20). *Why do we do this? Because we can*. Twitter.
34 Buffardi, L. E., & Campbell, W. K. (2008). Narcissism and social networking web sites. *Personality and Social Psychology Bulletin*, 34(10), 1303–1314.
35 Mehdizadeh, S. (2010). Self-presentation 2.0: Narcissism and self-esteem on Facebook. *Cyberpsychology, Behavior, and Social Networking*, 13(4), 357–364.
36 Rogers, M. K. (2006). A two-dimensional circumplex approach to the development of a hacker taxonomy. *Digital Investigation*, 3(2), 97–102.
37 Hutchings, A. (2014). Crime from the keyboard: Organised cybercrime, co-offending, initiation and knowledge transmission. *Crime, Law and Social Change*, 62(1), 1–20.
38 Rankmyhack.com [Archive.org].
39 Mitnick, K. D., & Simon, W. L. (2003). *The art of deception: Controlling the human element of security*. John Wiley & Sons.
40 Mitnick, K. (2011). *Ghost in the wires: My adventures as the world's most wanted hacker*. Hachette UK.
41 Gaia, J., Sanders, G., Sanders, S., Upadhyaya, S., Wang, X., & Woo, C. (2021). Dark traits and hacking potential. *Journal of Organizational Psychology*, 21(3). 23–46.
42 Skinner, W. F., & Fream, A. M. (1997). A social learning theory analysis of computer crime among college students. *Journal of Research in Crime and Delinquency*, 34(4), 495–518.
43 Norbury, A., & Husain, M. (2015). Sensation-seeking: Dopaminergic modulation and risk for psychopathology. *Behavioural Brain Research*, 288, 79–93.
44 Csikszentmihalyi, M. (1990). *Flow: The psychology of optimal experience*. Harper & Row.
45 Wu, T. C., Scott, D., & Yang, C. C. (2013). Advanced or addicted? Exploring the relationship of recreation specialization to flow experiences and online game addiction. *Leisure Sciences*, 35(3), 203–217.
46 Voiskounsky, A. E., & Smyslova, O. V. (2003). Flow-based model of computer hackers' motivation. *CyberPsychology & behavior*, 6(2), 171–180.
47 Young, R., Zhang, L., & Prybutok, V. R. (2007). Hacking into the minds of hackers. *Information Systems Management*, 24(4), 281–287.
48 Bandura, A. (2016). *Moral disengagement: How people do harm and live with themselves*. Worth Publishers.
49 Chua, Y. T., & Holt, T. J. (2016). A cross-national examination of the techniques of neutralization to account for hacking behaviors. *Victims & Offenders*, 11(4), 534–555.

50 Holt, T. J., & Kilger, M. (2008). Techcrafters and makecrafters: A comparison of two populations of hackers. *Proceedings of the 2008 WOMBAT Workshop on Information Security Threats Data Collection and Sharing*, 67–78.
51 Chng, S., Lu, H. Y., Kumar, A., & Yau, D. (2022). Hacker types, motivations and strategies: A comprehensive framework. *Computers in Human Behavior Reports*, 5, 100167.
52 Akers, R. (2017). *Social learning and social structure: A general theory of crime and deviance*. Routledge.
53 Sykes, G. M., & Matza, D. (1957). Techniques of neutralization: A theory of delinquency. *American Sociological Review*, 22, 664–670.
54 Hinduja, S. (2007). Neutralization theory and online software piracy: An empirical analysis. *Ethics and Information Technology*, 9(3), 187–204.
55 Minor, W. W. (1980). The neutralization of criminal offense. *Criminology*, 18(1), 103–120.
56 Bossler, A. M. (2021). Neutralizing cyber attacks: Techniques of neutralization and willingness to commit cyber attacks. *American Journal of Criminal Justice*, 46(6), 911–934.
57 Cohen, S. (2000). Human rights and crimes of the state: the culture of denial. In J. Muncie, E. McLaughlin, & M. Langan (Eds.), *Criminological perspectives. A reader* (pp. 489–507). Sage Publications.
58 Zain, N., & Javaid, T. (2025). Neutralization techniques and fraud justification: How cybercriminals evade accountability. https://www.researchgate.net/profile/Salman-Ali-39/publication/390236422_Neutralization_Techniques_and_Fraud_Justification_How_Cybercriminals_Evade_Accountability/links/67e561b243ec6369e202664a/Neutralization-Techniques-and-Fraud-Justification-How-Cybercriminals-Evade-Accountability.pdf
59 Wallach, M. A., Kogan, N., & Bem, D. J. (1964). Diffusion of responsibility and level of risk taking in groups. *The Journal of Abnormal and Social Psychology*, 68(3), 263.

8 Deceptive Tactics in Cybercrime

Stone Age Minds, Space Age Threats

The human mind, despite millions of years of evolutionary refinement, remains spectacularly ill-equipped for the digital world's endless cascade of persuasive demands. The cognitive architecture of humans evolved to navigate the physical world, where dangers announced themselves through sensory cues that brains learned to instantly process to survive. The same mental shortcuts that allowed early humans to survive saber-toothed tigers are exploited by the adversary to perpetrate schemes in the digital world. Consider for a moment the cognitive heuristics that laid the foundation for survival in the times of early humans, including the need to trust familiar faces, quickly respond to urgent warnings, follow authority figures during times of stress, and believe the cues provided by the sensory inputs around oneself. These psychological processes proved so essential to survival that they are hardwired into one's neural structure and operate beyond conscious awareness. Software patches for the human brain, unfortunately, are not readily available, which represents a reality that allows the adversary to distort the very fabric of the digital world by facilitating behavioral resonance in targets as a means to perpetrate their schemes. The adversary orchestrates synchronized exploits across multiple psychological systems to overwhelm cognitive defenses to push targets into harmful outcomes that feel reasonable at the time of execution. The asymmetry between minds adapted for the Stone Age and technology designed for the space age underscores the importance of understanding weaponized affective vulnerability engineering (WAVE) theory and its applications for the future of cybersecurity.

The WAVE of Social Engineering

As initially introduced in Chapter 2, social engineering involves manipulation techniques used by the adversary to circumvent technical defenses by attacking a target's cognitive processes. By exploiting cognitive biases rather than technical vulnerabilities, the adversary is positioned to hijack the target's mental models to accomplish their objectives, such as obtaining sensitive data or financial benefits. When explored through the lens of WAVE theory, the evidence indicates that the adversary orchestrates behavioral resonance in a target through the simultaneous exploitation of multiple cognitive processes. The ubiquity of digital communication transformed persuasion from an interpersonal art into an industrial process. Where once a fraudster might spend weeks cultivating a single target, artificial intelligence now enables the creation of thousands of personalized deception campaigns in minutes.[1] This notion extends beyond attack automation. It represents the enablement of the adversary to exploit affective vulnerabilities through triggers calibrated to a specific target. As communication preferences and functionality evolved at the societal level, so too did the adversary's tactics. Social engineering campaigns evolved to incorporate a variety of formats beyond spray and pray, blast phishing campaigns. The adversary now leverages precision spear-phishing and whaling attacks, angler phishing, callback phishing, smishing, and quishing. In the early 2020s, the popularization of large language models (LLMs) facilitated the production of automated, personalized copy for targets in seconds.[2] The adversary may feed collected attributes and data into an LLM to produce realistic contextually relevant campaigns that enhance click rates by over 50% compared to traditional, generic phishing campaigns.[3] This represents an application of the adversary essentially instituting A/B testing with LLMs to optimize psychological resonance.

In practice, the 2023 MGM Resorts attack exemplifies WAVE theory. Although surface analysis of the attack focuses on the social engineering tactics leveraged by the adversary (e.g., authority bias exploitation through executive impersonation, artificial urgency created via board presentation deadlines), WAVE theory reveals deeper orchestration at work. The adversary synchronized authority manipulation (i.e., executive impersonation) with temporal pressure (i.e., urgent deadlines) and contextual legitimacy (i.e., insider knowledge of board meetings) to create behavioral resonance that overwhelmed rational thought.[4] The cost associated with these types of incidents demonstrates how WAVE-driven psychological manipulation often results in damages exceeding the impact of sophisticated technical exploits or serves as a precursor to them.[5] Understanding executive psychology through WAVE theory also demonstrates the efficacy of WAVE attacks. Many executives operate under perpetual cognitive overload, managing frequent high-stakes decisions while processing multiple information streams at the same time.[6] This creates chronic, predictable vulnerability states (e.g., an overreliance on System 1 processing) to which the adversary synchronizes attacks as a means to maximize the potential of success for a campaign. Beyond authority and temporal manipulation lies the primal notion that scarce resources are more valuable, which is a concept readily exploited by the adversary.

Scarcity, FOMO, and Exclusivity

The FOMO represents a potent psychological bias that the adversary may exploit to instigate target behaviors.[7,8] By synchronizing scarcity indicators with time pressure and social proof, sophisticated attacks facilitate behavioral resonance that bypasses a target's cognitive processing and reduces a target's scrutiny of a request. In legitimate marketing contexts, this may take the form of time-bound promotions that generate a sense of urgency in a target to prompt specific action prior to the expiration of the deadline (e.g., flash sales with a countdown clock). Evidence indicates that in legitimate circumstances countdown clocks boost conversion rates by a statistically significant amount.[9] Within the context of cybercrime, this concept is exploited by the adversary by fostering a false sense of urgency in targets (e.g., password expiration deadlines, imminent account cancellations). Analysis of this practice through the lens of WAVE theory reveals why this psychological mechanism proves so effective. Scarcity exploitation creates neurological stress responses that prioritize immediate action over deliberative analysis (i.e., tunnelling).[10] In practice, this represents the hijacking of System 1 processing to circumvent System 2 through the invention of affective pressure on a target's cognitive processing.

The notion of exclusivity (e.g., wait-lists, invitation-only events) exploits social proof to stoke perceived scarcity. The artificial suppression of one's ability to engage in an event or purchase a product intensifies the perceived value of the transaction in the mind of the target. Exclusivity also plays on the notion of social recognition and peer competition by fostering a sense of social comparison in the target, resulting from the perceived increase in social standing that results from obtaining an exclusive item. Within the context of non-fungible tokens (NFTs), schemes may exploit scarcity bias through offering limited-edition collections or airdrops. Mint pages also often involve whitelist wallet addresses. Research indicates that 98% of NFTs launched in 2024 experienced minimal activity, if any, trading since launch, indicating the cyclical nature of hype and FOMO-driven activities.[11] Gated access and exclusivity, whether implied or real, exploit scarcity in the mind of the target to drive impulsive behaviors through artificially generated urgency. While the exploitation of scarcity bias uses FOMO to elicit desired outcomes in a target, an even more fundamental cognitive process may be exploited by the adversary based on one's need to maintain a coherent view of the world around them.

Confirmation Bias

The drive for individuals to seek out and value information that aligns with beliefs they already hold while also discounting contradictory evidence is known as confirmation bias.[12] This bias was essential to survival by supporting rapid decision-making processes based on recognized patterns. Today, however, this evolutionary shortcut transforms digital environments into belief manipulation laboratories. Social media algorithms represent the most pervasive example of confirmation bias at scale by feeding content to users based on material with which the user previously engaged. For example, engaging with content espousing specific political views induces the underlying recommendation algorithm to cultivate content for that user that aligns with that political perspective.[13] In practice, this narrows the varying views that a user consumes and intensifies the user's original beliefs. Evidence indicates that this formation of echo-chambers on social media platforms leads individuals to leave applications when faced with opposing views, further exacerbating in-group bias and radicalization.[14]

Evidence packs, also known as evidence collages (i.e., coordinated collections of fabricated materials designed to create the illusion of independent confirmation across multiple sources), are deployed to support false claims.[15] This entails manufacturing evidence that mimics reference materials to corroborate a perspective across multiple points of proof. The power in this practice comes from the synchronized presentation of statements to overwhelm one's capacity to verify information. Given that targets are more likely to trust subsequent claims without scrutiny, this becomes a powerful component of propaganda campaigns in the digital world.[16] The Pizzagate conspiracy in 2016 demonstrates how evidence packs exploit confirmation bias in the digital world.[17] The campaign included interconnected social media posts, doctored images, and fabricated documents that appeared to corroborate claims that a Washington D.C. pizzeria was linked to human trafficking. The campaign synchronized visual evidence (e.g., manipulated images), authoritative documentation (e.g., fabricated reports), social proof (e.g., coordinated sharing), and emotional urgency (e.g., claims related to child endangerment) to foster behavioral resonance that bypassed rational analysis. The self-reinforcing cycle culminated in real-world violence when an armed individual investigated the premises, demonstrating how engineered digital manipulation may translate into consequences in the physical world.[18] This phenomenon also proves dangerous because it exploits the evolved capacity for collaborative truth-seeking. Humans naturally validate information through social consensus (i.e., consensus heuristic).[19] While this survival mechanism proved essential in tribal contexts, it proves detrimental in the digital world as evidence packs weaponize the collaborative instinct by manufacturing artificial consensus across multiple apparent sources and creating synchronized social proof manipulation.

When false content spreads across multiple platforms and receives endorsement from various sources, it triggers a neurological response where repeated exposure to claims increases perceived truthfulness regardless of actual accuracy (i.e., the illusory truth effect).[20] Each exposure to false information increases familiarity, which human brains interpret as truthfulness. Individuals may confront the same false claim from multiple sources, leading to the interpretation of repetition as validation. Research shows that once repetition-validation loops establish false beliefs across multiple psychological systems, contradictory evidence often triggers defensive responses rather than analytical reconsideration.[21] The implications extend far beyond individual deception to threaten the epistemological foundations of democratic discourse via manufactured consensus. The analysis of confirmation bias through the lens of WAVE theory underscores why traditional media literacy approaches prove insufficient against sophisticated psychological manipulation. Teaching people to fact-check individual claims misses the reality of the digital world. While evidence packs and echo chambers weaponize the need for coherent worldviews, the next evolution of WAVE-driven attacks leverages advancing technologies to corrupt the very mechanisms through which we perceive and process information.

Digital Deception Tactics in Social Engineering Campaigns

Traditional social engineering campaigns operated similarly to confirmation bias exploitation, with both relying on volume and repetition at scale. The adversary, however, has evolved beyond the crude approach that defined early social engineering campaigns to now deploy increasingly sophisticated deception techniques that exploit human cognitive processing patterns and corrupt digital communication practices. The sophistication becomes apparent when considering the idea that modern deception campaigns synchronize technological capabilities with psychological vulnerabilities to create technological behavioral resonance. Phishing toolkits now supply collections of authentic corporate assets (e.g., logos, color codes, typography), enabling pixel-perfect impersonations of trusted brands. Given that individuals prioritize visual information processing over technical indicators (e.g., website addresses), this practice often leads to successful social engineering campaigns.[22] The Anthem healthcare data breach of 2015 illustrates sophisticated visual deception in action. The adversary created phishing sites and emails impersonating Anthem's corporate branding, including correct fonts, logos, and color schemes.[23] Despite sophisticated technical security controls, employees clicked on malicious links because the visual presentation appeared authentic, which led to the compromised personal information of approximately 80 million individuals.

Urgency cues represent another key aspect of successful social engineering campaigns. Time-bound threats in subject lines or email bodies push impulsive responses in targets that bypass deliberative processing. By compelling immediate action, the adversary forces information processing to take place through System 1 thinking rather than System 2 thinking of a target. Evidence indicates that phishing campaigns incorporating time-bound pressure produce significantly higher click-through rates than campaigns with neutral messaging.[24] When taken in tandem, the evidence indicates that urgency cues force information processing through System 1 thinking while visual authenticity exploits pattern-matching shortcuts, which creates synchronized cognitive pressure to overwhelm deliberate processing.

While these principles demonstrate sophisticated WAVE orchestration, these campaigns still rely on the adversary initiating contact with targets. The next iteration in social engineering reverses this dynamic in a type of social engineering known as angler phishing. In angler phishing attacks, the adversary generates false social media accounts to appear as a legitimate help resource for customers of a legitimate company. This allows the adversary to directly engage with targets and supply malicious links directly to individuals with real questions or complaints meant for the legitimate company. The sophistication of angler phishing becomes apparent when analyzed through WAVE principles. Angler phishing works on a psychological level because research shows that individuals seeking support are predisposed to trust the entity offering it due to the concept of contextual trust.[25] Customer service replies appear legitimate as a result of brand recognition and authority heuristics that automatically engage when the target processes the response. This self-initiation bias also leads a target to perceive the action as more trustworthy given that the target began the exchange, rather than an exchange driven by the adversary. Additionally, the synchronization of helpful timing (e.g., appearing when help is needed) with authoritative presentation (e.g., profiles appearing official) and solution-oriented messaging (e.g., addressing specific problems) creates behavioral resonance that makes skeptical evaluation psychologically difficult.

Callback phishing further upends the typical social engineering campaign paradigm by shifting control to the target. The furtherance of the scam depends on the target placing the call to the adversary, which reverses the traditional social engineering campaign dynamics. This creates an illusion of control for the target that reduces perceived risk while simultaneously exploiting loss aversion and temporal urgency. Targets feel empowered by initiating contact (i.e., agency illusion), urgency pressure motivates immediate action (i.e., temporal manipulation), and gradual information elicitation exploits foot-in-the-door effects (i.e., compliance escalation). These campaigns demonstrate WAVE's adaptive orchestration principle through carefully structured escalation sequences. Initial contact establishes urgency through imminent account closure or security breach notifications, while callback instructions create the illusion that targets control the interaction. Once voice contact establishes authority and rapport, adversaries slowly ratchet up information requests in sequences that WAVE theory identifies as synchronized vulnerability exploitation. Each compliance step creates psychological commitment that makes subsequent requests feel consistent with previous decisions, while urgency framing positions each escalation as necessary to avoid impending loss.

The ubiquity of smartphones enabled a new threat vector for adversarial exploitation via SMS-based social engineering campaigns (i.e., smishing).[26] Smishing campaigns exploit the unconscious application of reduced skepticism to communications reaching personal devices that function as extensions of intimate psychological space, which is known as intimacy bias. Personal mobile devices occupy a unique psychological territory as constant companions that mediate our most private communications. This creates effective vulnerabilities for the adversary to manipulate. The smishing campaigns impersonating government agencies (e.g., Toll Scams, Census-themed scams) demonstrate sophisticated psychological synchronization by combining authority bias (e.g., impersonation of a government agency), intimacy bias (e.g., SMS delivery), and temporal urgency (e.g., compliance deadlines) to create behavioral resonance that overcame rational verification instincts in targets through synchronized trust exploitation.

Interestingly, the widespread adoption of HTTPS encryption created an unintended psychological vulnerability through the mental association of visual security indicators with comprehensive trustworthiness. What was designed as a narrow technical signal became a broad trust heuristic that the adversary now weaponizes. Using free SSL certificates from services like Let's Encrypt, the adversary generates phishing domains that bypass browser warnings and exploit inherent trust responses from targets. Evidence indicates that over half of phishing sites now incorporate SSL certificates.[27] Research additionally found that nearly all (90%) of users misunderstood the meaning of the padlock icon.[28] In other words, technical authority indicators (e.g., padlock icons) combine with professional visual design (e.g., aesthetic legitimacy) and urgent messaging (e.g., temporal pressure) to create behavioral resonance that bypasses conscious analysis.

Attention-grabbing content, forced urgency, and social proof messaging combine to overwhelm available cognitive resources and force information processing in a target through heuristic pathways rather than analytical ones. The cognitive load associated with modern work environments creates particularly vulnerable conditions. Individuals juggling multiple communication methods, deadlines, and tasks lack available working memory for in-depth scrutiny of suspicious messages. When coupled with WAVE-orchestrated campaigns that present visual and emotional triggers activating automatic response pathways, targets find themselves cognitively unprepared for sophisticated psychological manipulation. In fact, recent findings illustrate that targets who believed rapid responses to email were highly important were found to be more likely to comply with social engineering campaigns marked as urgent.[29] It stands to reason that workplace cultures prioritizing response times create cognitive environments with the ideal conditions for synchronized psychological exploitation. Thus, a broader framework to shift society away from the infinite workday and acceptance of continuous partial attention as the standard necessitates fundamental changes in organizational culture and technological design to prioritize human cognitive limitations rather than maximizing engagement metrics. Individual and organizational adaptations, however, only represent the beginning of the transformation required to address WAVE-driven psychological manipulation.

Conclusion

Technology-enabled deception evolved beyond simple social engineering tactics into sophisticated psychological orchestration campaigns that exploit the evolutionary mismatch between human cognition and digital environments. WAVE theory provides the framework for understanding this evolution. From scarcity exploitation that hijacks our fear of missing out to confirmation bias manipulation that transforms us into accomplices in our own deception, the adversary of today succeeds through the coordinated exploitation of affective vulnerabilities rather than isolated manipulation techniques. This synchronized orchestration creates behavioral resonance. Beyond this, the same cognitive shortcuts that enabled early humans to survive in the harsh realities of ancient life remain present despite technological evolution creating asymmetries ripe for exploitation by the adversary. Reactive security approaches and technical controls that assume rational decision-making prove inadequate against attacks designed to bypass rational analysis through the weaponization of emotions. As discussed throughout this chapter, the same WAVE principles that enable manipulation of individual targets also scale to societal-level influence campaigns that threaten democratic discourse, social cohesion, and collective decision-making processes. Chapter 9 examines how these individual psychological vulnerabilities aggregate into powerful social catalysts that reshape entire communities and institutions. Beyond personal financial loss or data theft, WAVE-driven manipulation campaigns now target the psychological foundations of social trust, shared reality, and collective agency. The battle for human psychological autonomy evolved from protecting individual users to preserving the cognitive foundations of democratic society itself, revealing how modern information warfare exploits the same evolutionary psychology that makes us human to systematically undermine the social bonds that make civilization possible.

Reflection Questions

1. How does artificial urgency influence decision-making in daily digital interactions?
2. What fundamental changes in interface design, organizational culture, or regulatory frameworks are necessary to better align digital environments with human cognitive limitations?
3. What are the long-term implications for shared truth and collective decision-making of exploits such as evidence packs, confirmation bias exploitation, and manufactured consensus?
4. How might WAVE theory change approaches to cybersecurity training and defense strategies as compared to traditional awareness programs?

Skill Builder Labs

Application Scenario: Analyze a Multi-Vector WAVE Attack

You receive three simultaneous notifications (e.g., an urgent IT email threatening two-hour account suspension with a credential verification link, social media posts from colleagues about security updates, and a bank SMS about suspicious activity requiring immediate action). Using WAVE theory, take the following steps:

- Identify the synchronized psychological vulnerabilities exploited across these multiple touchpoints.
- Map how the adversary orchestrates behavioral resonance through timing, authority indicators, social proof, and scarcity pressure.
- Develop a decision framework that could help identify when multiple psychological systems are being simultaneously targeted.

Mini-Research Activity: Mapping Evidence Pack Construction

Objective

Review the psychological underpinnings of evidence packs.

Instructions

1. Select a recent conspiracy theory that gained traction online.
2. Trace how the narrative was supported through coordinated messages across multiple platforms.
3. Document any psychological manipulation techniques used (e.g., doctored images, fabricated documents, coordinated testimonials, and repetition patterns).
4. Analyze how the campaign exploited cognitive processes to make information feel truthful.

Deliverable

Construct a psychological manipulation analysis report documenting how a selected conspiracy theory exploited cognitive processes to bypass analytical evaluations, including the specific principles from WAVE theory that apply.

References

1. Yu, J., Yu, Y., Wang, X., Lin, Y., Yang, M., Qiao, Y., & Wang, F. Y. (2024). The shadow of fraud: The emerging danger of ai-powered social engineering and its possible cure. *arXiv preprint arXiv:2407.15912*.
2. Schmitt, M., & Flechais, I. (2024). Digital deception: Generative artificial intelligence in social engineering and phishing. *Artificial Intelligence Review, 57*(12), 324.
3. Kim, H., Song, M., Na, S. H., Shin, S., & Lee, K. (2025). When {LLMs} go online: The emerging threat of {Web-Enabled}{LLMs}. In *34th USENIX security symposium (USENIX Security 25)* (pp. 1729–1748). USENIX.
4. Barker, J. (2024). *Hacked: The secrets behind cyber attacks*. Kogan Page Publishers.
5. Salahdine, F., & Kaabouch, N. (2019). Social engineering attacks: A survey. *Future Internet, 11*(4), 89.
6. Ganster, D. C. (2005). Executive job demands: Suggestions from a stress and decision-making perspective. *Academy of Management Review, 30*(3), 492–502.
7. AlAmeeri, A. A., & AlMourad, M. B. (2025, April). Impact of social engineering on social media users. In *2024 International conference on IT innovation and knowledge discovery (ITIKD)* (pp. 1–5). IEEE.
8. Alutaybi, A., Al-Thani, D., McAlaney, J., & Ali, R. (2020). Combating fear of missing out (FoMO) on social media: The FoMO-R method. *International Journal of Environmental Research and Public Health, 17*(17), 6128.
9. Tiemessen, J., Schraffenberger, H., & Acar, G. (2023, April). The time is ticking: The effect of limited time discounts on consumers' buying behavior and experience. In *Extended abstracts of the 2023 CHI conference on human factors in computing systems*. Association for Computing Machinery, New York, NY, USA, Article 277, 1–11.
10. Civai, C., Elbaek, C. T., & Capraro, V. (2024). Why scarcity can both increase and decrease prosocial behaviour: A review and theoretical framework for the complex relationship between scarcity and prosociality. *Current Opinion in Psychology, 60*, 101931.
11. Miller, L. (2025). *State of 2024 NFT Drops*. NFTEvening.
12. Wason, P. C. (1960). On the failure to eliminate hypotheses in a conceptual task. *Quarterly Journal of Experimental Psychology, 12*(3), 129–140.

13 Workman, M. (2018). An empirical study of social media exchanges about a controversial topic: Confirmation bias and participant characteristics. *The Journal of Social Media in Society*, *7*(1), 381–400.
14 Modgil, S., Singh, R. K., Gupta, S., & Dennehy, D. (2024). A confirmation bias view on social media induced polarisation during Covid-19. *Information Systems Frontiers*, *26*(2), 417–441.
15 Krafft, P. M., & Donovan, J. (2020). Disinformation by design: The use of evidence collages and platform filtering in a media manipulation campaign. *Political Communication*, *37*(2), 194–214.
16 Pennycook, G., Cannon, T. D., & Rand, D. G. (2018). Prior exposure increases perceived accuracy of fake news. *Journal of Experimental Psychology: General*, *147*(12), 1865.
17 Tangherlini, T. R., Shahsavari, S., Shahbazi, B., Ebrahimzadeh, E., & Roychowdhury, V. (2020). An automated pipeline for the discovery of conspiracy and conspiracy theory narrative frameworks: Bridgegate, Pizzagate and storytelling on the web. *PloS One*, *15*(6), e0233879.
18 Bleakley, P. (2023). Panic, pizza and mainstreaming the alt-right: A social media analysis of Pizzagate and the rise of the QAnon conspiracy. *Current Sociology*, *71*(3), 509–525.
19 Ross, L., Greene, D., & House, P. (1977). The "false consensus effect": An egocentric bias in social perception and attribution processes. *Journal of Experimental Social Psychology*, *13*(3), 279–301.
20 Hasher, L., Goldstein, D., & Toppino, T. (1977). Frequency and the conference of referential validity. *Journal of Verbal Learning and Verbal Behavior*, *16*(1), 107–112.
21 Udry, J., & Barber, S. J. (2024). The illusory truth effect: A review of how repetition increases belief in misinformation. *Current Opinion in Psychology*, *56*, 101736.
22 Posner, M. I., Nissen, M. J., & Klein, R. M. (1976). Visual dominance: An information-processing account of its origins and significance. *Psychological Review*, *83*(2), 157.
23 Bailey, B. (2015). *Anthem: Hackers tried to breach system as early as Dec. 10*. U.S. News.
24 Butavicius, M., Taib, R., & Han, S. J. (2022). Why people keep falling for phishing scams: The effects of time pressure and deception cues on the detection of phishing emails. *Computers & Security*, *123*, 102937.
25 Nissenbaum, H. (2004). Privacy as contextual integrity. *Washington Law Review*, *79*, 119.
26 Agarwal, S., Suarez-Tangil, G., & Vasek, M. (2025). An overview of 7726 user reports: Uncovering SMS scams and scammer strategies. *arXiv preprint arXiv:2508.05276*.
27 PhishLabs. (2019). *More than half of phishing sites now use HTTPS*.
28 von Zezschwitz, E., Chen, S., & Stark, E. (2022, May). "It builds trust with the customers"-exploring user perceptions of the padlock icon in browser UI. In *2022 IEEE Security and Privacy Workshops (SPW)* (pp. 44–50). IEEE.
29 Stylianou, I., Bountakas, P., Zarras, A., & Xenakis, C. (2025). Suspicious minds: Psychological techniques correlated with online phishing attacks. *Computers in Human Behavior Reports*, *19*, 100694.

9 Psychological Catalysts and Impacts

When the Expert Becomes the Target

Dr. Sarah Chen, a cybersecurity professor at a large public university, stared at her phone screen in disbelief. The text message appeared to come from her bank, warning that her account showed suspicious activity and required immediate verification to prevent closure. Without thinking, she clicked the link and entered her credentials. Moments later, the adversary absconded with $47,000 from her savings account. Dr. Chen spent the 15 years that preceded this incident teaching students to recognize phishing attempts, published dozens of papers on social engineering defense mechanisms, and quite literally wrote the textbook on cyber awareness training. It is not hyperbole to state that Dr. Chen was capable of identifying a fake website from across a crowded lecture hall. And yet, while juggling three conference calls, grading exams, and worrying about her father's recent cancer diagnosis, Dr. Chen's extensive experience did not protect her from an all too common social engineering scam. This incident reveals a fundamental truth ignored by traditional cybersecurity approaches. Susceptibility independently operates from technical knowledge. The same cognitive limitations that enable manipulation by the adversary affect cybersecurity experts and novices alike. Intelligence, education, and professional experience provide incomplete protection against attacks designed to exploit the basic psychological processes governing most decisions.

Through the lens of weaponized affective vulnerability engineering (WAVE) theory, Dr. Chen's experience illustrates how adversaries create behavioral resonance by synchronizing technical deception with psychological pressure. The attack succeeded through precise timing that exploited her momentary cognitive vulnerability. The adversary weaponized her stress, her trust in familiar communication channels, and her divided attention to create a perfect storm of exploitation. This chapter explores the psychological factors that determine cybercrime susceptibility, the cascading impacts that extend far beyond immediate financial losses, and the feedback loops that either build resilience or perpetuate vulnerability, the understanding of which proves essential for developing defensive strategies supported by human psychology.

Target Susceptibility Factors

Demographics and Psychographics

Age creates vulnerability windows that adversaries exploit with precision timing. Popular perception paints older adults as primary cybercrime targets, yet research reveals a more complex picture. While popular perception paints older adults as the primary targets of digital deception, research reveals a more nuanced picture where both ends of the age spectrum demonstrate concerning vulnerability levels, albeit for different reasons. There is ample evidence in the literature that older adults experience what is clinically referred to as age-related cognitive decline.[1,2,3] Neurological changes affect executive functioning and episodic memory, which impairs the analytical scrutiny required for effective fraud detection. Meanwhile, younger individuals who are between 12 and 29 years old demonstrate cybercrime susceptibility rates more than three times higher than individuals who are over 65 years old.[4] This finding challenges the digital native mythology that permeates popular culture, positing that technological fluency translates into cybersecurity awareness. Analysis indicates that the younger demographic's vulnerability may stem from optimism bias, overconfidence, and social motivations that prioritize immediacy and peer approval over secure practices. Through the lens of WAVE theory, these age-related vulnerabilities represent distinct affective vulnerability states that adversaries weaponize. Romance scammers target older adults during periods of social isolation, synchronizing emotional manipulation with financial exploitation. Investment scammers target younger adults during career transitions, combining FOMO psychology with authority bias to create behavioral resonance that bypasses analytical thinking.

The intersection of personality traits with cybercrime vulnerability reveals uncomfortable truths about human psychology that transcend demographic categories. Impulsivity emerges as one of the strongest predictors of victimization across demographic categories. Individuals high in attentional impulsivity often struggle with deliberative processing, which may lead these individuals to less analytically based responses to social engineering attempts. In other words, motor impulsivity may manifest as difficulty inhibiting immediate reactions to urgent demands.[5] Research shows that higher impulsivity correlates with increased click rates on malicious links, which indicates that some individuals may possess a cognitive predisposition to cybercrime exploitation.[6] Anxiety presents an additional important paradox. While heightened vigilance might theoretically improve threat detection, anxious individuals demonstrate greater vulnerability to social engineering attacks.[7] Generalized anxiety heightens emotional reactivity while impairing the analytical scrutiny required for fraud detection. The result creates a population that is worried about digital threats while remaining vulnerable to the very dangers they fear. From a broader perspective, researchers studying the big five personality traits identified additional vulnerability patterns. Individuals scoring high on openness to experience demonstrate increased susceptibility to cybercrime, presumably due to their willingness to engage with novel digital experiences.[8] Conversely, higher emotional stability and conscientiousness generally reduce the likelihood of exploitation, though these protective effects may still be overwhelmed by situational pressures or sophisticated targeting by the adversary.

Socioeconomic factors influence both victimization risk and impact severity through multiple mechanisms. Lower-income individuals may face higher risks from certain scam types while lacking resources for recovery when victimization occurs. However, higher-income individuals may face more sophisticated targeting due to their financial attractiveness while having better access to protective resources and recovery support. Furthermore, digital divide disparities create complex vulnerability patterns that extend beyond simple access issues. While limited technological exposure increases susceptibility to basic deceptions, the relationship between digital literacy and cybercrime vulnerability follows an interesting curve. Individuals with moderate technical knowledge often face elevated risks because they possess enough confidence to disable security measures while lacking sufficient expertise to recognize sophisticated threats.[9] Moreover, trust norms vary significantly across cultural contexts, creating differential exploitation opportunities for the adversary.[10] Cultures with high power distance show increased susceptibility to social engineering attacks that exploit hierarchical authority patterns, while materialistic values increase vulnerability to investment fraud schemes across both individualistic and collectivistic societies.[11,12]

Situational Vulnerabilities

In addition to demographic attributes, personality traits, and cultural attitudes, situational factors represent another potential vulnerability exploited by the adversary. For example, individuals entering retirement or beginning college report elevated levels of stress, identity shifts, and routine disruptions, diminishing deliberative processing while heightening emotional reactivity (i.e., tunneling).[13] During these transitional periods, people often delegate financial oversight, neglect digital hygiene, or embrace new technologies without understanding associated risks, which create windows of opportunity that skilled adversaries recognize and exploit.[14]

Decision fatigue represents one of the most exploitable psychological states present in digital environments. The constant stream of requests, notifications, and content sent to individuals each day creates cognitive exhaustion that progressively degrades judgment quality.[15] The adversary exploits this phenomenon by timing attacks for peak decision fatigue periods, such as late in the afternoon before a holiday, around key deadlines (e.g., year-end, tax reporting deadlines), when mental resources are likely depleted. Multitasking additionally amplifies cognitive vulnerability by fragmenting attention across competing priorities. The combination of time pressure, emotional stress, and divided attention created optimal conditions for exploitation. WAVE theory explains why this timing proves so effective. Thus, cognitive depletion creates synchronized vulnerability across multiple psychological systems. Attention narrows, risk assessment capability deteriorates, and pattern recognition defaults to familiar shortcuts. The adversary exploits this convergence by presenting urgent requests that feel routine to slip past a target's fatigued cognitive filters.

Social isolation creates psychological vulnerabilities that technology-dependent threat actors exploit through romance scams, friendship fraud, and social support schemes. Individuals experiencing social isolation demonstrate increased susceptibility to digital relationships that bypass normal verification processes, leading them to trust anonymous correspondents more readily than face-to-face acquaintances.[16] In other words, research shows that loneliness overwhelms analytical judgment and facilitates exploitation. This is supported by reporting statistics, as well. The COVID-19 pandemic provided a natural experiment in isolation-based vulnerability. Reported losses to romance scams increased by 52% during 2020.[17] Thus, it stands to reason that loneliness may overwhelm analytical judgment, as individuals prioritize emotional connection over rational skepticism about suspicious requests. Social isolation may also cause an uptick in cybercrime exploitation as a result of an inability for a target to connect with trusted individuals who would advise against engaging in suspicious interactions. However, this is not without its own drawbacks as caregiver burden creates additional vulnerability in a target. This is done through stress, social isolation, and financial pressure that diminish defensive capabilities in adult children managing elderly parent care. These individuals often become targets for follow-on scams exploiting emotional investment and crisis-response psychology.

Crisis periods generate acute vulnerability spikes that, at least in part, explain the prevalence of disaster-themed cybercrime campaigns. Natural disasters, terrorist attacks, and public health emergencies create emotional states characterized by fear, urgency, and reduced analytical thinking. For example, the public notifications made after significant data breaches generate follow-on scams (e.g., malicious ads touting free credit monitoring services) while natural disasters may spawn fraudulent schemes exploiting related fears and economic anxiety (e.g., COVID-19 Investment Scams). Beyond crisis response periods, the adversary may exploit times of heightened stress within an organization. For instance, research shows that the adversary regularly executes social engineering campaigns during periods of reported outages of services (e.g., technology disruptions), as well as when public announcements are made about company changes (e.g., merger announcements, widespread layoffs).[18,19]

As discussed in previous chapters, the adversary may also artificially impose time pressure tactics to exploit fundamental features of human decision-making psychology. Under time constraints, individuals default to System 1 thinking patterns that prioritize speed over accuracy, emotional reaction over analytical processing, and familiar patterns over careful verification. By incorporating urgency elements into social engineering campaigns, the adversary is positioned to successfully manipulate targets by artificially manufacturing situational vulnerabilities, which often compounds already present factors. The SolarWinds supply chain attack demonstrated how the adversary may leverage situational factors to manipulate targets. As organizations rushed to assess and respond to the potential compromise, follow-on social engineering campaigns were reported with the adversary allegedly impersonating vendors, IT staff, and government agencies to send messages concerning fraudulent security updates and account verification requests. The frequency and success of follow-on attacks illustrate how the adversary may exploit situational factors to amplify vulnerability in targets.

The Cyber Hygiene Paradox

The relationship between technical knowledge and cybersecurity vulnerability defies simple linear assumptions. While basic digital literacy provides some protection against elementary scams, moderate technical knowledge often creates a dangerous middle where confidence exceeds competence.[20] Individuals with intermediate skills, for example, often disable security features they perceive as obstacles while lacking expertise to recognize sophisticated threats or the downstream impact of these decisions.[21] This version of the Dunning-Kruger effect manifests in cybersecurity contexts when individuals with limited knowledge demonstrate inflated confidence in their scam detection abilities.[22] This psychological bias proves particularly dangerous because overconfident users actively resist security measures they perceive as unnecessary, with research demonstrating that self-assessed cybersecurity knowledge negatively correlates with actual protective behavior effectiveness.[23] In other words, the evidence indicates that overconfidence in one's abilities to detect cybercrime attempts reduces one's vigilance and analytical scrutiny while increasing one's willingness to take risks.

Common misconceptions about cybersecurity compound this issue by creating predictable exploitation opportunities for the adversary. Consider the fact that many users believe antivirus software provides comprehensive protection. This belief leads individuals to engage in riskier behaviors that they may not have otherwise engaged in under false assumptions that they may afford to do so, given the security features they use.[24] As discussed in earlier chapters, individuals may also incorrectly assume that websites that look legitimate are safe due to a failure to understand how easily the adversary may replicate familiar interfaces and communication patterns. This phenomenon of overconfidence in security features extends to individual behaviors where people implement visible security measures that provide minimal actual protection while neglecting less obvious and more effective practices. Password complexity requirements exemplify this pattern. In response to password requirements, users may create elaborate passwords that they store in unsecure locations (e.g., Post-it notes on their office computer screen) or reuse the same complex password across multiple, sensitive accounts, which in practice negates the intended security benefits of the complex passssword.[25]

The current iteration of cybersecurity awareness training programs does little to support the long-term success of targets. As a result of the forgetting curve phenomenon, evidence indicates that knowledge retention significantly drops if not reinforced, with some studies even indicating that individuals forget approximately half of the new information within one hour of exposure if not actively reviewed.[26,27] Within the context of cybersecurity training, it is clear that traditional one-off training sessions provide minimal lasting protection for entities. Knowledge transfer problems also compound this issue when training scenarios fail to provide relevant context. For example, users who identify obvious phishing examples in training environments often struggle to identify sophisticated social engineering campaigns that blend legitimate and malicious elements.[28] Taken in tandem with the notion of overconfidence, research suggests that the disconnect between training and reality may expand false confidence in targets and increase vulnerability rather than reducing it even within a short time after the training. When exploited by the adversary, the resulting manipulation exacts damage extending far beyond immediate financial losses.

Psychological Impact on Survivors

Emotional Trauma

The immediate psychological impact of cybercrime resembles acute trauma responses.[29] Survivors often report shock, disbelief, and cognitive disruption that impairs decision-making and heightens vulnerability to additional exploitation attempts. The emotional trajectory follows a predictable pattern increasingly recognized in literature as cyber trauma. In the context of cyber trauma, initial shock gives way to intense anger, with many survivors reporting fury directed both at perpetrators and themselves. The self-directed anger represents a particularly cruel aspect of cybercrime psychology, where survivors blame themselves for trusting individuals who exploited them in an emotional response combining feelings of violation with self-recrimination that survivors of traditional crime also exhibit. Shame and embarrassment compound the psychological damage associated with cybercrime. It stands to reason that feelings such as these contribute to the majority of survivors of cybercrime incidents not seeking support.[30] Romance scam survivors, for example, report experiencing acute humiliation that challenges fundamental assumptions about human relationships and their own judgment capabilities.[31] Evidence also indicates that cybercrime survivors exhibit psychological response patterns aligned with individuals who suffered domestic abuse (e.g., self-blame, isolation, difficulty trusting future partners).[32]

Moreover, chronic psychological outcomes develop in substantial proportions of survivors of cybercrime. Nearly a quarter of survivors report depression, which may extend several years after the initial incident.[33] Additionally, survivors of severe cyber harassment display post-traumatic stress disorder (PTSD) symptoms at rates comparable to survivors of physical trauma. Over half of survivors also report experiencing sleep disruption with intrusive thoughts creating chronic insomnia patterns.[34] Thus, the evidence indicates that the combination of these symptoms of survivors of cybercrime incidents (e.g., hypervigilance, anxiety, rumination, insomnia) creates patterns that serve to increase susceptibility to further exploitation. In other words, studies show that a potential self-reinforcing cycle of cybercrime exploitation exists.[35]

Financial Trauma

The financial devastation accompanying cybercrime creates cascading psychological effects that extend far beyond immediate monetary losses. Direct financial theft often represents only the beginning of economic impact, as survivors face additional costs for credit monitoring, legal consultation, and identity restoration services. Beyond the individual impact on recovery, individuals employed by organizations targeted by the adversary face individual ramifications, as well. This may include outcomes from increased financial insecurity associated with potential job loss to productivity losses during recovery efforts, as organizations may be forced to switch to tedious manual processes when technology systems are unavailable.[36,37] The associated damage to a survivor's credit score highlights another insidious long-term financial implication of cybercrime (e.g., identity theft). These individuals may face frequent revictimization through loan rejections, employment difficulties, and housing challenges as a result of the incident in a psychological phenomenon known as financial PTSD. Financial PTSD may manifest as an individual develops hypervigilance around money management, intrusive thoughts about financial security, and avoidance behaviors that impair normal economic functioning.

Survivors may also exhibit trust erosion as the individuals demonstrate a loss of confidence in banking systems, payment platforms, and financial institutions. This institutional mistrust creates additional economic consequences as survivors forego beneficial financial products and services due to generalized fear. Digital payment platform abandonment represents another common response any survivors also report reverting to only transacting cash.[34] This technological regression creates practical hardships in an increasingly digital world while increasing an individual's vulnerability to crime in the physical world. For instance, survivors who abandon electronic payment methods may carry larger amounts of cash, making these individuals an attractive target for traditional robbery (e.g., mugging). All the while, this shift does not address the initial source of the trauma. Beyond avoiding digital payment platforms, platform avoidance behaviors may manifest in deactivating social media accounts and avoiding digital services to an extent that fosters social isolation and economic disadvantage. While some digital minimization provides genuine security benefits, extreme avoidance may adversely impact the quality of one's life to an extent outweighing any potential protective effects. Moreover, decision paralysis reportedly affects survivors who may become unwilling to make financial decisions due to generalized fear of the potential for additional exploitation as a result of prior cybercrime victimization.[38] This form of financial trauma provides one of the more significant implications as it may prevent survivors from participating in beneficial investment opportunities (e.g., retirement planning activities). Beyond the emotional and economic devastation associated with cybercrime lies the disruption to a survivor's concept of self.

Selfhood Trauma

Cybercrime impacts more than one's emotional and financial well-being. It assaults fundamental aspects of one's identity and self-concept. The persistence of digital artifacts creates ongoing psychological wounds. Fraudulent social media posts, unauthorized transactions, and defamatory content (e.g., unapproved sexual abuse images) may remain accessible long after remediation, leading to sustained psychological impact on a survivor. Survivors often describe feeling haunted by the adversary and unable to fully reclaim their authentic presence in the digital world. This psychological impact also influences surviors' relationships with others, both at the time of the incident and afterwards. Survivors of romance scams, for example, often face significant strain when pursuing future romantic relationships as a result of the exploitation.[39] Damage to one's concept of self in terms of their professional identity may also occur as a result of cybercrime incidents associated with an individual's role at work. The psychological burden proves especially prevalent for individuals in technology roles who may perceive successful exploitation by the adversary as a professional failure. Organizations may inadvertently compound this trauma through blame attribution and disciplinary responses when not always appropriate.[40] Employees deemed responsible for creating a cybersecurity incident that caused widespread organizational impact may face termination, demotion, or public shaming that destroys any future career prospects.

The erosion of technological self-efficacy represents another dimension of selfhood trauma. Survivors who previously identified themselves as technologically competent report significant shame stemming from a fear of peers viewing the individual as incompetent. The cognitive dissonance between a self-concept of proficient with technology and the experience of surviving a cybercrime incident may initiate lasting internal uncertainty about one's abilities if not appropriately addressed. Through the lens of WAVE theory, selfhood trauma represents an important aspect of potential future revictimization. Survivors who doubt their own judgment become more susceptible to future manipulation. The shame and isolation that follow cybercrime attacks create affective vulnerability states that adversaries may exploit through follow-on campaigns, turning the psychological damage resulting from a successful attack into a weapon that continues working long after the initial attack succeeds. This psychological weaponization creates self-perpetuating cycles where initial victimization may either build resilience through appropriate recovery or generate vulnerability states that increase the likelihood of repeated exploitation.

Self-Perpetuating Cycle of Chronic Exploitation

The circular relationship between the psychological factors that increase susceptibility consisting of the psychological symptoms of exploitation reveals a key concept of WAVE theory. Successful attacks cultivate the precise psychological conditions enabling future exploitation. The cognitive mechanisms underlying this cyclical vulnerability operate through interconnected pathways involving trust assessment impairment, executive functioning degradation, and social isolation amplification. Research demonstrates that cybercrime victimization damages the cognitive and emotional processes essential for effective detection of manipulation attempts. In fact, survivors of cybercrime typically exhibit learned helplessness characteristics, such as pervasive beliefs that protective actions prove fundamentally futile. The resulting feelings of hopelessness erode motivation for protective behaviors and create a self-fulfilling prophecy where reduced vigilance enables subsequent exploitation.

The psychological architecture of this response centers on attribution patterns that determine recovery trajectories. Survivors who internalize responsibility for a cybercrime attack may develop chronic doubt about their judgment capabilities, in turn making them more susceptible to manipulation of their diminished confidence. The relationship between executive functioning and susceptibility also proves relevant to this discussion as cybercrime victimization impairs the deliberative processing that is essential for effective detection. This cognitive degradation creates a self-reinforcing cycle where initial exploitation damages the mental processes required to prevent future exploitation, which resembles depression-maintenance cycles where negative attributions create self-fulfilling prophecies.[41] In other words, survivors who believe they are vulnerable to cyber exploitation subsequently demonstrate reduced vigilance, decreased security investment, and increased risk-taking behaviors that fulfill their negative expectations.

Behavioral Adaptations

An important notion as to why traditional cybercrime recovery processes fail stems becomes evident through an analysis of the adaption patterns exhibited by survivors that these approaches fail to address. Survivors of cybercrime often develop behavioral adaptations that create new categories of risk while attempting to address previous vulnerabilities. Hypervigilance represents one common adaptation that paradoxically increases exploitation risk. Hypervigilant behaviors include excessive account monitoring, repeated security log checking, and obsessive scrutiny of communications may also escalate into chronic anxiety disorders. Survivors who develop compulsive security behaviors often experience chronic stress and decision fatigue that impair the analytical judgment necessary for effective threat detection as the constant state of elevated alertness creates cognitive exhaustion. While some increased vigilance provides genuine security benefits, maladaptive hypervigilance (i.e., compulsive) responses often impair daily functioning and strain social relationships due to constant preoccupation.[42] The manifestation of risk compensation represents the opposite extreme as survivors adopt riskier behaviors after implementing specific security measures. In a phenomenon resembling the Peltzman effect in traffic safety (i.e., individuals drive more aggressively after installing safety equipment), evidence indicates individuals often engage in riskier behaviors after implementing security controls under the assumption that their new security measures provide sufficient protection.[43,44] This compensation effect proves problematic because it combines technical protection with behavioral vulnerability. Another iteration of a maladaptive response includes when survivors avoid digital services entirely rather than learning to safely use them (i.e., technology abandonment).

Ripple Effects within Communities

Cybercrime consequences extend far beyond direct survivors to affect families and communities through secondary trauma and collective efficacy erosion. Family members of survivors often experience their own psychological distress while providing support during recovery processes. Family systems experience secondary trauma that creates household-level vulnerability patterns. Cybercrime victimization generates financial stress, trust erosion, and behavioral restrictions that damage family functioning while creating the precise psychological conditions that adversaries target in relationship-based fraud schemes. Family members develop anxiety about digital security that often manifests as either excessive restriction or compensatory risk-taking, both of which create exploitable vulnerabilities.[45] Adolescent children of survivors, for instance, may be restricted from normal online activities, which potentially creates social isolation and educational disadvantages. Many spousal relationships additionally report facing strain when financial consequences create economic stress or intimacy violations occurred as part of the cybercrime incident. Reports indicate that trust issues often emerge around spousal monitoring of digital behaviors or as blame dynamics develop around responsibility for the incident with studies indicating that divorce rates increase following cybercrime incidents, although causation versus correlation remains unclear.[46]

Outside of impacts within familial units, cybercrime incidents may also facilitate trauma within organizations. For example, productivity losses may extend beyond technical disruption to include increased distraction and decreased morale. Fear may also develop after organizations experience breaches that involve employee complicity or negligence as workplace surveillance increases and interpersonal trust decreases. Career consequences stemming from a cybercrime incident may also impact colleagues and supervisors who face additional scrutiny. In turn, the psychological burden of potential adverse career outcomes feeds organizational stress. Moreover, public confidence in organizations also declines following high-profile breaches, which may cause further organizational stress. Despite this seemingly intractable cycle of self-perpetuating vulnerability, research indicates that these destructive patterns may be interrupted through recovery approaches treating the root cause instead of the symptoms.

Recovery Pathways

Effective cybercrime recovery requires interventions that interrupt the self-perpetuating psychological cycles that create chronic vulnerability rather than simply addressing immediate technical or financial consequences. WAVE theory posits that successful recovery approaches must restore the cognitive and emotional processes damaged by cybercrime victimization through building resilience and acknowledging limitations without surrendering to them. This approach includes attribution retraining, executive functioning restoration, and trust calibration. Attribution retraining is an essential prong of recovery to cybercrime incidents. Given that survivors must develop an accurate understanding of cybercrime sophistication, this reframing emphasizes adversary capability rather than personal failing. This cognitive restructuring proves essential for maintaining the analytical confidence necessary for future threat assessment while avoiding the learned helplessness that enables repeat exploitation. Research demonstrates that survivors who attribute successful attacks to external, unstable, and specific causes maintain better security behavior engagement compared to those who internalize responsibility for sophisticated manipulation.[47] Executive functioning restoration requires structured interventions that rebuild deliberative processing capabilities while addressing the chronic stress and decision fatigue that cybercrime generates. Given that cognitive rehabilitation approaches that combine stress management with analytical skill development prove more effective than traditional trauma treatment for maintaining cybersecurity vigilance, the goal of this prong involves restoring the mental processes essential for threat detection while preventing the cognitive exhaustion that facilitates vulnerability. Trust calibration represents another essential recovery component that addresses the relationship between trustworthiness assessment and exploitation susceptibility. This requires understanding how cybercrime damages the psychological mechanisms individuals use to evaluate relationship authenticity, then providing structured practice with verification processes that work within rather than against normal social functioning.

Interventions and Support Mechanisms

With few survivors of cybercrime reportedly seeking treatment from mental health professionals, there is a clear gap in care for those experiencing clinically significant distress.[47,48,49] Identified barriers include shame, perceived stigma, lack of insurance coverage for cybercrime trauma, and therapist unfamiliarity with forensic cyberpsychology. This service deficit may also occur because standard therapeutic approaches prove inadequate for addressing the unique psychological dynamics of cybercrime. Traditional trauma treatment often focuses on processing discrete events rather than building resilience against ongoing threats. Effective cybercrime therapy must implement the three-pronged recovery approach through structured clinical interventions.

Narrative rebuilding represents a crucial component of attribution retraining as part of the psychological recovery process for survivors. This practice necessitates that survivors work to develop coherent explanations for their experiences that restore agency and competence perceptions. Successful recovery narratives typically emphasize the exploit rather than focusing on personal failings. In other words, encouraging survivors to identify external factors rather than internal deficiencies is an important component of this practice. Clinical approaches to address executive functioning restoration include mindfulness exercises, working memory enhancement protocols, and structured decision frameworks to support survivors without creating unnecessary cognitive overload. The integration of mindfulness concepts with a focus on deliberative processing proves more effective than either approach implemented in isolation. Peer mentoring programs that pair cybercrime survivors with individuals who have successfully navigated recovery provide a valuable approach to addressing trust calibration. These relationships provide both practical guidance and psychological support for mentors and mentees.

In summary, individual recovery efforts prove most effective when also supported by community interventions. Peer support forums provide valuable insights into natural coping mechanisms and recovery patterns among survivors of cybercrime. Adaptive responses include seeking social support, engaging in problem-focused coping, and maintaining perspective about personal responsibility versus adversary culpability. Furthermore, community education programs that incorporate survivor experiences prove more effective than traditional awareness training for a variety of reasons (e.g., illustrating survivors as agents working toward justice rather than as passive recipients of harm into active). This is an important message to send to other survivors as a means to disrupt the vulnerability cycle. By countering the perceived hopelessness that enables victimization cycles while providing a realistic assessment of both threat sophistication and defensive capability, this approach is an important way to disrupt cybercrime by addressing the psychological as well as technical aspects of cybercrime.

Conclusion

The psychological impact of cybercrime creates cascading effects that reshape individual and community behaviors. The evidence presented throughout this chapter demonstrates that cybercrime succeeds through weaponized affective vulnerability engineering that exploits fundamental features of human psychology and social connection. Through the lens of WAVE theory, the self-perpetuating nature of cybercrime susceptibility provides an important concept about the ways in which the adversary may manipulate the responses of survivors. Understanding this cyclical vulnerability reveals why traditional cybersecurity approaches that focus exclusively on technical protection prove inadequate against contemporary cybercrime. The principles discussed in this chapter underscore why cybersecurity cannot remain a purely technical discipline. The most sophisticated technical controls in the world often prove useless when attention is not given to the mind behind the screen. Integrating psychological understandings with technical capability to protect both systems and the human beings who operate them proves critical to future defensive strategies. Chapter 10 explores how these psychological insights translate into practical strategies that acknowledge both the capabilities and limitations of human psychology against the adversary.

Reflection Questions

1 What situational vulnerabilities (e.g., stress, transitions, decision fatigue, social isolation) increase susceptibility to social engineering attacks?
2 What specific clinical interventions might help break the cycle of revictimization?
3 What proactive measures could organizations take to address these secondary psychological impacts and prevent the erosion of collective resilience?
4 What collective actions could buffer community-level ripple effects?

Skill Builder Labs

Application Scenario: Craft a support plan for a cybercrime survivor

Design a plan to support a 78-year-old grandmother who lost $15,000 to a romance scam. Take the following steps:

- Conduct an emotional triage assessment.
- Assess any ongoing contact with the adversary.
- Document all evidence and explore recovery options.
- Implement safeguards and secure all accounts.
- Address psychological factors and social needs.
- Establish protocols for the future.

Mini Research Activity: Forensic Cyberpsychology Incident Analysis

Objective

Apply WAVE theory to cybercrime incidents.

Instructions

1 Select a recent cybercrime incident.
2 Analyze the psychological vulnerability factors that enabled the attack.
3 Examine how the incident demonstrates WAVE theory.
4 Review the cascading psychological effects on survivors.
5 Evaluate how the incident created conditions for future exploitation.
6 Assess what recovery approach would interrupt the self-perpetuating cycle.

Deliverable

Compose an investigative summary of the selected incident, including an emphasis on how psychological vulnerabilities create self-perpetuating cycles of exploitation.

References

1 Salthouse, T. A. (2009). When does age-related cognitive decline begin? *Neurobiology of Aging*, *30*(4), 507–514.

2 Glisky, E. L. (2007). *Changes in cognitive function in human aging.* In D. R. Riddle (Ed.), *Brain aging: Models, methods, and mechanisms* (pp. 3–20). CRC Press/Taylor & Francis.
3 Harada, C. N., Love, M. C. N., & Triebel, K. (2013). Normal cognitive aging. *Clinics in Geriatric Medicine, 29*(4), 737.
4 U.S. Federal Trade Commission. (2024). *Consumer sentinel network data book.*
5 Dalley, J. W., Everitt, B. J., & Robbins, T. W. (2011). Impulsivity, compulsivity, and top-down cognitive control. *Neuron, 69*(4), 680–694.
6 Hadlington, L. (2017). Human factors in cybersecurity; examining the link between Internet addiction, impulsivity, attitudes towards cybersecurity, and risky cybersecurity behaviours. *Heliyon, 3*(7), e00346.
7 Ghaiumy Anaraky, R., Cartwright, M., & Nov, O. (2025, April). The role of auditory environments and anxiety in detecting phishing emails. In *Proceedings of the extended abstracts of the chi conference on human factors in computing systems* (pp. 1–10).
8 Van de Weijer, S. G., & Leukfeldt, E. R. (2017). Big five personality traits of cybercrime victims. *Cyberpsychology, Behavior, and Social Networking, 20*(7), 407–412.
9 Diaz, A., Sherman, A. T., & Joshi, A. (2018). Phishing in an academic community: A study of user susceptibility and behavior. arXiv. *arXiv preprint arXiv:1811.06078.*
10 Dietz, G., Gillespie, N., & Chao, G. T. (2010). Unravelling the complexities of trust and culture. *Organizational Trust: A Cultural Perspective,* 3–41. Cambridge University Press.
11 Prabowo, H. Y. (2024). When gullibility becomes us: Exploring the cultural roots of Indonesians' susceptibility to investment fraud. *Journal of Financial Crime, 31*(1), 14–32.
12 Bullee, J. W., Montoya, L., Junger, M., & Hartel, P. (2017). Spear phishing in organisations explained. *Information & Computer Security, 25*(5), 593–613.
13 Dirkin, G. R. (1983). Cognitive tunneling: Use of visual information under stress. *Perceptual and Motor Skills, 56*(1), 191–198.
14 Montañez, R., Golob, E., & Xu, S. (2020). Human cognition through the lens of social engineering cyberattacks. *Frontiers in Psychology, 11,* 1755.
15 Hirshleifer, D., Levi, Y., Lourie, B., & Teoh, S. H. (2019). Decision fatigue and heuristic analyst forecasts. *Journal of Financial Economics, 133*(1), 83–98.
16 Bellucci, G., & Park, S. Q. (2024). Loneliness is associated with more trust but worse trustworthiness expectations. *British Journal of Psychology, 115*(4), 641–664.
17 U.S. Federal Trade Commission. (2021). *Consumer sentinel network data book 2020.*
18 Tran, T., Do, B. G., Ngo, A., Krishtipati, S., Dang, N. A., & Sarkar, S. (2024). The impacts of layoffs announcement on cybersecurity breaches. PACIS 2024 Proceedings. 10. AIS.
19 Clement, N. (2023, July). M&A Effect on data breaches in hospitals: 2010–2022. In *Proceedings of the 22nd workshop on the economics of information security, Geneva, Switzerland* (pp. 5–8).
20 Lackner, S., Francisco, F., Mendonça, C., Mata, A., & Gonçalves-Sá, J. (2019). Some scientific knowledge is a dangerous thing: Overconfidence grows non-linearly with knowledge. *arXiv preprint arXiv:1903.11193.*
21 De Kimpe, L., Walrave, M., Verdegem, P., & Ponnet, K. (2022). What we think we know about cybersecurity: An investigation of the relationship between perceived knowledge, internet trust, and protection motivation in a cybercrime context. *Behaviour & Information Technology, 41*(8), 1796–1808.
22 Dunning, D. (2011). The Dunning–Kruger effect: On being ignorant of one's own ignorance. In Edited by James M. Olson Mark P. Zanna *Advances in experimental social psychology* (Vol. 44, pp. 247–296). Academic Press.

23 Beautement, A., Sasse, M. A., & Wonham, M. (2008). The compliance budget: Managing security behaviour in organisations. In *Proceedings of the 2008 new security paradigms workshop*. Association for Computing Machinery, New York, NY, USA, 47–58.
24 Butavicius, M., Parsons, K., Lillie, M., McCormac, A., Pattinson, M., & Calic, D. (2020). When believing in technology leads to poor cyber security: Development of a trust in technical controls scale. *Computers & Security, 98*, 102020.
25 Gaw, S., & Felten, E. W. (2006, July). Password management strategies for online accounts. In *Proceedings of the second symposium on Usable privacy and security*. Association for Computing Machinery, New York, NY, USA, 44–55.
26 Ebbinghaus H. (1880). *Urmanuskript "Ueber das Gedächtniß"*. Passavia Universitätsverlag.
27 Murre, J. M., & Dros, J. (2015). Replication and analysis of Ebbinghaus' forgetting curve. *PloS One, 10*(7), e0120644.
28 Kumaraguru, P., Sheng, S., Acquisti, A., Cranor, L. F., & Hong, J. (2008, October). Lessons from a real world evaluation of anti-phishing training. In *2008 eCrime researchers summit* (pp. 1–12). IEEE.
29 Budimir, S., Fontaine, J. R., Huijts, N. M., Haans, A., Loukas, G., & Roesch, E. B. (2021). Emotional reactions to cybersecurity breach situations: Scenario-based survey study. *Journal of Medical Internet Research, 23*(5), e24879.
30 Bidgoli, M., & Grossklags, J. (2016, June). End user cybercrime reporting: What we know and what we can do to improve it. In *2016 IEEE International Conference on Cybercrime and Computer Forensic (ICCCF)* (pp. 1–6). IEEE.
31 Coluccia, A., Pozza, A., Ferretti, F., Carabellese, F., Masti, A., & Gualtieri, G. (2020). Online romance scams: Relational dynamics and psychological characteristics of the victims and scammers. A scoping review. *Clinical Practice and Epidemiology in Mental Health: CP & EMH, 16*, 24–35.
32 Mechanic, M. B., Weaver, T. L., & Resick, P. A. (2008). Mental health consequences of intimate partner abuse: A multidimensional assessment of four different forms of abuse. *Violence against Women, 14*(6), 634–654.
33 Balcombe, L. (2025). The mental health impacts of internet scams. *International Journal of Environmental Research and Public Health, 22*(6), 938.
34 U.K. Home Office. (2025). *Understanding the cyber crime and fraud victim journey*.
35 McDowell, J. (2023). Exploring the relationship between self-esteem, financial egocentrism, and fraud susceptibility in cyber-enabled fraud schemes involving crypto assets. Doctoral Dissertations and Projects. 5008.
36 Abbou, B., Kessel, B., Ben Natan, M., Gabbay-Benziv, R., Dahan Shriki, D., Ophir, A., ... & Dudkiewicz, M. (2024). When all computers shut down: The clinical impact of a major cyber-attack on a general hospital. *Frontiers in Digital Health, 6*, 1321485.
37 Lee, J., & Choi, S. J. (2021). Hospital productivity after data breaches: Difference-in-differences analysis. *Journal of Medical Internet Research, 23*(7), e26157.
38 Brands, J., & van Wilsem, J. (2021). Connected and fearful? Exploring fear of online financial crime, Internet behaviour and their relationship. *European Journal of Criminology, 18*(2), 213–234.
39 Whitty, M. T., & Buchanan, T. (2016). The online dating romance scam: The psychological impact on victims–both financial and non-financial. *Criminology & Criminal Justice, 16*(2), 176–194.
40 Renaud, K., Searle, R., & Dupuis, M. (2021, October). Shame in cyber security: Effective behavior modification tool or counterproductive foil? In *Proceedings of the 2021 new security paradigms workshop*. Association for Computing Machinery, New York, NY, USA, 70–87.

41 Moorey, S. (2010). The six cycles maintenance model: Growing a "vicious flower" for depression. *Behavioural and Cognitive Psychotherapy, 38*(2), 173–184.
42 Kimble, M., Boxwala, M., Bean, W., Maletsky, K., Halper, J., Spollen, K., & Fleming, K. (2014). The impact of hypervigilance: Evidence for a forward feedback loop. *Journal of Anxiety Disorders, 28*(2), 241–245.
43 Peltzman, S. (1975). The effects of automobile safety regulation. *Journal of Political Economy, 83*(4), 677–725.
44 Kearney, W. D., & Kruger, H. A. (2016). Theorising on risk homeostasis in the context of information security behaviour. *Information & Computer Security, 24*(5), 496–513.
45 Button, M., Blackbourn, D., Sugiura, L., Shepherd, D., Kapend, R., & Wang, V. (2021). Victims of cybercrime: Understanding the impact through accounts. In Weulen Kranenbarg, M., Leukfeldt, R. (eds) *Cybercrime in context: The human factor in victimization, offending, and policing* (pp. 137–156). Springer International Publishing.
46 Gibbs, T. (2025). From trust to Trauma: The psychological and relational impact of cyber-enabled cybercrimes. *RAIS Journal for Social Sciences, 9*(1), 231–239.
47 Monteith, S., Bauer, M., Alda, M., Geddes, J., Whybrow, P. C., & Glenn, T. (2021). Increasing cybercrime since the pandemic: Concerns for psychiatry. *Current Psychiatry Reports, 23*(4), 18.
48 Serfaty, M., Billings, J., Vickerstaff, V., Lee, T., Buszewicz, M., & Satchell, J. (2024). Help-seeking in older crime victims: A mixed-methods study in collaboration with the Metropolitan Police Service. *PLOS Mental Health, 1*(3), e0000082.
49 Mumford, E. A., Rothman, E. F., Maitra, P., & Sheridan-Johnson, J. (2023). US young adults' professional help-seeking in response to technology-facilitated abuse. *Journal of Interpersonal Violence, 38*(11–12), 7063–7088.

10 Mitigating Cybercrime through Psychological Insights

A Digital Fortress with Open Doors

The security team at Global Manufacturing Inc. installed state-of-the-art endpoint detection, implemented multi-factor authentication (MFA), and deployed machine learning threat analytics across their 50,000-employee network. Their quarterly penetration test scored 98% on technical controls. Six weeks later, a single email convinced their CFO to wire $4.2 million to a fraudulent account. The email contained no malware. It bypassed no firewalls. It exploited no zero-day vulnerabilities. Instead, it weaponized the CFO's trust in routine business communication, her cognitive shortcuts under time pressure, and her reluctance to question apparent authority during a stressful acquisition deadline. This incident reveals the central paradox of modern cybersecurity. Organizations build digital fortresses with walls capable of withstanding sophisticated adversarial attacks on technical controls. Yet, the adversary waltzes in through the front door by convincing someone to hold it open for them. This is not an indictment of this approach. Technical controls are an important component of a comprehensive cybersecurity program. They are, however, only one part.

From a socio-technical perspective, Global Manufacturing's breach illustrates why traditional cybersecurity approaches fail when treated as purely technical problems. Although organizations implement cascading security features across multiple layers (i.e., defense in depth), the alignment of these technical controls facilitates exploitable gaps. For instance, an employee may receive a phishing email during a stressful deadline after participating in annual cybersecurity training that occurred over six months ago, while the email mimics familiar corporate communication. While each layer may have properly functioned in isolation, the synergy of these defenses created an exploitable gap. This represents the Swiss Cheese Model, positing that security controls may fail if holes in defenses align across multiple layers.[1,2] Research into human factors in cybersecurity acknowledges that attacks occur due to exploits across human and technology by drawing on socio-technical systems theory to highlight how these factors interact in an environment.[3] As discussed throughout this book, WAVE theory extends these foundational principles by unifying fragmented insights from multiple disciplines into a coherent framework for understanding how the adversary manipulates targets to

DOI: 10.4324/9781003649199-10

bridge engineering and psychology. This interplay of human and technical factors is why user experience principles are increasingly integrated into security design approaches.

UX Design Interventions

The integration of user experience principles into security design represents the overdue acknowledgment that humans will circumvent security measures that make their lives difficult.[4] To develop effective cybersecurity systems, one must understand cognitive biases, decision-making patterns, and human behavior. The evolution of MFA provides an important example of this. Early implementations required users to memorize multiple passwords, carry hardware tokens, and navigate confusing authentication sequences that resembled digital obstacle courses. These systems failed because they ignored the idea that people resort to shortcuts that undermine security when working memory becomes overwhelmed (i.e., cognitive load theory).[5] MFA implementations now integrate streamlined controls (e.g., biometric authentication, push notifications) to make secure login feel effortless instead of punitive, including making security measures more usable rather than more restrictive to increase an organization's cybersecurity posture.[6] In fact, organizations implementing thoughtful UX design report higher adoption rates and reduced user resistance to security measures.[7]

WAVE theory explains this success through the resonance disruption principle. When security interfaces work with natural cognitive patterns, they prevent the cognitive overload exploited by the adversary to perpetrate an attack. This idea is exemplified by just-in-time (JIT) approaches, which deliver security guidance precisely when users need it. Instead of annual security training provided only once per year, JIT approaches leverage contextual micro-learning sessions as brief reminders triggered by risk indicators using a principle known as the spacing effect, which proves more effective than annual training sessions.[8] Importantly, the shift to JIT approaches highlights important shifts in organizational culture and leadership necessary to strengthen an organization's cybersecurity program.

Organizational Culture Interventions

Organizational culture shapes cybersecurity behavior more powerfully than most technical controls, although this reality rarely receives proportional attention in security budgets. Culture operates through unwritten rules, social expectations, and leadership modeling that can either reinforce or undermine formal security policies. Interestingly, research shows that employees are significantly more likely to follow cybersecurity policies when senior leaders visibly support them.[9] In other words, the old-school approach (i.e., rules for me vs. thee) damages more than organizational morale. Furthermore, evidence indicates that the most effective security programs mix intrinsic motivators (e.g., ego, achievement) with extrinsic incentives (e.g., penalties for negligence). The 2017 Equifax breach underscores this point, given that the root cause of the breach was identified as a complacent organizational culture around cybersecurity.[10] Similarly, the 2013 Target breach revealed a culture that prioritized business operations over security vigilance, despite multiple intrusion alerts from security tools, employees felt disempowered to act, and incident warnings went unheeded during the peak holiday shopping season.[11] Findings such as these demonstrate how weak cultures around cybersecurity outweigh technical controls.

Psychological safety also plays a crucial role in security culture formation. When executives share personal anecdotes and normalize security mistakes as learning opportunities, they create environments where security vigilance becomes culturally expected rather than individually mandated.[12] WAVE theory reveals why cultural approaches succeed where individual training fails. Strong security cultures create social proof mechanisms that counteract manipulation by the adversary. To put it another way, it becomes harder for the adversary to facilitate the behavioral resonance necessary for successful attacks when the organizational culture reinforces secure behaviors. In fact, research shows that companies where employees viewed security as shared responsibility showed faster incident detection, better containment protocols, and reduced overall impact.[13] While organizational culture provides a system of stop signs to enhance overall safety while driving, it is ultimately the drivers who decide whether to hit the brakes. This reality requires targeted behavioral interventions to ensure employees make protective choices when the moment calls for it.

Behavioral Interventions

As in earlier chapters, traditional cybersecurity training programs operate by delivering annual sessions and expecting behavioral change to persist until the next one, which demonstrates an approach that ignores psychological science's understanding of memory, habit formation, and skill retention. Annual cybersecurity training sessions that cram comprehensive content into a single session basically guarantee minimal retention of actionable knowledge, given that humans forget over two-thirds of new information within one day of learning it in a phenomenon known as the forgetting curve, proving there are better approaches to cybersecurity.[14] For example, research shows that learning by failure, in a controlled and safe way, inoculates employees against social engineering attacks by boosting their vigilance.[15] The rise of organizations leveraging phishing simulations as part of their cybersecurity programs highlights the increasing understanding of this approach. Additionally, programs combining spaced repetition (e.g., multiple tests) with personalized content delivery and real-time performance feedback were shown to dramatically reduce social engineering success rates for a sustained period.[16] Incorporating gaming elements (e.g., points, badges, and leaderboards) into cybersecurity programs also taps into intrinsic motivational factors (e.g., competitiveness) in individuals. In fact, findings show that gamified security training programs build security habits in individuals more effectively than traditional approaches.[17] From a WAVE perspective, the evidence indicates that cybersecurity behaviors are driven by cognitive processes, and effective interventions must also be psychological (e.g., repeated exposure, nudging). Thus, the psychological insight driving the success of programs such as these involves treating cybersecurity like any other complex skill that requires deliberate practice rather than one-time exposure. Although training approaches build long-term cybersecurity, organizations also need interventions (e.g., nudging) that guide correct decisions in the moment when cognitive shortcuts and time pressure make deliberate analysis difficult.

Nudge theory provides powerful tools for guiding human behavior without restricting choice.[18] In the context of cybersecurity, nudges leverage cognitive biases and decision-making shortcuts to steer users toward safer choices while preserving autonomy. Default settings represent perhaps the most powerful nudging tool available. When settings focused on user privacy are enabled by default, adoption rates are nearly perfect, and when privacy settings take an opt-in approach, participation falls to less than one-fourth of users.[19] Another iteration of nudging involves social proof nudges, which display behavioral norms to influence individual choices.[20] Within the realm of cybersecurity, this approach leverages pressure to conform to encourage adoption of protective behaviors.[21] Loss aversion messaging additionally exploits the psychological reality that people feel losses more intensely than equivalent gains (i.e., security warning messages emphasizing losing one's data prove more motivating than equivalent messages promising to protect one's data). According to WAVE theory, the alignment of choice architecture with natural psychological tendencies, these nudging creates environmental conditions that make secure choices feel obvious rather than forced. It is important to consider that, while training and nudging address human behavior through education and choice architecture, technology may also amplify these psychological insights by automatically detecting behavioral anomalies with speed and at scale.

Machine learning systems are capable of processing billions of data points to identify fraud patterns.[22] The incorporation of behavioral analytics into cybersecurity programs leverages machine learning pattern recognition capabilities to detect anomalies that indicate potential security threats.[23] These systems work by establishing baseline behaviors for normal user activity to allow deviations from that baseline that warrant additional investigation to be flagged. AI-driven forensic analysis additionally demonstrates high detection accuracy levels. Spam filtering is a common example of this, with many companies leveraging AI to filter suspicious emails with flagged manipulative language cues. A nuanced understanding of the psychology underpinning cybercrime scams proves essential to the development of more sophisticated detection systems from both technical and human perspectives. By analyzing behavioral patterns that indicate adversarial orchestration attempts, systems may identify the conditions enabling psychological manipulation before attacks succeed.

Policy and Legal Interventions

Cybercrime's transnational nature raises clear enforcement challenges, such as the adversary launching an attack from one country by routing traffic through several other countries to target entities in yet another jurisdiction. Unfortunately, international cooperation moves slowly, especially when compared to the agility of the adversary. While diplomats debate legal frameworks and jurisdictional issues, illicit organizations adapt their techniques in real-time. The result is a persistent cat-and-mouse game where the cats are arthritic and the mice have superpowers. International frameworks (e.g., The Council of Europe's Budapest Convention, the African Union's Malabo Convention) attempt to address these challenges. The Budapest Convention, formally known as The Council of Europe's Convention on Cybercrime, represents the primary international framework for cybercrime cooperation.[24] Adopted in 2001 and entering into force in 2004, the Budapest Convention treaty establishes common criminal law standards and provides mechanisms for mutual legal assistance. As of 2025, 80 states ratified the Budapest Convention, including several non-European countries, recognizing the utility for addressing transnational cyber threats. The Malabo Convention, formally known as the African Union Convention on Cyber Security and Personal Data Protection, was adopted in 2014 and entered into force in 2023.[25] The Malabo Convention treaty mandates the establishment of national data protection and cybersecurity authorities, harmonizes legal frameworks, and fosters cross-border cooperation among African states. Moreover, the Organization for Security and Co-operation in Europe (OSCE) confidence-building measures provide additional mechanisms for international cybersecurity cooperation.[26] The central challenge of international cooperation, therefore, lies not in the absence of legal frameworks. It lies in the complexity of diverse legal systems, cultures, and politics.

Despite the structural foundation for cooperation offered via international agreements, these treaties often overlook the human toll of cybercrime. Survivors of cybercrime reportedly experience heightened levels of anxiety and fear in online interactions after incidents.[27] Research shows survivors are also at an increased risk of developing maladaptive coping mechanisms, as well as depression and PTSD. This reality underscores the need for legal frameworks to mandate trauma-informed responses to cybercrime incidents rather than leaving support measures to organizational discretion. Effective frameworks increasingly require organizations to provide credit monitoring services, identity restoration support, and clear guidance on risk mitigation. Such provisions reflect an emerging recognition that psychological trauma from identity compromise demands comprehensive care, as well as technical remediation. The United Kingdom's General Data Protection Regulation (GDPR) exemplifies how psychological principles may be embedded in regulatory frameworks to improve security outcomes.[28] This includes privacy-by-default requirements to leverage status quo bias as a means to improve population-level privacy protection, as well as consent mechanisms to address cognitive limitations in privacy decision-making. From a WAVE perspective, legal frameworks and survivor assistance programs must address the environmental conditions that make future manipulation possible. By providing survivors with trauma-informed care, it is possible to disrupt the vulnerability cycles that adversaries exploit for repeated targeting.

Given the increasing gap between regulatory intent and behavioral reality, organizations often implement technical compliance measures to satisfy regulatory requirements while failing to address underlying psychological factors that drive security behavior, in part because they are not mandated to do so. Future regulatory approaches must incorporate psychological insights at multiple levels to bridge this implementation gap. At the individual level, effective regulations may mandate user interface designs that leverage psychological principles to promote secure behaviors. At the organizational level, effective regulations may address the social factors shaping security behavior within institutions. The international dimension presents perhaps the greatest opportunity for psychological insight integration. Current treaty frameworks assume rational actor models that poorly reflect how entities actually respond to incidents. A psychologically informed approach to international cooperation, recognizing cultural differences in risk perception, authority relationships, and social trust, may improve the effectiveness of collaboration across jurisdictions. While essential for the future, the integration of psychological insights into cybersecurity policy faces several implementation challenges requiring careful consideration. Regulatory agencies often lack the interdisciplinary expertise needed to evaluate behavioral interventions, as well as the rapid evolution of both cybercrime and psychology research that makes keeping regulations current and evidence-based difficult. It is clear, however, that the most effective future cyber regulations will combine robust technical standards with deep psychological insights to create nuanced approaches addressing both the technological and human dimensions of cybercrime, which requires new forms of expertise to bridge the gap between technology and psychology.

Conclusion

Global Manufacturing's $4.2 million loss reveals the fundamental flaw in treating cybersecurity as a purely technical problem. No amount of endpoint protection, machine learning analytics, or MFA defends against the adversary capable of weaponizing human psychology to elicit a desired response in a target. Cybersecurity programs and legal frameworks must account for the mind behind the screen. Through the lens of WAVE theory, these approaches succeed because they disrupt the behavioral resonance orchestrated by the adversary. The future of cybersecurity lies in recognizing that every technical control ultimately depends on human behavior. The most sophisticated firewall becomes worthless if someone disables it out of frustration. The strongest encryption fails if people share passwords to avoid inconvenience. The most advanced threat detection proves useless if alerts are ignored or misunderstood. Effective cyber defense requires abandoning the illusion that humans may be engineered out of security systems. Instead, security systems that work with human psychology must be engineered and acknowledge cognitive exploits. Humans, when properly accounted for, are not the weakest link in cybersecurity. This understanding proves more urgent as we consider the next wave of technological innovations. As discussed in Chapter 11, the adversary of tomorrow will not only manipulate existing vulnerabilities. They will engineer new ones. The emerging trends discussed in Chapter 11 are not distant science fiction scenarios. They are emerging realities that demand we move beyond reactive cybersecurity toward predictive protection informed through the application of WAVE theory.

Reflection Questions

1 What specific design principles make protective behaviors feel natural rather than forced?
2 When implementing nudges (e.g., default privacy settings, social proof messaging), how can organizations avoid crossing into manipulative persuasion?
3 Which psychological factors make some individuals naturally resistant to social engineering while others remain vulnerable?
4 How can international cybercrime cooperation frameworks account for cultural differences without compromising security effectiveness?

Skill Builder Labs

Application Scenario: Design a Phishing Simulation Program

Design a phishing simulation program for a large law firm with 1,000 employees across multiple offices. Take the following steps:

- Design a rollout strategy minimizing psychological reactance.
- Develop progressive difficulty levels to apply controlled failure principles.
- Plan communication that uses social proof to normalize security vigilance.

Mini Research Activity: Nudge Design for Social Engineering Prevention

Objective

Design and test behavioral interventions that reduce susceptibility.

Instructions

1 Identify a specific social engineering attack vector.
2 Design different nudges that could prevent this attack.
3 Create a simple A/B test to measure effectiveness.
4 Consider potential unintended consequences of each intervention.
5 Develop implementation recommendations that incorporate WAVE principles.

Deliverable

Craft an implementation plan to address the selected social engineering attack vector, including supporting rationale and WAVE theory integration.

References

1. Reason, J. (1990). The contribution of latent human failures to the breakdown of complex systems. *Philosophical Transactions of the Royal Society of London. B, Biological Sciences, 327*(1241), 475–484.
2. Grandhi, S. R., & Still, J. D. (2025). Deciphering human error: Improving cybersecurity reporting. In *Proceedings of the human factors and ergonomics society annual meeting* (p. 10711813251358790). SAGE Publications.
3. Schaltegger, T., Ambuehl, B., Bosshart, N., Bearth, A., & Ebert, N. (2025). Human behavior in cybersecurity: An opportunity for risk research. *Journal of Risk Research, 28*(8). 1–12.
4. Adams, A., & Sasse, M. A. (1999). Users are not the enemy. *Communications of the ACM, 42*(12), 40–46.
5. Hjeij, M., & Vilks, A. (2023). A brief history of heuristics: How did research on heuristics evolve?. *Humanities and Social Sciences Communications, 10*(1), 1–15.
6. U.K. National Cyber Security Centre. *People-centered security, Accessibility as a cyber security priority.* NCSC.
7. Felt, A. P., Ainslie, A., Reeder, R. W., Consolvo, S., Thyagaraja, S., Bettes, A., ... & Grimes, J. (2015, April). Improving SSL warnings: Comprehension and adherence. In *Proceedings of the 33rd annual ACM conference on human factors in computing systems.* Association for Computing Machinery, New York, NY, USA, 2893–2902.
8. Skinner, T., Taylor, J., Alam, A., & Ali, R. (2021, October). Does learning method matter in cyber security behaviour? Spaced Vs. massed e-learning. In *2021 8th International Conference on Behavioral and Social Computing (BESC)* (pp. 1–6). IEEE.
9. Kuo, K. M., Talley, P. C., & Lin, D. Y. M. (2021). Hospital staff's adherence to information security policy: A quest for the antecedents of deterrence variables. *INQUIRY: The Journal of Health Care Organization, Provision, and Financing, 58*, 00469580211029599.
10. U.S. 115th Congress, House of Representatives, Committee on Oversight and Government Reform, Majority Staff Report. (2018). *The Equifax data breach.*
11. U.S. Senate, Committee on Commerce, Science, and Transportation. (2014). *A kill chain analysis of the 2013 target data breach* [Staff Report].
12. Benetti, P. J., Kanse, L., Fruhen, L. S., Parkes, K. R., & Stephenson, E. K. (2024). Leader safety storytelling: A qualitative analysis of the attributes of effective safety storytelling and its outcomes. *Safety Science, 178*, 106618.
13. Ahmad, A., Desouza, K. C., Maynard, S. B., Naseer, H., & Baskerville, R. L. (2020). How integration of cyber security management and incident response enables organizational learning. *Journal of the Association for Information Science and Technology, 71*(8), 939–953.
14. Ebbinghaus H (1880) Urmanuskript "Ueber das Gedächtniß". Passavia Universitätsverlag.
15. Gutierrez, C. N., Kim, T., Della Corte, R., Avery, J., Goldwasser, D., Cinque, M., & Bagchi, S. (2018). Learning from the ones that got away: Detecting new forms of phishing attacks. *IEEE Transactions on Dependable and Secure Computing, 15*(6), 988–1001.
16. Kumaraguru, P., Cranshaw, J., Acquisti, A., Cranor, L., Hong, J., Blair, M. A., & Pham, T. (2009, July). School of phish: A real-world evaluation of anti-phishing training. In *Proceedings of the 5th symposium on usable privacy and security.* Association for Computing Machinery, New York, NY, USA, Article 3, 1–12.
17. Scholefield, S., & Shepherd, L. A. (2019, June). Gamification techniques for raising cyber security awareness. In *International conference on human-computer interaction* (pp. 191–203). Springer International Publishing.

18 Thaler, R. H., & Sunstein, C. R. (2009). *Nudge: Improving decisions about health, wealth, and happiness*. Penguin.
19 Johnson, E. J., Bellman, S., & Lohse, G. L. (2002). Defaults, framing and privacy: Why opting in-opting out1. *Marketing Letters*, *13*(1), 5–15.
20 Sharma, K., Zhan, X., Nah, F. F. H., Siau, K., & Cheng, M. X. (2021). Impact of digital nudging on information security behavior: An experimental study on framing and priming in cybersecurity. *Organizational Cybersecurity Journal: Practice, Process and People*, *1*(1), 69–91.
21 Venema, T. A., Kroese, F. M., Benjamins, J. S., & De Ridder, D. T. (2020). When in doubt, follow the crowd? Responsiveness to social proof nudges in the absence of clear preferences. *Frontiers in Psychology*, *11*, 1385.
22 Manzoor, M. F., & Aslam, M. F. (2025). Enhancing banking fraud detection: Role of machine learning and deep learning methods. *Premier Journal of Artificial Intelligence*, *1*. 1–13.
23 Jain, V., & Mitra, A. (2025). Real-time threat detection in cybersecurity: Leveraging machine learning algorithms for enhanced anomaly detection. In M. Almaiah & Y. Maleh (Eds.), *Machine intelligence applications in cyber-risk management* (pp. 315–344). IGI Global Scientific Publishing.
24 Council of Europe. (2001). *Convention on Cybercrime* (ETS No. 185). Council of Europe Treaty Office.
25 African Union. (2014). *African union convention on cyber security and personal data protection (Malabo Convention)*.
26 Organization for Security and Co-operation in Europe. (2013, December 3). *Decision No. 1106: Initial set of OSCE confidence-building measures to reduce the risks of conflict stemming from the use of information and communication technologies (PC. DEC/1106)*.
27 Borwell, J., Jansen, J., & Stol, W. (2022). The psychological and financial impact of cybercrime victimization: A novel application of the shattered assumptions theory. *Social Science Computer Review*, *40*(4), 933–954.
28 European Commission, Regulation (EU) 2016/679 of the European Parliament and of the Council of 27 April 2016 on the protection of natural persons with regard to the processing of personal data and on the free movement of such data, and repealing Directive 95/46/EC (General Data Protection Regulation, GDPR).

11 Anticipating the Future of Cybercrime

The Oracle's Dilemma

In ancient Greece, the Oracle at Delphi was renowned for providing rulers with accurate prophecies, albeit cryptically delivered. King Croesus, for example, sought advice on attacking Persia. As legend holds, the Oracle told the king that he would destroy a great empire. The Oracle did not, however, mention that the great empire that would be destroyed would be that of King Croesus.[1] The sentiment holds true for forensic cyberpsychologists today who face a similar predicament, who must predict the future of cybercrime with enough precision to guide defensive strategies while avoiding the preparation of yesterday's threats with tomorrow's budgets. This chapter explores how adversaries will weaponize emerging technologies against human psychology, why traditional defensive approaches remain inadequate, and how the comprehensive theory of WAVE guides proactive defense strategies in anticipating evolving threats rather than simply reacting.

AI as the Perpetrator

The current conversation around AI in cybersecurity primarily focuses on technical capacities (e.g., automated threat detection, behavioral analytics, adaptive response systems). While important, this misses a more foundational shift. The integration of artificial intelligence into adversary operations represents perhaps the most significant evolution in threat capabilities since the invention of the computer itself. Contemporary adversaries discovered that machine learning technologies, which were originally designed to enhance human productivity, may be weaponized.

LLMs now enable the adversary to automate personalized social engineering campaigns on an industrial scale.[2] Where traditional mass phishing relied on generic templates, AI-enhanced phishing campaigns now generate thousands of unique messages targeting specific organizations while incorporating current events, personal relationships, and professional context that would require extensive manual research to achieve without LLM support. The Lazarus Group, linked to the DPRK, exemplifies this evolution. Their early campaigns relied on generic phishing templates translated poorly into multiple languages, which included clear tells to savvy targets. By 2024, their operations incorporated AI-generated content.[3]

DOI: 10.4324/9781003649199-11

This exceeds the notion of simple automation at scale, instead representing psychological engineering at scale. Research shows that AI-enhanced phishing campaigns achieve click-rates far exceeding those of traditional phishing campaigns.[4] AI transformed social engineering campaigns from spray and pray operations into psychological sniper attacks. The next iteration will consist of campaigns in which the AI does more than support the adversary. AI embodies it. As the capabilities of agentic AI continue to grow at an exponential rate, the adversary will leverage agents to collect intelligence, take action on the information, and adapt to evade detection in real-time.

The botnet incidents demonstrate coordinated fleets of compromised IoT devices sharing reconnaissance data while dynamically reallocating tasks to introduce the notion of swarm intelligence in cybercrime.[5] Traditional botnets operated through simple command-and-control hierarchies, executing predetermined tasks with minimal adaptation. The new generation may demonstrate emergent, autonomous behaviors where individual nodes contribute to collective decision-making processes that exceed the sum of their parts. One subset might conduct credential stuffing attacks while another simultaneously launches denial-of-service operations against security infrastructure, with the coordination enabling attacks that appear to originate from multiple, unrelated adversaries. From a WAVE perspective, swarm-based attacks exploit human limitations in pattern recognition and attribution analysis. Security teams struggle to distinguish between coincidental parallel attacks and coordinated campaigns when artificial intelligence simultaneously orchestrates deception across multiple vectors. In turn, the psychological burden of defending against adaptive threats creates decision fatigue that adversaries may exploit through precisely timed escalation.

Although thwarted, the 2024 Ferrari deepfake incident provides a glimpse into a potential future.[6] An employee received what appeared to be a video call from the company's CEO, complete with familiar vocal patterns, background details from the executive's actual office, and discussion of confidential projects that only insiders would know.[6] The attack only failed because the employee requested additional verification through established protocols. Through the lens of WAVE theory, deepfakes represent the weaponization of our neurological predisposition to trust sensory evidence. Human brains inherently process facial expressions, vocal patterns, and body language as reliable indicators of identity and intent.[7,8] Deepfake technology exploits these evolutionary mechanisms. As deepfakes permeate throughout every facet of society and the liar's dividend becomes common parlance, the future may hold a reality in which truth may be dismissed as fabrication.[9] This is a situation ripe for exploitation by the adversary. For example, the adversary may flood targets with obvious deepfakes to undermine trust in authentic evidence with the goal of sowing deliberate confusion rather than convincing deception.

Data-Driven Attacks

Consider the implications of the surveillance economy discussion in Chapter 5 within the context of cybercrime. Every target's digital footprint provides material for eventual manipulation. The adversary possesses the capability to transform seemingly innocuous personal data into precisely targeted psychological manipulation campaigns foreshadowing a potential future of cybercrime where data informs attack methodologies. The image of the lone hacker typing away in a dark basement gave way to a reality of industrialized scam compounds. Primarily located in Southeast Asia, these facilities operate as large-scale factories where individuals who were exploited and trafficked are forced to perpetrate social engineering campaigns against targets under the threat of violence.[10] As the sophistication of these operations continues to increase, the future likely holds a world in which the adversary possesses the capability to construct detailed profiles to inform targeted scripts that adapt to an individual's specific vulnerabilities. The next generation of these scam compounds will likely evolve to apply data analytics to human manipulation. Operating as veritable factories of fraud, these facilities may weaponize every conceivable data point to feed sophisticated behavioral playbooks designed for exploitation, including leveraging AI-enhanced analysis to uncover optimal strategies that evolve in real-time.

From a forensic cyberpsychology perspective, understanding these operations requires mapping how stolen data translates into persuasive narratives. The relationship between data and script represents a critical nexus for the future of targeted manipulation. For instance, knowledge that a target recently lost a family member might trigger a bereavement-themed scam, while data indicating financial stress may activate debt consolidation fraud campaigns. This script-data matching process reveals how the adversary may weaponize data against targets to transform personal information into psychological ammunition. The psychological impact on survivors will extend beyond immediate financial loss. Repeated, tailored targeting undermines trust in digital communications. Through the lens of WAVE theory, these operations will exploit our fundamental need for social connection by corrupting the very channels through which we seek community and support, further exacerbating perceived intimacy violations through normalization.

Perhaps the most insidious potential iteration of cybercrime entails the intentional corruption of information rather than its theft. Data poisoning attacks target the integrity of systems by injecting malicious information into them.[11] In the context of machine learning systems, this may entail injecting fraudulent data into training datasets to create vulnerabilities that may remain dormant for months or years before impact. Unlike traditional cyberattacks that announce their presence through system disruption, data poisoning operates behind the scenes to corrupt the decision-making process at the foundation. For example, researchers discovered that financial fraud detection systems were compromised through poisoned training data that taught algorithms to overlook specific money laundering patterns.[12] Similarly, attempted infiltration of medical diagnostic datasets sought to introduce biases that would cause AI systems to misdiagnose certain conditions.[13] These attacks represent the weaponization of a target's trust in data-driven systems by exploiting the increasing reliance on algorithmic decision-making.

From a forensic cyberpsychology perspective, data poisoning attacks require analysis of motivational layering that exceeds traditional cybercrime frameworks.

The determination as to whether the corruption represents sabotage for its own sake, profit-driven manipulation designed to enable other illicit activities, or ideologically motivated attempts to undermine trust in technological systems requires the nuanced analysis only achievable through WAVE theory. The long-term nature of these attacks represents a new frontier in cybercrime where digital trust is weaponized and signals a maturation of threat actor strategy. By eroding a target's ability to trust the underlying data at a time when society continues to grow increasingly reliant on AI-enhanced decisions, the successful execution of data poisoning attacks allows the adversary to threaten societal confidence in systems underpinning modern reality. As the adversary erodes trust in centralized data systems, the emergence of decentralized alternatives provides a potential promising solution as a means to circumvent the need for trust in the digital world. While blockchain technology may solve certain technical trust problems, it also introduces novel vectors that align with WAVE theory's emphasis on exploiting human cognitive limitations.

Blockchain Technology and the Decentralized Paradox of Trust

DeFi protocols created a parallel financial system where traditional regulatory oversight proves largely ineffective. Smart contract vulnerabilities enable code-is-law heists where the adversary exploits programming flaws to steal funds.[14,15] In the future, the adversary may combine exploits targeting legal ambiguity in the world of DeFi. The immutable nature of blockchain technology also means successful exploits cannot necessarily be reversed, which facilitates a one-way wealth transfer difficult to compare to traditional finance (TradFi). The next generation of DeFi exploits will likely evolve beyond simple flash loan attacks to incorporate algorithmic manipulation of human psychology. The adversary may deploy AI-driven analysis of market sentiment and behavioral patterns to identify optimal timing for smart contract exploits that maximize psychological impact while minimizing the technical sophistication required. Rug-pull schemes also exploit decentralized governance structures. In the current state, illicit groups create legitimate-appearing DeFi projects, attract investor funds through social media marketing, then drain treasuries through pre-programmed mechanisms. The 2023 AnubisDAO incident exemplified this approach when the adversary stole over $60 million within hours while maintaining the appearance of a legitimate organization.[16] It stands to reason that rug-pull schemes will evolve to exploit increasingly sophisticated decentralized governance structures. To accomplish this, the adversary may create elaborate deception campaigns that exploit genuine community trust. From a WAVE perspective, these operations may also weaponize the psychological need for financial autonomy and community belonging. At its core, the DeFi model exploits human cognitive biases toward group consensus and authority diffusion, making individual responsibility determination nearly impossible when theft occurs through collective decision-making processes that the adversary may manipulate from within the group.

Currently, privacy coins like Monero offer transaction privacy exceeding traditional cash while enabling global transfers at digital speeds. Cryptocurrency mixing services (e.g., Tornado Cash) allow individuals to obfuscate the source and destination of funds even on public blockchains. The Lazarus Group, for instance, laundered hundreds of millions of dollars through cryptocurrency mixers.[17] The next evolution of privacy coins and mixing technologies will offer transaction anonymity that exceeds anything currently possible while enabling instantaneous global transfers. Future iterations may incorporate quantum-resistant cryptography that makes transaction analysis mathematically impossible even for advanced surveillance states. Nation-state adversaries will likely leverage these capabilities to conduct financial warfare at unprecedented scales with the strategic objective of destabilizing entire economic systems through untraceable wealth transfers that exploit the psychological foundations of monetary trust. Through the lens of WAVE theory, this represents the weaponization of our dependence on pattern recognition for fraud detection. The human brain's inability to process the complexity of algorithmic transaction obfuscation may create additional blind spots for the adversary to exploit in conducting financial crimes at a global scale.

Tokenized identity systems of the future may also provide unforeseen fraud categories where compromising blockchain records legitimizes fraudulent goods, services, and credentials throughout entire distribution networks. Unlike traditional identity theft affecting individuals, future tokenized identity fraud will compromise organizational hierarchies through cascading authentication failures that undermine trust in digital signatures. The adversary may target foundational identity verification systems to corrupt the authenticity of everything from pharmaceutical supplies to voting systems. The psychological impact of future tokenized identity attacks will extend beyond immediate fraud execution to accomplish strategic execution of foundational trust collapse. From a WAVE perspective, this will exploit the neurological tendency to delegate complex verification tasks to technological systems, which creates psychological dependencies that the adversary weaponizes through systematic corruption of blockchain-based verification systems. This will mark a fundamental shift in the adversary's strategy, pivoting from attacking centralized systems to corrupting decentralized trust mechanisms. Despite this potential shift, quantum computing remains the existential threat on the horizon capable of rendering all current cryptographic foundations obsolete and forcing society to reconceptualize cybersecurity.

Quantum Horizon

Quantum computing represents an existential threat to contemporary cryptographic systems that makes concerns about Y2K appear quaint by comparison. The timeline for cryptographic obsolescence, however, remains frustratingly uncertain. Expert predictions range from never to next year, depending on which quantum research breakthrough occurs during that news cycle. Despite the uncertainty around when quantum computing will reach the inflection point, the adversary remains active, already exploiting the future potential. The idea of HNDL attacks, for example, represents perhaps the most psychologically sophisticated threat vector in cybercrime history. Intelligence agencies and illicit organizations may already be collecting encrypted communications for future decryption when quantum computers become available. This type of attack creates a temporal vulnerability, exploiting human cognitive limitations around long-term risk assessment capabilities, as current communications appearing secure may in fact become retroactively compromised. In other words, HNDL attacks require society to reconceptualize privacy and confidentiality. From a WAVE perspective, HNDL attacks weaponize the tendency to undervalue future consequences relative to present benefits (i.e., temporal discounting). Despite the threat of HNDL attacks, organizations continue to transmit sensitive information through channels that may become transparent to quantum-enabled adversaries, driven by the psychological comfort that current encryption provides apparent security.

In another application of the notion, the uncertainty around quantum computing itself becomes a weapon for the adversary to exploit via quantum anxiety. Quantum anxiety already manifests in organizational overinvestment in theoretical post-quantum technologies while neglecting immediate security vulnerabilities, which demonstrates how future threats may compromise present-day security through psychological misdirection. Future post-quantum cryptography implementation will face the classic security challenge of replacing functional systems with theoretical improvements under conditions of extreme uncertainty. NIST's selection of algorithms like CRYSTALS-Kyber and CRYSTALS-Dilithium represents humanity's attempt to build mathematical defenses against computational capabilities that do not currently exist.[18] The performance implications of these systems (e.g., exponentially larger key sizes, increased computational requirements) create entirely new categories of resource-based vulnerabilities that adversaries may exploit during the transition period. Organizations will face difficult choices about when to initiate expensive migrations to address quantum threats that may arrive tomorrow, or never. A process that will likely foster decision paralysis, which will be exploited by the adversary. Furthermore, future quantum-safe cryptography may introduce new categories of implementation vulnerabilities that current security frameworks cannot yet anticipate. The mathematical complexity of future iterations of post-quantum algorithms may soon exceed human cognitive capacity for verification. Through the lens of WAVE theory, this represents the ultimate delegation of security decisions to a technological authority whose correctness cannot be independently verified, posing the potential for the creation of vulnerabilities that may be exploited for decades before detection.

Proactive Defense Strategies

The accelerating sophistication of threat actor operations demands a reconceptualization of defensive strategies to future-proof responses. The reactive approach to cybersecurity today (e.g., patching vulnerabilities after discovery, responding to incidents after detection, updating policies after exploitation) will prove woefully inadequate against the adversary of tomorrow. Through the lens of WAVE theory, effective defense requires anticipating how future technologies will be weaponized against human cognitive limitations while building adaptive capacity for threats.

Effective preparation requires structured foresight methodologies, identifying weak signals and stress-testing defensive strategies.[19] The 2019 emergence of deepfake technology in illicit forums exemplifies weak-signal detection failure.[20] Although academic research demonstrated proof-of-concept voice synthesis capabilities as early as 2016, security organizations largely ignored these developments, including in user-awareness training.[21] From a WAVE perspective, this represents the weaponization of institutional cognitive bias toward familiar threat categories. Security teams focus disproportionately on variations of existing attacks while dismissing novel threat vectors that exploit psychological mechanisms in new ways. Effective weak-signal detection requires overcoming confirmation bias through structured analytical techniques. The Analysis of Competing Hypotheses methodology forces security teams to consider alternative threat scenarios beyond their organizational experience. Intelligence fusion centers increasingly employ devil's advocate protocols where team members are specifically assigned to challenge prevailing threat assessments, counteracting groupthink that leads to strategic surprise.

Red-team exercises adopt adversarial thinking to challenge assumptions and reveal planning blind spots. These workshops bring together diverse stakeholders to brainstorm how adversaries might exploit emerging technologies for strategic objectives. The methodology deliberately seeks uncomfortable scenarios to force organizations to confront assumptions and identify adaptive capacity requirements. Traditional red-team exercises focus on technical penetration testing within current threat environments. Future-oriented threat-casting expands this methodology to explore how adversaries might weaponize technologies still in development. From a forensic cyberpsychology perspective, effective threat-casting requires understanding adversarial motivation beyond immediate financial gain. Future exercises must explore ideological motivations, state-sponsored objectives, and emerging illicit business models that may drive threat evolution. Exercises simulating deepfake attacks against organizational leadership consistently demonstrate decision paralysis when employees cannot verify authentic communications from compromised channels. Through the lens of WAVE theory, these scenarios exploit hierarchical trust relationships that human psychology evolved to navigate in small groups but prove maladaptive in complex organizational environments where authority verification becomes technically challenging.

Threatcasting (i.e., science fiction prototyping) leverages narrative techniques to explore interaction effects between emerging technologies and human behavior.[22] Detailed stories about technology misuse can identify policy stress points before investing in potentially vulnerable systems. Fictional scenarios reveal unintended consequences that traditional risk assessment might overlook while providing memorable examples, enhancing communication across stakeholder groups (e.g., incorporating speculative scenarios involving AI-generated disinformation campaigns to anticipate regulatory gaps before platform deployment). These narrative exercises revealed how adversaries might exploit definitional ambiguities in policies through edge cases that technical specifications failed to address. From a WAVE perspective, science fiction prototyping exposes how adversaries weaponize human cognitive limitations in policy interpretation and enforcement. Science fiction prototyping also provides safe environments for exploring extreme scenarios that organizational culture might otherwise suppress without triggering organizational panic.

Beyond preparing as a means to enhance security before a disaster, organizations may benefit from preparing as a means to respond to a disaster (i.e., resilience engineering). This approach acknowledges that sophisticated adversaries will inevitably succeed and encourages organizations to design systems that maintain essential functions during compromise, which transforms cybersecurity from binary success/failure metrics to graduated response capabilities. For instance, organizations tracking Mean Time to Detection and Mean Time to Recovery (i.e., resilience metrics) demonstrate faster threat containment and reduced impact.[23] Resilience metrics measure adaptive capacity under stress through indicators like decision-making quality degradation, team coordination and effectiveness during incidents, as well as psychological recovery rates following security breaches. Moreover, chaos engineering deliberately introduces controlled failures to test response capabilities before adversaries discover them.[24] Future chaos exercises must incorporate psychological stressors that adversaries weaponize during attacks. From a WAVE perspective, chaos exercises reveal how adversaries exploit human psychological limitations during crisis situations. Resilience metrics must also measure collective psychological recovery following sophisticated social engineering campaigns. Organizations experiencing targeted manipulation attacks demonstrate measurable trust degradation that affects security culture for months after technical remediation. Future resilience engineering requires psychological inoculation programs that build cognitive resistance to manipulation through controlled exposure to chaos variables (e.g., information uncertainty, time pressure, confusion) to improve human decision-making under conditions that adversaries deliberately create.

Self-healing technologies automatically detect, isolate, and remediate threats without human intervention.[25] At the broadest level, AI-driven patch management systems illustrate this idea by analyzing vulnerability information and prioritizing remediation based on actual threat intelligence rather than generic severity scores. These systems address human cognitive limitations in processing complex technical information under time pressure while reducing decision fatigue that adversaries exploit during incident response. Future self-healing architectures may incorporate psychological threat modeling that anticipates how adversaries weaponize human decision-making processes to mitigate future threats prior to actualization. Future systems may incorporate behavioral economics principles to present vulnerability information in formats that overcome cognitive biases affecting risk perception and implementation prioritization in a synergized approach.

Conclusion

The evolution of cybercrime toward psychological manipulation at an industrial scale demands defensive strategies that address human cognitive limitations alongside technical vulnerabilities. Through the lens of WAVE theory, effective proactive defense requires anticipating how adversaries will weaponize emerging technologies against human psychology while building adaptive capacity for threats that transcend traditional cybersecurity frameworks. Future defense strategies must acknowledge that the human element represents both the greatest vulnerability and the most powerful defensive capability. Psychological resilience, cognitive diversity, and collaborative intelligence provide defensive advantages that technical solutions alone cannot achieve. The organizations that thrive in the evolving threat environment will be those that integrate psychological science into cybersecurity practice while building human-centered defensive capabilities that adapt faster than adversarial innovation cycles. The convergence of artificial intelligence, quantum computing, and decentralized technologies creates threat possibilities that exceed current defensive imagination. Proactive defense requires embracing uncertainty while building adaptive capacity for scenarios that challenge fundamental assumptions about cybersecurity. Through structured foresight, resilience engineering, and collaborative innovation, defenders can build strategic advantages that persist even as specific threat techniques evolve. The future of cybersecurity lies not in predicting exact threats but in building psychological and technical resilience that adapts to whatever adversaries devise.

Reflection Questions

1 Which future technology feels most underestimated in current cybersecurity plans?
2 How might you be unconsciously preparing to defend against yesterday's threats with tomorrow's budgets?
3 What weak signals in current technology trends, human behavioral changes, or adversarial innovations might your organization be overlooking?
4 How could your organization better leverage human psychological strengths while building defenses against the weaponization of human cognitive limitations?

Skill Builder Labs

Scenario: Draft a Five-Year Threatcast for AI

Develop a five-year plan threatcast assuming increasing AI advancement and adversary sophistication. Take the following steps:

- Establish the current AI threat baseline.
- Map AI advancement trajectories and identify emerging attack vectors.
- Profile adversarial adoption patterns and projected impact scenarios.
- Develop defense strategies and a review cadence.

Mini Research Activity: Compare Blockchain Forensics Tools

Objective

Compare the efficacy of two blockchain forensics tools.

Instructions

1. Obtain access to two blockchain forensic tools (e.g., open-source programs, free trials).
2. Analyze the capabilities and limitations of the platforms for investigating illicit cryptocurrency transactions.
3. Test both platforms using publicly available case studies or sample transaction data.
4. Compare approaches to address clustering, transaction graph analysis, and cross-chain tracking while evaluating accuracy and coverage.
5. Document strengths, weaknesses, and use cases for each tool.
6. Consider how the adversary may adapt techniques to evade detection.
7. Select a tool and assess resources required for implementation.
8. Develop a high-level plan to implement the tool at a law enforcement agency.

Deliverable

Design a product analysis report of the two blockchain forensic tools, including rationale supporting a recommendation and a corresponding implementation plan.

References

1. Herodotus. (1931). *Herodotus, with an English translation by ad godley*. Book I, Chapter 53. W. Heinemann.
2. Gallagher, S., Gelman, B., Taoufiq, S., Vörös, T., Lee, Y., Kyadige, A., & Bergeron, S. (2024). Phishing and social engineering in the age of llms. In Kucharavy, A., Plancherel, O., Mulder, V., Mermoud, A., Lenders, V. (eds), *Large language models in cybersecurity: threats, exposure and mitigation* (pp. 81–86). Springer Nature Switzerland.
3. Microsoft Threat Intelligence. (2024). *Staying ahead of threat actors in the age of AI*.
4. Heiding, F., Lermen, S., Kao, A., Schneier, B., & Vishwanath, A. (2024). Evaluating large language models' capability to launch fully automated spear phishing campaigns: Validated on human subjects. *arXiv preprint arXiv:2412.00586*.
5. Mims, N. A. (2025). The botnet problem. In Vacca, J. (ed), *Computer and information security handbook* (pp. 261–272). Morgan Kaufmann.
6. Galletti, S., & Pani, M. (2025). How Ferrari hit the brakes on a deepfake CEO. *MIT Sloan Management Review (Online)*, 1–5. https://www.proquest.com/docview/3166295448?fromopenview=true&pq-origsite=gscholar&sourcetype=Scholarly%20Journals
7. Morton, J., & Johnson, M. H. (1991). CONSPEC and CONLERN: A two-process theory of infant face recognition. *Psychological Review*, *98*(2), 164.
8. Deen, B., Koldewyn, K., Kanwisher, N., & Saxe, R. (2015). Functional organization of social perception and cognition in the superior temporal sulcus. *Cerebral Cortex*, *25*(11), 4596–4609.
9. Schiff, K. J., Schiff, D. S., & Bueno, N. (2022). The liar's dividend: Can politicians use deepfakes and fake news to evade accountability. *American Political Science Review*, *100*(1), 1–20.
10. Franceschini, I., Li, L., & Bo, M. (2023). Compound capitalism: A political economy of Southeast Asia's online scam operations. *Critical Asian Studies*, *55*(4), 575–603.

11 Kure, H. I., Sarkar, P., Ndanusa, A. B., & Nwajana, A. O. (2025). Detecting and preventing data poisoning attacks on AI models. *arXiv preprint arXiv:2503.09302*.
12 Paladini, T., Monti, F., Polino, M., Carminati, M., & Zanero, S. (2023). Fraud detection under siege: Practical poisoning attacks and defense strategies. *ACM Transactions on Privacy and Security*, *26*(4), 1–35.
13 Alber, D. A., Yang, Z., Alyakin, A., Yang, E., Rai, S., Valliani, A. A., ... & Oermann, E. K. (2025). Medical large language models are vulnerable to data-poisoning attacks. *Nature Medicine*, *31*(2), 618–626.
14 Atzei, N., Bartoletti, M., & Cimoli, T. (2017, March). A survey of attacks on ethereum smart contracts (sok). In *International conference on principles of security and trust* (pp. 164–186). Springer Berlin Heidelberg.
15 van der Laan, J. (2022). Smart contracts and "Code is Law"-some additional considerations. *International Journal of Blockchain Law* 4. 27–33.
16 Cong, L. W., Grauer, K., Rabetti, D., & Updegrave, H. (2023). The dark side of crypto and Web3: crypto-related scams. *Available at SSRN 4358572*.
17 Arbabi, A., Shojaeinasab, A., & Najjaran, H. (2025). Mixing services in Bitcoin and Ethereum ecosystems: A review. *IET Blockchain*, *5*(1), e70021.
18 U.S. National Institute of Standards and Technology, Computer Security Resource Center. (2024). *Announcing approval of three federal information processing standards (FIPS) for Post-Quantum Cryptography*.
19 Ansoff, H. I. (1975). Managing strategic surprise by response to weak signals. *California Management Review*, *18*(2), 21–33.
20 Ajder, H., Patrini, G., Cavalli, F., & Cullen, L. (2019). *The state of deepfakes: Landscape, threats, and impact*. DeepTrace.
21 Thies, J., Zollhofer, M., Stamminger, M., Theobalt, C., & Nießner, M. (2016). Face2face: Real-time face capture and reenactment of rgb videos. In *Proceedings of the IEEE conference on computer vision and pattern recognition* (pp. 2387–2395). IEEE.
22 Johnson, B. D., Vanatta, N., & Coon, C. (2022). Threatcasting. In *Threatcasting* (pp. 3–12). Springer International Publishing.
23 Lemon, J. (2024). *Sans 2024 detection and response survey*. SANS.
24 Konstantinou, C., Stergiopoulos, G., Parvania, M., & Esteves-Verissimo, P. (2021, October). Chaos engineering for enhanced resilience of cyber-physical systems. In *2021 Resilience Week (RWS)* (pp. 1–10). IEEE.
25 Frei, R., McWilliam, R., Derrick, B., Purvis, A., Tiwari, A., & Di Marzo Serugendo, G. (2013). Self-healing and self-repairing technologies. *The International Journal of Advanced Manufacturing Technology*, *69*(5), 1033–1061.

12 Conclusion

Why Security Awareness Training Often Falls Short

Psychological consistency creates opportunities alongside vulnerabilities. Authority bias, which makes employees susceptible to fraudulent directives from supposed executives, also strengthens compliance with legitimate security policies when properly implemented. Urgency bias, which pressures targets into hasty decisions, also accelerates deployment of critical security updates when appropriately channeled. The challenge involves working with these psychological realities rather than attempting to eliminate them, an impossible task given their evolutionary origins and continued utility in non-security contexts. Thus, traditional security awareness programs embody good intentions undermined by fundamental misunderstandings about human behavior. Most approaches treat cybersecurity as an information transfer problem. Rational decision-making will naturally follow the provision of knowledge to employees. This assumption overlooks substantial research demonstrating that knowledge alone rarely produces consistent behavioral change, particularly when viewed through the lens of WAVE theory. Research shows that security professionals with extensive technical knowledge and professional motivation to detect threats identified phishing emails only a portion of the time under normal conditions.[1] When subjected to time pressure that simulates realistic workplace environments, their detection accuracy further dropped, underscoring how even expert knowledge provides incomplete protection against sophisticated psychological manipulation. Organizations achieving meaningful reductions in successful attacks employ different approaches by focusing on environmental design rather than solely on individual education to reduce social engineering susceptibility.[2] By making secure behaviors easier than insecure alternatives, providing immediate feedback without public shaming, and leveraging social influence to reinforce positive security choices, these organizations fostered positive behavioral resonance. Furthermore, the concept of choice architecture (i.e., strategically designing decision environments to promote beneficial outcomes) offers more promising frameworks than traditional awareness training.[3] Rather than expecting perfect rational decision-making under affective pressure, effective programs acknowledge both cognitive limitations and emotional vulnerabilities to guide users toward secure choices through environmental cues and process design that account for manipulated emotional states. This approach exhibits the importance of WAVE-informed cybersecurity programs.

Perhaps the most significant insight emerging from this analysis concerns the different rates of change between technological capabilities and human psychological vulnerabilities. Although cybersecurity tools have exponentially advanced over the years, the cognitive biases and behavioral patterns that adversaries exploit remain consistent across decades. In fact, phishing emails from 1996 exploited the same psychological principles (e.g., authority, urgency, reciprocity, social proof) as contemporary deepfake video campaigns. While the underlying emotional triggers remain constant, adversaries now possess tools to engineer these triggers with surgical precision based on individual psychological profiles. This pattern creates both encouragement and frustration for security practitioners. While an understanding of stable psychological vulnerabilities enables the development of countermeasures with lasting effectiveness, no amount of technological advancement completely eliminates these vulnerabilities. In other words, human psychology cannot be patched through software updates or upgraded through hardware replacement. Mitigating the threat posed by the adversary requires rethinking how organizations approach cybersecurity through the lens of WAVE theory to address the psychological element persisting across each new technological iteration.

Emerging Challenges Reshaping Security Assumptions

Machine learning capabilities now enable adversaries to conduct personalized psychological manipulation at scales that previously required extensive human resources. The adversary is capable of launching attack campaigns targeting thousands of individuals simultaneously with customized content based on social media analysis, purchasing patterns, and behavioral profiling.[4] Traditional security awareness becomes inadequate when the adversary may generate infinite variations of manipulated content tailored to individual psychological profiles. This challenge extends beyond recognizing generic social engineering indicators to now include detecting manipulation techniques that feel authentically personal and contextually appropriate. Although defensive AI applications offer promising countermeasures through behavioral analytics and adaptive threat detection capabilities, these same systems introduce new vulnerabilities through adversarial machine learning techniques that manipulate defensive algorithmic decision-making. The resulting arms race between offensive and defensive AI creates environments where the advantage constantly shifts between adversaries and defenders.

Beyond this, quantum computing represents both a future cryptographic threat and a current psychological challenge affecting cybersecurity decision-making today. Uncertainty surrounding quantum development timelines creates cognitive overload among security professionals who must make long-term cryptographic decisions based on incomplete information, while fear-based narratives around quantum threats create affective vulnerabilities that adversaries may exploit.[5] Post-quantum cryptography standards require implementation choices with decades-long implications, while quantum threat materialization is estimated to occur anywhere from five to fifty years in the future. This temporal uncertainty affects resource allocation, technology adoption, and strategic planning in ways that traditional risk management frameworks handle poorly. While security teams already report increased stress levels, the requirement to balance immediate operational needs against theoretical future threats that may never materialize further compounds well-documented issues (e.g., burnout).[6] The psychological concept of quantum anxiety influences technology decisions even when actual quantum capabilities remain years from practical deployment, creating emotional states where decision-makers are susceptible to manipulation by vendors, consultants, and the adversary who may exploit these fears. Beyond quantum applications, organizations struggle with investment decisions that must account for threats that may never exist while maintaining protection against current attacks that definitely do. This planning challenge extends beyond technical considerations to organizational psychology and resource management under uncertainty.

Brain–computer interface technologies approaching commercial viability introduce cybersecurity challenges that transcend traditional boundaries between digital and biological systems.[7] Direct neural connections to digital networks create potential attack vectors that could influence human cognition, memory, and decision-making processes. This represents a substantial manifestation of WAVE theory, given that the theoretical possibility of neural hacking attacks targeting thought processes represents a qualitative shift in cybersecurity that current frameworks cannot adequately address. Neural interfaces may enable direct manipulation of emotional states, fear responses, and trust mechanisms without the need for external sensory input. Research into neural data protection and cognitive privacy remains nascent while commercial brain–computer interface development rapidly accelerates. The convergence of neural interfaces with WAVE theory techniques may enable unprecedented levels of psychological manipulation that bypass all traditional defensive measures. Although these technologies may also enable new defensive capabilities through neural-based authentication and threat detection systems that leverage difficult to manipulate brain patterns, they raise profound questions about mental autonomy and cognitive privacy that legal and ethical frameworks are also not prepared to effectively handle. This is particularly true considering the potential for neural-level affective manipulation that these technologies may create. Thus, the challenge extends beyond technical implementation to fundamental questions about human agency and the acceptable boundaries of security monitoring when consciousness itself becomes part of the digital landscape, which is a quandary only WAVE theory stands ready to address.

Ethical Considerations That Demand Attention

Advanced cybersecurity capabilities increasingly require extensive behavioral monitoring and analysis that challenges traditional privacy expectations. Balancing collective security needs with individual autonomy demands careful consideration of how protective measures affect human dignity and democratic values. Current informed consent mechanisms prove inadequate for modern cybersecurity complexity. Many individuals lack the technical knowledge necessary to understand what they are consenting to when accepting terms of service for products that monitor behavior, analyze communications, and make access decisions.[8] Addressing how surveillance capabilities that enable effective cybersecurity may also become tools for oppression without appropriate constraints and oversight mechanisms provides another important aspect of future technology (i.e., the same behavioral monitoring that protects against insider threats may violate employee privacy when implemented without adequate safeguards). Explainable artificial intelligence additionally becomes essential when automated systems make decisions affecting human opportunities and access to services. Algorithmic decision-making that cannot provide coherent justifications philosophically undermines basic principles of accountability.

As discussed throughout this book, society faces fundamental questions about balancing personal autonomy with collective needs extending beyond individual choice. Poor cybersecurity decisions increasingly affect other users through network effects and shared infrastructure vulnerabilities.[9] Different populations also require different approaches to this balance, especially when considering varying susceptibility to affective manipulation. Children, older adults, individuals with cognitive limitations, and other vulnerable groups may benefit from more restrictive security measures, while technically sophisticated users may prefer greater control over their risk tolerance and security configurations. Thus, the challenge involves designing adaptive systems to accommodate emerging threats and varying user preferences while maintaining baseline security requirements that protect broader digital ecosystems.[10] Expressly, individual autonomy must be balanced against collective welfare in ways that preserve democratic values while ensuring effective protection against sophisticated psychological manipulation.

Synthesizing the Evidence

Throughout this book, one pattern emerged: the notion that psychology serves as the foundational element of cybercrime. Psychological factors shape domains (e.g., adversary tactics, target vulnerabilities, defensive effectiveness) in ways that persist, regardless of technological advancement. WAVE theory unifies concepts by moving beyond isolated principles fragmented across multiple disciplines (e.g., psychology, computer science, criminology, engineering, economics) into a singular explanatory model that works on multiple levels (e.g., micro, meso, macro). The evolution of attack methodologies over recent years demonstrates the consistent exploitation of emotional and psychological susceptibilities through deliberately constructed manipulation frameworks, which is a cornerstone of WAVE theory. Despite the increasing technical sophistication of exploitation capabilities, the adversary continues to favor psychological manipulation tactics. WAVE theory represents an evolution beyond the principles upon which it builds by focusing specifically on the tendency of the adversary to combine affective vulnerabilities (i.e., the emotional triggers and psychological states used by the adversary to circumvent rational decision-making processes) to facilitate behavioral resonance in targets. In so doing, WAVE theory transforms forensic cyberpsychology from an application of isolated insights by providing a systems-level theory explaining how the adversary exploits human emotion in digital environments that scales from implications for individuals to organizations to geopolitics.

Reflection Questions

1 Where should the line between collective security and individual privacy be drawn?
2 With AI enabling personalized psychological manipulation at scale, how might organizations defend against attacks tailored to individual psychological profiles?
3 How might organizations balance preparing for uncertain future threats (e.g., quantum computing) with addressing current definite threats?
4 What are ways that WAVE theory may be integrated into emerging technologies to enhance cybersecurity?

References

1 Carroll, F., Adejobi, J. A., & Montasari, R. (2022). How good are we at detecting a phishing attack? Investigating the evolving phishing attack email and why it continues to successfully deceive society. *SN Computer Science, 3*(2), 170.
2 Waelchli, S., & Walter, Y. (2025). Reducing the risk of social engineering attacks using SOAR measures in a real-world environment: A case study. *Computers & Security, 148*, 104137.
3 Thaler, R. H., & Sunstein, C. R. (2009). *Nudge: Improving decisions about health, wealth, and happiness*. Penguin.
4 Ai, L., Kumarage, T., Bhattacharjee, A., Liu, Z., Hui, Z., Davinroy, M., ... & Hirschberg, J. (2024). Defending against social engineering attacks in the age of llms. *arXiv preprint arXiv:2406.12263*.
5 Alessa, A. S., Hammoudeh, M., & Singh, H. (2025). A Peek into the post-quantum Era—PQA PQC: What will happen in 2030. In Mohammad Hammoudeh, Clinton M. Firth, Harbaksh Singh, Christoph Capellaro, Mohamed Al Kuwaiti *Quantum technology applications, impact, and future challenges* (pp. 163–180). CRC Press.
6 Chen, H., Liu, M., & Lyu, T. (2022). Understanding employees' information security–related stress and policy compliance intention: The roles of information security fatigue and psychological capital. *Information & Computer Security, 30*(5), 751–770.
7 Maiseli, B., Abdalla, A. T., Massawe, L. V., Mbise, M., Mkocha, K., Nassor, N. A., ... & Kimambo, S. (2023). Brain–computer interface: Trend, challenges, and threats. *Brain informatics, 10*(1). Article 20.
8 Luger, E., Moran, S., & Rodden, T. (2013, April). Consent for all: Revealing the hidden complexity of terms and conditions. In *Proceedings of the SIGCHI conference on Human factors in computing systems*. Association for Computing Machinery, New York, NY, USA, 2687–2696.
9 Palleti, V. R., Adepu, S., Mishra, V. K., & Mathur, A. (2021). Cascading effects of cyber-attacks on interconnected critical infrastructure. *Cybersecurity, 4*(1), 8.
10 Pekaric, I., Groner, R., Witte, T., Adigun, J. G., Raschke, A., Felderer, M., & Tichy, M. (2023). A systematic review on security and safety of self-adaptive systems. *Journal of Systems and Software, 203*, Issue C. 111716.

Index

accessibility and inclusive UX 41–42
adaptive feedback loops 2
advanced persistent threat (APT) campaigns 47
adversary 31–32, 34–35, 140
aesthetic bias 41
AI, in cybersecurity 139–140
algorithmic biases 62
algorithmic decision-making 153
angler phishing 108
AnubisDAO incident (2023) 142
anxiety 35, 41, 58, 62, 115
Apple ecosystem 41
artificial intelligence (AI) 6, 139–140
attention engineering 45–46
attention regulation research 43
authority heuristics 5, 108

behavioral/behavioral: adaptations 122–123; interventions 132–133; resonance analysis 7
blockchain technology 142–143
brain–computer interface technologies 152
Budapest Convention (2001) 16, 134
business email compromise (BEC) 2, 18

California Privacy Rights Act (CPRA) 48
callback phishing 105, 109
class-action litigation 48
cognitive: biases 43–44, 151; diversity 147; impacts of technology 42–43; load theory 40; rehabilitation 124; resources 4; vulnerabilities 43
collaborative intelligence 147
collective intelligence 56
Computer Fraud and Abuse Act 1986 (CFAA) 16
confirmation bias 44
content surveillance 61

Conti ransomware operation 31
COVID-19 pandemic 55–57
credibility heuristics 4
criminal specialization 92
cryptocurrencies 92
Csíkszentmihályi, Mihály 97
cultural elements 35
cybercrime: adversary behavior 34–35; behavioral interventions 132–133; and cognition 15–16; cross-border policing and MLAT limits 77–78; ecosystems 8; financial drivers 90–92; fundamentals 15–16; globalization (1990s–2010s) 73–75; ideological drivers 92–94; IoT and Edge Threats 81–84; offensive and defensive AI 81–82; patterns 34; personal drivers 94–98; policy and legal interventions 133–135; professionalization and industrialization (2010s–2020s) 75–77; Proto-Hacks (1960s–1980s) 71–73; Quantum-Era Risks 84–85; rationalizing behavior 98; statistics 18; Stuxnet and State Operations 78–79; Target and Equifax Data Breaches 79–81; technology-dependent cybercrime 26–27; technology-enabled cybercrime 27–28; UX design interventions 131; victimization 8
cybercrime-as-a-service (CaaS) 31
cybercrime attack lifecycle: objective execution 30; target compromise 29–30; target selection 28–29
cybercrime ecosystem: adversary 31–32; defenders 32; targets 33–34
cybercrime organizations 31, 34
cyber-deviance 16
cyber-enabled crime 16, 27–28
cyber-enhanced crime 15

Cyber Hygiene Paradox 118–119
cyberpsychology: defined 3–4; evolution of 12–15; research methods in 18–20
cybersecurity: AI in 139–140; block chain technology 142–143; data-driven attacks 140–142; DeFi protocols 142–143; ethical considerations 152–153; frictionless and ethical design in 48–49; Oracle's dilemma 139; psychological manipulation in 5; quantum computing 143–144

darknet hacking forums 96
dark patterns 45
data localization 65
data minimization 20
data-wipe attack 27
DDoS attack 17
decentralized finance (DeFi) protocols 92, 142–143
decision-making online 5
deepfake technology 6, 59
DeepMind 55
Democratic Congressional Campaign Committee (DCCC) 29
Democratic National Committee (DNC) 29
Democratic People's Republic of Korea (DPRK) 30
denial-of-service operations 140
digital: amnesia 42; behavior 3; communications 5, 17, 18; defenses 1; detox 61; environments 3, 4; identity vulnerability assessment 21–22; interfaces 5; platforms 5, 65; psychology 3
Digital Equipment Corporation 97
Doe, Jane 1
domain name system (DNS) 26
Dunning-Kruger effect 118

economic disparity 34
election interference 5
emotional distress 7
Environmental, Social, and Governance (ESG) reporting 64
Equifax breach (2017) 30, 42, 131
European Union's Digital Services Act 47
evidence packs 107
evolution, of cyberpsychology: web 1.0 (digital self-emergence) 12–14; web 2.0 (social connectivity and algorithms) 14
exploitation: adversary 140; self-perpetuating cycle of 121–123; technical sophistication of 153

facial recognition technology 61
fear of missing out (FOMO) 5
Federal Communications Commission 57
Ferrari deepfake incident (2024) 140
financial fragility 33
financial trauma 120
flow theory 97
Foldit 57
forensic cyberpsychology 3, 141
free security software 44

Galaxy Zoo 56
GameStop trading phenomenon 5
General Data Protection Regulation (GDPR) 134
generative artificial intelligence (GenAI) 31
globalization (1990s–2010s) 73–75
group polarization 5

Herrick, Matthew 95
HNDL attacks 143–144
HTTPS encryption 109
human cognitive abilities 4
human-computer interactions 3
Human Genome Project 56
human psychology 15

IBM Watson oncology system 58
Individual Vulnerability Model 2
influencers 32
interface psychology: aesthetic bias 41; technology capabilities and user expectations 40
international cooperation agreements 48
Internet of Things (IoT): devices 60; and Edge Threats 81–84
internet psychology 3

just-in-time (JIT) approaches 131

Knowledge Deficit Assumption 2

large language models (LLMs) 105
large-scale emergencies 91
law enforcement 7
Lazarus Group 139, 143
LulzSec 93, 96

machine learning systems 133
maladaptive coping strategies 45
malicious interface design 43–44
Malware 17
mass phishing 139
media coverage 35

MGM Resorts attack (2023) 105
Mirai malware 89
misconceptions, cyber security 118
Mitchell, Ricky Joe 95
Mitnick, Kevin 97
modern cybercrime 36
money mules 31, 32
moral disengagement theory 98

Nielsen, Jakob 40
non-fungible tokens (NFTs) 106
non-verbal communication 4
NotPetya 27
nudge theory 133

offenses: technology-dependent cybercrimes 16–17; technology-enabled crimes 17–18
online: attention 3; behavior 4; trust 4
open network architectures 33
open-source intelligence (OSINT) harvesting 29
operational security (OpSec) 20–21
Operation Egypt 93
Operation Payback campaign (2010) 93
Operation Tunisia 93
organizational culture interventions 131–132
organizational hierarchies 31
organizational psychology 18
Organization for Security and Co-operation in Europe (OSCE) 134
organized crime groups 91

Pacific Bell 97
password requirements 49
personal health information (PHI) 33
phishing emails 91
physical surveillance 25
pig butchering scams 28, 41
Pizzagate conspiracy 107
political activism 94
post-quantum cryptography (PQC) algorithm 84
post-traumatic stress disorder (PTSD) 119
privacy coins 92
Privacy Zuckering 45
proactive defense strategies 144–146
profit-driven manipulation 142
Prometheus Paradox 62
Proto-Hacks (1960s–1980s) 71–73
psychological: ramifications 61–62; resilience 147; safety 132; vulnerabilities 1

quantum computing 84–85, 143–144, 151

RaaS platform 99
RankMyHack.com 97
ransomware 17, 21, 26–27
ransomware-as-a-Service (RaaS) 31, 98
regulators 32
regulatory frameworks 47–48
remote work technology 56
research methods, in cyberpsychology: mixed methods in 19–20; qualitative research 19–20; quantitative research 19
resilience metrics 146
robust OpSec 18
romance scammers 27, 43
Rosetta Project 57
Routine Activity Theory (RAT) 6
Russian Foreign Intelligence Service 94

sampling strategies 47
security: assumptions 151–152; awareness programs 150–151; fatigue 48; interface design 41
self-healing technologies 146
selfhood trauma 121
sextortion scams 28
situational vulnerabilities 116–118
Skill Builder Labs 9
small and medium-sized businesses (SMBs) 33
smishing (SMS phishing) 90
smishing campaigns 109
Social Cognitive Theory (SCT) 5–6
social engineering campaigns 29–30, 43; digital deception tactics in 108–110
social: identities 14; isolation 117, 123; norms 6
social media intelligence (SOCMINT) 29
social proof mechanisms 5
status quo bias manipulation 50
Stuxnet and State Operations 78–79
Stuxnet worm 94
survivors: emotional trauma 119–120; financial trauma 120; selfhood trauma 121
Swiss Cheese Model 130

target 33–34; cognitive processes of 15; compromise 29–30; credibility heuristics in 4; demographics and psychographics 115–116; digital fraud 27; and Equifax Data Breaches 79–81; selection 28–29

158 *Index*

task-switching research 46
Technical Primacy Bias 2
technical vulnerabilities 1, 7
technological innovation 8; cyber warfare and disinformation 59–60; digital divides and cultural paradoxes 57–58; economic drivers of 58–59; ethical frameworks 63–64; governance frameworks 62–63; legal frameworks 64–65; psychological ramifications 61–62; surveillance economy and anonymity collapse 60–61
technology-dependent cybercrimes 26
technology service providers 32
Theory of Planned Behavior (TPB) 6
threat casting 145
Todd, Amanda 95
Tornado Cash 32
trust indicators 41
Twitter Bitcoin 4

United Kingdom's Computer Misuse Act 1990 16
U.S. National Security Agency (NSA) 61

vishing (voice phishing) 90
vulnerability scanning 29

weaponized affective vulnerability engineering (WAVE) theory 1, 2; confirmation bias 106–107; in cybercrime cases 22; cyberpsychological foundation of 4–5; scarcity, FOMO, and exclusivity 105–106
weaponized interface design: attention engineering 45–46; dark patterns 45
web psychology 3

For Product Safety Concerns and Information please contact our EU representative GPSR@taylorandfrancis.com
Taylor & Francis Verlag GmbH, Kaufingerstraße 24, 80331 München, Germany